Understanding Digital Societies

Understanding Digital Societies

Edited by Jessamy Perriam and Simon Carter

Los Angeles I London I New Delhi
Singapore I Washington DC I Melbourne

Published by

SAGE Publications Ltd, 1 Oliver's Yard, 55 City Road, London EC1Y 1SP

SAGE Publications Inc, 2455 Teller Road, Thousand Oaks, California 91320

SAGE Publications India Pvt Ltd, B1/I 1 Mohan Cooperative Industrial Area, Mathura Road, New Delhi 110 044

SAGE Publications Asia-Pacific Pte Ltd, 3 Church Street, #10-04 Samsung Hub, Singapore 049483

in association with

The Open University, Walton Hall, Milton Keynes MK7 6AA

First published 2021

This publication forms part of the Open University module DD218 *Understanding digital societies*. Details of this and other Open University modules can be obtained from Student Recruitment, The Open University, PO Box 197, Milton Keynes MK7 6BJ, United Kingdom (tel. +44 (0)300 303 5303; email general-enquiries@open.ac.uk).

Alternatively, you may visit the Open University website at www.open.ac.uk where you can learn more about the wide range of modules and packs offered at all levels by The Open University.

Edited and designed by The Open University.

Typeset by The Open University.

Paperback printed and bound in the UK by Page Bros Group Ltd.
Hardback printed and bound in the United Kingdom by Ashford Colour Press Ltd.

Paperback ISBN 978-1-5297-3257-3   Hardback ISBN 978-1-5297-3258-0   eBook ISBN 978-1-5297-3387-7

1.1

Contents

Preface

Understanding Digital Societies is a stand-alone book designed to offer an introduction to how sociology can make sense of the character, history, challenges and opportunities encountered in digital societies. The book forms the primary study materials for the Open University module DD218 *Understanding digital societies*, which aims to demonstrate the insights that sociology offers into everyday life, society and technology in a contemporary context across four substantive sections: 'Everyday life and the digital'; 'Society, technology, citizens and cities'; 'Humans and machines'; and 'Uses and abuses of the digital'. The book explores how ideas about societies both create and respond to technologies. It also investigates how new collectives are assembled and mobilised through digital technologies and considers how the same technologies can divide individuals and groups and give rise to new patterns of inequality.

Although *Understanding Digital Societies* was written in the late 2010s and early 2020s, we were mindful to produce a text that could help examine digital technology regardless of the technologies and platforms that were in use at the time. Supported by a diverse range of contemporary and historical examples, the book demonstrates that sociological concepts and a sociological understanding of everyday life can help us make sense of ever-changing digital societies. The approach of this book also takes account of how sociology has been shaped by other disciplines and intellectual approaches, including cultural studies, science and technology studies, history, religious studies, criminology and anthropology.

Module teams produce Open University teaching materials. These teams involve contributors from The Open University as well as other UK-based and international institutions, module and project managers, tutors, external assessors, editors, designers, audio and video producers and administrators. Academics on the DD218 *Understanding digital societies* module team were based mainly in the Sociology department of The Open University's School of Social Sciences & Global Studies, within the Faculty of Arts and Social Sciences. But the module team drew upon the expertise of colleagues from other universities and institutions to construct a module with interdisciplinary foundations and appeal. While the book editors have primary responsibility for the content of this book, the assignment of editors' names to this book does not adequately convey the collective nature of production at The Open University. We would like to thank all our colleagues in the broader module team for their intellectual energy, hard work and good humour. Particular thanks are due to Androulla Corbin, who has, among many other things been a resourceful, professional and efficient Curriculum Manager and Liz McFall, who was the main driving force in the early stages of the module.

Simon Carter

Jessamy Perriam

Contributors

Simon Carter is a sociologist working at The Open University with interests in Science and Technology Studies, health and medicine and science engagement. He originally was a research chemist working in the automotive industry and then in environmental protection. After studying at The Open University, his career took a different direction when he returned to full time higher education to complete a PhD at Lancaster University. After this, Simon mainly specialised in the sociology of health and illness, and medical sociology.

Rhys Crilley is a Leverhulme Trust Early Career Researcher in the Department of Politics and International Relations at the University of Glasgow. His current research explores narratives of nuclear weapons, and he works on the intersections of popular culture, social media and global politics with a specific interest in war and legitimacy. Rhys has published over twenty journal articles in outlets such as *International Studies Review, Journalism, International Affairs* and *Millennium*. He is currently working on writing his first monograph. He tweets at @rhyscrilley.

Umut Erel, Professor of Sociology, has widely researched and published on migration, gender, ethnicity and racism. She is also interested in participatory, arts-based and collaborative methods.

Marie Gillespie is Professor of Sociology at The Open University. Her teaching and research interests revolve around migration, media and communication. She has published widely on the mediation of war, peace and security, forced migration and digital connectivity, cultural and digital diplomacy. Books include: *Social Media, Religion and Spirituality*; *Diasporas and Diplomacy: Cosmopolitan Contact Zones at the BBC World Service* and *Drama for Development: Cultural Translation and Social Change*.

John Maiden is a Senior Lecturer in Religious Studies at The Open University. His main research interests are global evangelical, charismatic and pentecostal Christianity.

Liz McFall is Director of Data Civics and Chancellor's Fellow based in the Edinburgh Futures Institute and Sociology at the University of Edinburgh. She co-edited *Markets and the Arts of Attachment* (2017), wrote *Devising Consumption: Cultural Economies of Insurance, Credit and Spending* (2014) and *Advertising: A Cultural Economy* (2004) and edits the *Journal of Cultural Economy*. She is co-founder of AWED, a collective that make films and installations exploring the orchestration of civic sentiments and data techniques, most recently *Closes and Opens: A History of Edinburgh's Futures*.

Jessamy Perriam is Assistant Professor in the Technologies in Practice research group and the Centre for Digital Welfare at the IT University of Copenhagen. She was previously Lecturer in Sociology at The Open University. Her research is situated within Science and Technology Studies and Sociology, and focuses on public sector digital transformation, failure, cybersecurity and public demonstrations of expertise.

Peter Redman is a Senior Lecturer in Sociology at The Open University. He is on the editorial board of the journal *Psychoanalysis, Culture & Society* and co-edits the Palgrave book series 'Studies in the Psychosocial'.

David G. Robertson is a Lecturer in Religious Studies at The Open University, co-founder of the Religious Studies Project, and co-editor of the journal *Implicit Religion*. His work applies critical theory to the study of alternative and emerging religions, 'conspiracy theory' narratives and the disciplinary history of the study of religions. He is the author of *UFOs, the New Age and Conspiracy Theories: Millennial Conspiracism* (Bloomsbury, 2016) and co-editor of *After World Religions: Reconstructing Religious Studies* (Equinox, 2016) and the *Handbook of Conspiracy Theories and Contemporary Religion* (Brill, 2018). Twitter: @d_g_robertson.

Paul-François Tremlett is a Senior Lecturer in Religious Studies at The Open University. He has conducted ethnographic research in Manila, Taipei, Hong Kong and London focusing on religious and secular conceptions of urban space. His interests include the classical social theory of religion, postmodernism and processes of rapid social and religious change.

Darren Umney is a writer and researcher whose work weaves together interests in cultural geography, social history, post-war architecture, cartography and design. Born in North Buckinghamshire, his particular curiosity around the conception and construction of new towns is probably based on the experience of one being built through the middle of his formative years.

Sophie Watson is Professor of Sociology at The Open University. Her research interests currently concern city water cultures, and street markets as spaces of mobilities, materialities, public space and inclusion. Her recent books are *Spatial Justice in the City* (Routledge, 2019) and *City Water Matters: Cultures, Practices and Entanglements of Urban Water* (Palgrave Macmillan, 2019).

Introduction

Simon Carter and Jessamy Perriam

Contents

Setting the scene

Welcome to *Understanding Digital Societies*. We hope that you will enjoy reading this book and that it will enable you to understand how society and technology relate to one another in the world around us. This relationship will be framed using three sociological threads, and a wealth of examples will contextualise the issues being discussed to demonstrate how sociology can be used to help make sense of our world as it relates to the digital.

How do the social and the technical shape each other?

This book is about the relationships between society and technology and about how the social and the technical shape one another. For example, do technological developments change society? Alternatively, could the opposite be true? Thus, it is common to refer to periods of prehistory as the Stone Age, Bronze Age and Iron Age. The use of this classification implies that these societies were solely shaped by the technologies they used. So, it could be argued that the Bronze Age replaced the Stone Age because its technology was better – bronze tools were far more efficient than stone ones. Progress was seen to be determined by technology.

It could equally be argued that it was not just the technology that determined progress, but rather a range of social, economic and political factors determined the transformation from the Stone to the Bronze Age. These included developments such as the establishment of inter-regional trade networks in copper and tin; changes in society that allowed the emergence of metalworking and metallurgy as a specialist form of work; and the creation of systems of exchange that both supported trade and an increasing division of labour (Given *et al.*, 2001). Alternatively, it may be that social and technical change are so intimately entwined that it makes little sense to speak of one without the other. Throughout this book, as we consider different digital societies, we will be considering the question of how do the social and the technical shape each other?

You may think that we are currently entering a digital age. While it may be helpful to think about technologies in reference to the times and places they were developed within, it is simplistic to think that once

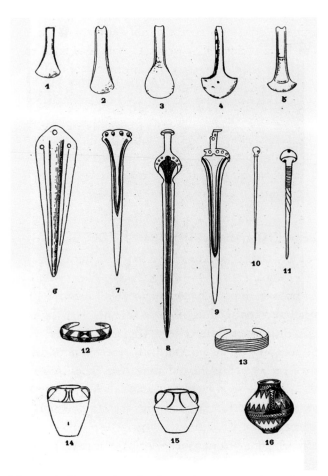

Figure 1 Bronze Age implements, ornaments and pottery (Period II).

that era is over its technology becomes obsolete, replaced with something new. We are not restricted to using technologies that only come from one era. Take plumbing, for example. In its simplest form, plumbing is an ancient technology with clay sewer pipes being used in Mesopotamia around 6,000 years ago. Many people today use and take these for granted each day alongside more recent digital technologies that allow us to connect to the internet.

Communities using any technology may do so because they work best for the tasks that they want to achieve, while others do not have access to these tools. For instance, to stay with the plumbing example, in 2015 around 844 million people worldwide still lacked even a basic drinking water service and 2.3 billion people still lacked even a basic sanitation service (World Health Organization, 2017). Similarly, with digital technologies, some people with access to digital technologies may refuse to use them for a variety of reasons. Others may wish to access digital services but have no access to the internet – in 2016 around 55% of the world's population had no access to the internet (World Economic Forum and The Boston Consulting Group, 2016). How might we consider varying levels of access to, or use of, digital technologies across different individuals and communities?

Social worlds

Sociology is defined differently by groups of academics around the world, but it is helpful to begin to think of sociology in terms of social worlds. The concept of the social world emerged from what is now commonly called the Chicago School of Sociology. The University of Chicago founded the first sociology department in 1892. One important and influential perspective to come out of this department was the idea that people's conduct toward both things and other people is based on the meanings that we give to them. These meanings are gained from how we relate to and react to the *people and things* around us. These exchanges between people, groups and things are often called social interactions by sociologists, and it is by interactions like these that people give meaning to everyday activities. A 'social world' can then broadly be understood as a group of people who share certain perspectives, understandings and meanings, and these are used to coordinate behaviours based on some shared interest or common task.

Social worlds can be informal and mundane and, at their simplest, they are the everyday interactions between *people and things* doing activities together. The routines, customs, rules (both informal and sometimes formal) and shared meanings that are established eventually constitute the character and distinctiveness of different social worlds. New members of a social world have to learn by participating in the social world. As Geoffrey Bowker and Susan Leigh Star (1999) have observed:

> We are all in this sense members of various social worlds—communities of practice—that conduct activities together. Membership in such groups is a complex process, varying in speed and ease, with how optional it is and how permanent it may be. One is not born a violinist, but gradually becomes a

member of the violin playing community of practice through a long period of lessons, shared conversations, technical exercises, and participation in a range of other related activities

(Bowker and Star, 1999, p. 294).

To take a slightly different example, we could look at the social world of art. We could ask 'Who does art?' The obvious answer is that an individual known as an artist does art. However, it could also be reasoned that a far wider range of people are involved in art than just the artist. This was the view taken by the sociologist Howard Becker in his book *Art Worlds* (1982).

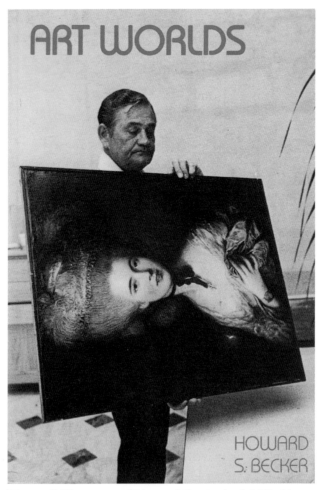

Figure 2 The cover of Howard Becker's *Art Worlds*

The cover of Becker's book shows a bored-looking porter carrying a picture in a gallery. For Becker, this porter is as much part of the social world of art as the painter. Art is, in this view, a collective activity or social world made up of a variety of people and objects. They include the museum or gallery curator who decides which art to display; the academics or popular critics who define the conventions, categories and the cultural value of art in journals and popular media; the auction houses and buyers who assess and ascribe economic worth to art; and the many caretakers, restorers and porters who store, care for and display works of art. All these individuals and things make up the social world of art:

> Works of art, from this point of view, are not the products of individual makers, "artists" who possess a rare and special gift. They are, rather, joint products of all the people who cooperate via an art world's characteristic conventions to bring works like that into existence. Artists are some sub-group of the world's participants who, by common agreement, possess a special gift.
>
> (Becker, 1982, p. 35)

Studying social worlds gives sociology a distinctive approach to understanding society. It allows us ways of seeing the world that moves beyond taken-for-granted assumptions and in doing so, provides deeper, and sometimes more challenging, ways of knowing social life. Sociology is distinct from many other disciplines in that it starts with the belief that groups, cultures and institutions, and considers that their connections can and should be direct objects of study. And it also recognises that these objects of study are more than just the sum of the individual parts that make them up – they are more than just aggregations of individual actors.

Social relationships

A social world then is a concept to help us understand how groups of people – collectivities of various sorts – share and make meaning out of doing things together. Everyday life is made up of many overlapping social worlds. Some are informal, others are more formal structures, and most are a mixture of the informal and formal. Of interest to sociologists is: how do these different social worlds overlap and cooperate? And what happens when social worlds conflict with each other?

To help us answer questions like these, sociologists tend to examine social relationships. For sociologists, the idea of a social relationship is used to try and explain how individuals arrange themselves into groups much like the worlds of art described above. Social relationships can be intimate and personal, such as family ties and friendship groups. However, they can also be impersonal and more dispersed.

For example, early social theorists such as Karl Marx considered the social relationships around those who own things (capitalists) and those who only own their capacity to do work (the working class). More recently, sociologists have explored what issues and values groups coalesce and what are the situations that make them do so, such as why people affiliate to certain political parties or interest groups. Social relationships are not limited to people; sociologists are also interested in the objects that we make and use or choose not to use – and how we relate to them.

How the book is organised

In *Understanding Digital Societies*, you will be focusing on the social relationships between individuals, digital objects and society. To do this, the book will introduce you to some sociological ideas that will help you understand these relationships. One of the first of these will be the idea of **social structures**. Simply put, a social structure is an arrangement of social relations that form a recognisable pattern of relationships that help make up a social world. For example, a grouping of intimate personal relations forms something we would all recognise as a family structure.

We will be exploring social relationships and structures more in Section 1 of the book where we will be talking in more detail about social media, but the issues associated with social relations and social worlds will be apparent and returned to throughout the book.

Throughout this book, we will be exploring the issues outlined here by using three *sociological threads*. These threads will each explore a pairing of concepts that sociologists often write about, and study. These are:

- Individuals and society

- People and things

- Power and inequality.

While these sociological threads intersect with areas of sociological interest such as race, class and gender, we will primarily be considering them by looking at digital technologies. Let us look at each of these in turn:

Individuals and society

Sociology is often understood as seeking to understand the various ways in which an individual interacts with society. In his 1959 book *The Sociological Imagination*, sociologist Charles Wright Mills (often referred to as C. Wright Mills) describes the relationship between individuals and societies as many 'personal troubles' contributing towards 'public issues' (Mills, 2000). Another way of putting this is that issues commonly seen as individual problems are often linked to wider social structures. For example, someone who is disadvantaged because of poverty may think that this is entirely due to failings on their part.

However, a sociologist could also point out that poverty is linked to wider social forces, such as the class structure, in the society in which a person lives. Even something as personal as the friends we have may seem like an individual choice. However, closer examination may reveal that while friendship is, to some extent, a personal choice, there are also many constraints and internalised societal values that shape our friendship choices.

People and things

Throughout the book, we will explore the relations between *people and things*. Sociologists, as well as being interested in social relations, are also interested in the material stuff that people surround themselves with and the meanings that this stuff has for members of various social worlds. Clothes, tools, gadgets, furniture and buildings all have meanings ascribed to them and help shape the way that society works. For example, if you were going for a job interview, you would probably choose clothes that conveyed a meaning of seriousness. So this outfit would be very different from the one you would select when playing or watching sport or doing the gardening on an allotment.

In various parts of the book we will explore the relationship between digital technology and people, and the work people need to do to manage these digital things. We will also pick this up again in Section 3 when we examine in more detail the wearable technologies people use to monitor their cycling and walking, often for health purposes. However, on the flip side of this, how might our use of technological things such as smartphones impact others? In Section 4 we will see that our use of technology can impact other people as well as the environment in detrimental ways.

Power and inequality

The final sociological thread we will consider in this book is *power and inequality*. In a broad sense, sociologists are interested in who holds more power than others and the inequalities that occur as a result. Sociologists look at how societies are organised and structured and how this can lead to hierarchies of gender, class and ethnicity. Inequalities can appear in many ways such as income and wealth inequality, unequal access to education or cultural resources, and

Figure 3 Wearable technology

differing treatments by power structures such as the police and judicial systems.

When we focus on inequalities while looking at digital societies, we want to ask whom technology empowers and disempowers, and who experiences inequality. In each part of the book, you will see examples of this, including wearable technology, migration technology, automation, and how computers use sets of rules in everyday life.

When exploring the sociological threads of *individuals and society*, *people and things*, and *power and inequality*, it should be remembered that these are tools to help you understand digital society. Often there will be some overlap between these threads. Thus, as noted previously, inequality or poverty is often experienced as a 'private trouble' for the individual, but if many individuals experience inequality, then this rapidly becomes a 'public issue' embedded in the political and economic structures of society.

Reading this book

Within *Understanding Digital Societies*, our aim is to equip you with the theoretical tools to help you examine and analyse issues that you notice in your everyday life. To do this we use examples throughout the book to highlight the main themes of *individuals and society, people and things,* and *power and inequality.*

Section 1 introduces you to the idea of the 'sociological imagination', as first advanced by C. Wright Mills – the idea that personal problems relate to societal issues – through the example of women cyclists in the Victorian era and inequalities faced in early consumer photography. We also examine how that relates to poverty and austerity in contemporary society. Within Section 1, you will also look at Erving Goffman's ideas about how people present themselves in everyday life (Goffman, 1959) to consider some of the theory used by social scientists to think about online interactions. We do this by drawing on examples of musicians interacting with fans on social media. We then think about 'capital' – what people choose to present of themselves and how that is understood by others. We do that by thinking about internet celebrities and influencers.

In Section 2, we think about how technology plays a part in various communities. We start by taking you to two places in the UK – Edinburgh and Milton Keynes – to unpack the concept of the smart city. We then travel with asylum seekers to observe how technology is considered both an aid and a danger to their journey. Later in Section 2 we also see how technology plays a large role in sustaining transnational communities, such as migrant workers keeping in touch with their families back home, and migrants connecting with their religious communities in their new location.

We shift focus in Section 3 to the relationships between *people and things.* The chapters in this section ask you to consider how we relate to technological objects in everyday life. To do this, we discuss some of the objects that already play a role in how we interact with the world around us (whether we are aware of it or not) such as GPS systems on your smartphone or in your car, and the automated systems that help pilots navigate and fly commercial jets. We also take a critical look at technology in the workplace, through the example of how technology governs workers in spaces like the Amazon warehouse. Finally, we describe how objects such as fitness trackers relate to our sense of well-being in comparison to that of others. Throughout this section of the book we want you to consider whether objects have **agency**. And if they do, how do they use that agency with humans?

Finally, Section 4 introduces the concept of '**social harm**' by considering various issues in digital societies such as environmental concerns, the rise of misinformation, cybersecurity, mental health and flaws in algorithms that govern our interactions with institutions and organisations. To be sure, we are not suggesting a technological determinist approach to digital societies by discussing social harm. We do, however, want to give you the theory and some examples to help you articulate and describe situations that could be considered harmful.

The team of authors and editors writing this book did so at a particularly tumultuous time in society. In many cases, this raised new issues for us to think about when putting this book together. During the time that we've worked on this book, we have heard about Cambridge Analytica and their use of social media data to target citizens to vote in certain ways without their explicit knowledge.

We have seen with increasing urgency how important it is to change our behaviour to avoid a climate catastrophe, an issue that has largely been brought to our attention by grassroots activists such as Greta Thunberg and Extinction Rebellion. We have also seen many more technologies welcomed into daily life with smart assistants such as Siri and Alexa; our personal data is becoming far more valuable to corporate entities. We also finalised this book in the midst of the Covid-19 pandemic, a global event which has highlighted power and inequality in new and serious ways. All this is to say, that at the time of writing this is where digital societies are currently at.

We are certain that there will be many other issues that will be at the forefront of your mind when you come to read this book. Our hope is that this book will give you the sociological tools necessary to be able to grapple with what is happening in digital societies in the years to come.

References

Becker, H.S. (1982) *Art worlds*. Berkeley, CA: University of California Press.

Bowker, G. and Star, S. (1999) *Sorting things out: classification and its consequences*. Cambridge, MA: MIT Press.

Goffman, E. (1959) *The presentation of self in everyday life*. New York, NY: Anchor Books.

Given, M., Kristiansen, K. and Rowlands, M. (1999) *Social transformations in archaeology: global and local perspectives*. London: Routledge.

Mills, C.W. (2000) *The sociological imagination*. New York, NY: Oxford University Press.

World Health Organization (2017) *Progress on drinking water, sanitation and hygiene*. Geneva: World Health Organization.

World Economic Forum and The Boston Consulting Group (2016) *Internet for all: a framework for accelerating internet access and adoption*. Geneva: World Economic Forum.

Section 1

Everyday life and the digital

Chapter 1

The digital sociological imagination

Jessamy Perriam

Contents

1 Introduction

How do the problems that we experience individually in everyday life compare with some of the broader issues happening around us in wider society?

This chapter introduces one of the main pieces of sociological theory you will be working with throughout the book. As described in the Introduction to the book, there are three main sociological threads that form the theoretical backbone of this book: *individuals and society*, *people and things* and *power and inequality*.

1.1 Teaching aims

The aims of this chapter are for you to:

- be introduced to the sociological imagination as a way of understanding *individuals and society*

- understand how technology figures in individual problems and broader society

- challenge notions that technology is new.

2 What is the sociological imagination?

The focus of this chapter is the sociological imagination, which is both the title of a book and an idea that outlines how individual problems relate to issues in broader society.

In 1959, C. Wright Mills wrote a book, *The Sociological Imagination*, to clarify his ideas on how social scientists could think about and **frame** sociology. In the first chapter of his book Mills describes the promise of sociology: how it can help everyone better observe and understand society. He describes how sociologists must pay attention to both 'personal troubles' and 'public issues'. This chapter of the text book will unpack what Mills meant and how we can apply his ideas to digital societies, as well as to contemporary issues in society more broadly.

Mills begins his description of the sociological imagination by describing the problem facing 'ordinary men'.

> What ordinary men are directly aware of and what they try to do are bounded by the private orbits in which they live; their visions and their powers are limited to the close-up scenes of job, family, neighborhood; in other milieux [social settings in which decisions are made], they move vicariously and remain spectators. And the more aware they become, however vaguely, of ambitions and of threats which transcend their immediate locales, the more trapped they seem to feel.
>
> Underlying this sense of being trapped are seemingly impersonal changes in the very structure of continent-wide societies. The facts of contemporary history are also facts about the success and the failure of individual men and women. When a society is industrialized, a peasant becomes a worker; a feudal lord is liquidated or becomes a businessman. When classes rise or fall, a man is employed or unemployed; when the rate of investment goes up or down, a man takes new heart or goes broke. When wars happen, an insurance salesman becomes a rocket launcher; a store clerk, a radar man; a wife lives alone; a child grows up without a father. Neither the life of an individual nor the history of a society can be understood without understanding both.
>
> (Mills, 2000, p. 3)

What is Mills describing here? He's talking about individuals and their daily life. When life is stable for an 'ordinary individual', that person rarely looks beyond the immediate circumstances of their career, their family or where they live. However, Mills suggests that society impacts individual lives more than the ordinary person realises. Changes in society impact individuals. The examples that he gives talk primarily about economic shifts from a society becoming industrialised, but he also discusses temporary societal shifts such as war, and how they impact individuals and families.

Who was C. Wright Mills?

Figure 1.1 American sociologist Charles Wright Mills pictured towards the end of his life in 1960.

Charles Wright Mills (1916–1962) was an American sociologist who produced the bulk of his work in the mid 20th century. His writing focused on the roles of governments, military and bureaucracy and their collective impact on inequality in society. Mills completed his PhD studies on the sociology of knowledge before the start of World War II.

Post World War II, Mills's writing focused on developing critical standpoints on social inequality, problems facing the middle class, and power held by the elite. Crucially, he often disagreed with sociologists of the same era and asserted that they were often too detached from the communities they claimed to study. He called for sociologists to be more concerned and involved with problems in everyday life, with the intention that sociologists should be activists, as well as researchers.

His most famous work is *The Sociological Imagination*, which is the focus of this chapter. *The Sociological Imagination* was written in 1959 and was intended to provide a way for people to observe and think about the relationship between individual experiences and world events or troubles.

Mills describes a framework for helping us, as social scientists, understand and observe how individuals relate to society. Although he wrote this text in the mid 20th century and uses some language and examples that might sound a bit outdated, are you able to identify examples of personal troubles and public issues?

The concept of the sociological imagination is helpful for when we ask questions about what is happening in digital societies and to whom.

2.1 Biography and history, troubles and issues

Mills sometimes describes his ideas with interchangeable terms. Instead of talking about 'public issues' he may refer to 'history'. And other times, when talking about 'personal troubles', he may use the term 'biography'. It may be more helpful for you to consider the sociological imagination in terms of personal 'biography' and a public 'history'.

Mills defines troubles and issues thus:

> *Troubles* occur within the character of the individual and within the range of his immediate relations with others; they have to do with his self and with those limited areas of social life of which he is directly and personally aware …

> *Issues* have to do with matters that transcend these local environments of the individual and the range of his inner life.

They have to do with the organization of many such milieux into the institutions of an historical society as a whole, with the ways in which various milieux overlap and interpenetrate to form the larger structure of social and historical life. An issue is a public matter: some value cherished by publics is felt to be threatened ...

... consider unemployment. When, in a city of 100,000, only one man is unemployed, that is his personal trouble, and for its relief we properly look to the character of the man, his skills, and his immediate opportunities. But when in a nation of 50 million employees, 15 million men are unemployed, that is an issue, and we may not hope to find its solution within the range of opportunities open to any one individual.

(Mills, 2000, pp. 8–9)

2.2 Reading *The Sociological Imagination* today

Some of the texts that you will read in *Understanding digital societies* were written during a time where it was more the norm to use phrases or terms that we might find offensive nowadays. C. Wright Mills's writing has quite a specific tone that is representative of a certain period. Sociological writing from the early to mid 20th century can sometimes be difficult to navigate as the reader is often assumed to be of a certain class, gender or education level. When *The Sociological Imagination* was written in 1959, far more men of middle and upper class backgrounds had access to higher education in comparison to women or those in the working class. This is reflected in the text, as Mills describes the sociological imagination with examples that seem to be rather masculine: they refer to an era where men were expected to be the breadwinners for the household. This approach might seem out of touch with contemporary living if you are part of a living situation where there are two or more incomes providing for the needs of the household. Although the examples that Mills and others sociologists of that era use to illuminate their ideas may seem outdated, the ideas themselves remain valuable in helping us examine the world around us. When reading these older sociological texts you should consider how their ideas could be used or challenged within the contemporary context.

Mills's description of the sociological imagination can be helpful when we examine what is happening in contemporary society. Mills describes the relations between history and biography, along with the relations between personal troubles and public issues. Essentially, Mills's sociological imagination shows us that problems we encounter individually can often be understood as contributing to the narrative of broader problems happening in society.

2.3 The sociological imagination and women's cycling

Daughter *(enthusiastically)*. "Oh, Mamma! I *must* Learn Bicycling! So delightful to go at such a pace!"
Mamma *(severely)*. "No thank you, my dear; you are *quite* 'fast' enough already!"

Figure 1.2 This cartoon from the late 1890s shows how it was considered controversial for women to be seen cycling in public.

One example of the relationship between individuals and society can be found in Kat Jungnickel's book *Bikes and Bloomers* (2018), where she investigates the difficulties faced by upper and middle class women in 1890s Britain who wished to take up cycling. In her **qualitative research** Jungnickel describes the biographies of women who took up cycling. Using archive material such as newspaper and magazine articles, **patents** and birth, death and marriage registrations, she found out that women cycling along the streets of suburban Victorian London in the 1890s faced extreme danger due to the fact that women's clothing often got caught in the bicycle's moving parts. They also faced abuse on the street by pedestrians and passers-by that believed women of that social standing should not take part in such physical activity (Figure 1.2).

Jungnickel's archive research looked at patent documents that were filed by women cyclists who invented new outfits that were safe for cycling. Many of these outfits were convertible – transforming from a full skirt into a pair of bloomers with a cape within seconds (Figure 1.3).

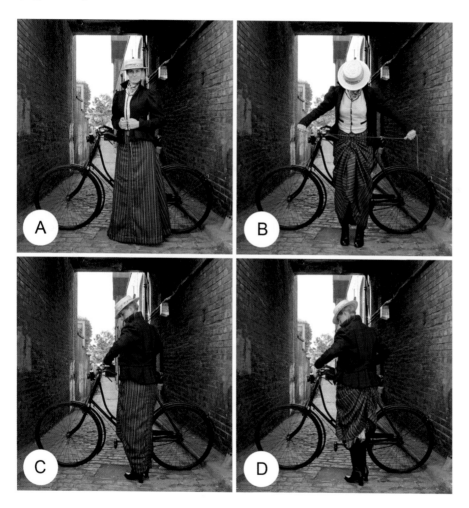

Figure 1.3 This photograph shows convertible cyclewear in action. This is a cycling outfit made in the 2010s, based on information available from patents. The wearer can adjust the skirt with drawstrings to allow the fabric to sit away from the moving parts of the bicycle.

While women overcame the physical dangers of cycling posed by their clothing, they still had the problem of public abuse when out on their bikes. Why was that so?

Let's consider Jungnickel's research through the lens of C. Wright Mills's sociological imagination (Figure 1.4). First, we identify the biography (or personal trouble) in the research. Women cyclists were in danger of injury from the combination of their bicycle's moving parts and their clothing. They were also dealing with verbal and physical abuse from people who objected to women cycling on public thoroughfares. In the diagram on the following page, you can see how women's convertible cyclewear could be considered an expression of the sociological imagination. If you follow the action of the illustration from bottom to top you can see how many reports of women being injured while cycling translates into the wider public issue of women's bicycle safety in the 1890s.

Now let's examine the history (or the public issues) at play in this research. The events described in *Bikes and Bloomers* take place in the late Victorian era where societal expectations of women were different to those in the twenty-first century. To be sure, we do not presently live in an era with no societal expectations of women, but they are very different expectations. As Jungnickel describes, in Victorian Britain there was a very narrow set of expectations placed on women:

> Ideas around citizenship and freedom of movement are closely aligned with power, gender and public and private space. In Victorian society, women's mobility was physically and ideologically shaped by social codes and behavioural norms and closely linked in their clothing ... Up until the mid nineteenth century, the moral responsibility of reproduction, the bearing of and caring for children, defined middle- and upper-class women's lives. There were strict gender and labour divisions in place, whereby 'men produced, women reproduced' [Russett (1989) quoted in original]. The lives of these women were deeply rooted in one particular place – the home. It was an inward-looking private and domestic role, distinctly different from that of the public life of men.

(Jungnickel, 2018, p. 31)

Figure 1.4 The Sociological Imagination and women's cycling history

From this excerpt, we can see that women's very public mobility on bicycles was at odds with the societal expectations of upper and middle class women to remain in caring roles within the home. Victorian women cyclists faced verbal and physical abuse because they were flouting the expectations that broader society had for them.

In her work, Jungnickel explains her focus on upper and middle class women, rather than working class women. The lived experiences of women in the Victorian era were clearly marked by class. Put simply, working class women could not afford the time or money to take part in leisure activities such as cycling, nor were they able to keep up with the fashion trends that Jungnickel describes. Working class women were quite often in the workforce while also carrying out emotional and domestic labour in the home.

3 Technological determinism and technological utopianism

Throughout this book, we will keep bumping into ideas connected to **technological determinism** and **technological optimism** (also known as **technological utopianism**). These terms describe two of the different perspectives or attitudes people may have towards technology. It is important as sociologists that we keep our analysis between these two perspectives.

A technological determinist perspective is a teleological idea that suggests that technology will take society to a distinctly positive or negative endpoint (Franklin, 2004). For example, some on the more pessimistic side of technological determinism might argue that technologies such as data collection and storage or facial recognition allow us to be more readily surveilled by those in positions of power or privilege. On the other end of the spectrum, a technological optimist perspective (also known as a technological utopian perspective) suggests that technology can be liberating and produces only positive outcomes for individuals and societies. As social scientists, our role is to acknowledge and highlight that technology could have good outcomes for some, while at the same time producing negative outcomes for others.

Kat Jungnickel's work on women and cycling shows this middle ground approach. From one perspective, cycling technology was a positive innovation for upper and middle class Victorian women, as it allowed them improved mobility and exercise. But the widespread introduction of cycling was not perfect either. From another perspective, some saw cycling technology as a challenge to the social norms of expected women's behaviour. From a practical perspective, despite the invention of the safety bicycle – a development of the bicycle closely resembling those we ride today – women still faced danger when cycling due to the fashion norms, with clothing becoming caught in moving parts. But is the bicycle to blame or the fashion? When considering the positive or negative impacts of technology, we need to approach the social, economic and political contexts within which the technology is used.

We will continue to revisit and challenge both technological optimist and technological determinist viewpoints throughout this book. You may notice this when we look at transnational use of technology, the introduction of AI and issues in technology use. But keep the words of Mills in mind when he wrote about the sociological imagination: 'Neither the life of the individual nor the history of a society can be understood without understanding both.' (Mills, 2000, p. 1) How might we extend this to include technology? Try this out for yourself: think about how social media platforms or digital devices such as tablets or smartphones have been discussed in both determinist or utopian ways.

3.1 Food banks and austerity

Figure 1.5 In the UK, food banks typically provide three days' worth of food to citizens who – for many reasons – find themselves unable to afford the essentials.

Now let's consider a modern example of a public issue: food bank use in the UK (Figure 1.5). An individual finds him or herself in a situation where – for a variety of reasons – they are unable to afford put food on the table. Many media sources have reported the increase in demand for food bank parcels, especially since the introduction of **austerity policies** by the UK government. This is coupled with an increase in the cost of living for items and services such as rent, food

and transport. Below is an extract from **empirical research** done by
Kayleigh Garthwaite, Peter Collins and Clare Bambra in 2015.

> David and Jenni came to the foodbank for the first time after
> David left work due to mental health problems. Both were
> currently not working but had lengthy histories of employment –
> David as a chef and Jenni in retail. The ongoing threat of
> austerity impacted upon David's health on a day-to-day basis:
>
> *It's just been stress cos I'm the worrier me, Jenni doesn't worry about*
> *nothing, it's me that worries. We'd come back home and I was half*
> *expecting the landlord to be there with all our stuff out on the front,*
> *like 'get out' type of thing y'know like you see on the telly when they*
> *repossess the house …*
>
> Similarly, David told me how he and his wife now shop in the
> cheap frozen food stores in the Town Centre, despite the fact that
> *'it's cheap but the quality isn't very good. We've had fish fingers from*
> *there and they were disgusting'.* Naomi and David were mindful of
> how their health needs should be aligned with their nutritional
> needs; the fulfilment of those requirements was the issue.
>
> (Garthwaite *et al.*, 2015. pp. 41–42)

Identifying personal troubles and public issues

■ In the extract above about food bank use there are many personal
troubles at play. Read through the extract again and try to identify:

- the personal troubles that David and Jenni face before using the
food bank
- the public, societal issues that relate to David and Jenni's personal
troubles
- the personal troubles that arise after David and Jenni begin to use
food banks and purchase lower quality food
- the public, societal issues that could arise with the increase in food
bank usage and poor nutrition.

4 Technology implicated in the sociological imagination

Figure 1.6 A Shirley card. Shirley cards were used by photographic laboratories to calibrate machines for printing photographs.

We will now explore how the sociological imagination can be used to observe and understand inequalities produced or reproduced by technology. We will look in particular at the example of the Kodak film photography company and the 'Shirley card' (Figure 1.6).

The Shirley card was an image that helped photographic laboratories calibrate their developing and printing machines to produce the most accurate colour levels. The 'Shirley' on the card was a photograph of a glamorous woman, looking at the camera with a beaming smile. The problem? Throughout most of the 20th century, Shirley's skin tone was that of a white person. This meant that the film developing process was not calibrated for images of people who had skin tones other than Shirley's almost porcelain white.

As a result, people with skin tones that differed from the Shirley card found that their holiday photographs and family memories contained images that were not as accurate as they had hoped. This extract from the NPR website explains more:

Reading 1.1 Mandalit Del Barco, *How Kodak's Shirley cards set photography's skin-tone standard*

For many years, this 'Shirley' card – named for the original model, who was an employee of Kodak – was used by photo labs to calibrate skin tones, shadows and light during the printing process.

'She was the standard,' Garcia says, 'so whenever we printed anything, we had to pull Shirley in. If Shirley looked good, everything else was OK. If Shirley didn't look so hot that day, we had to tweak something – something was wrong.'

Shirley cards go back to the mid-1950s, a time when Kodak sold almost all of the color film used in the U.S. After a customer used the film, he or she would bring the roll to a Kodak store to be printed. In 1954, the federal government stepped in to break up Kodak's monopoly.

...

Under DeMoulin's direction, Kodak came up with its S5 printer for independent photo labs. And to make sure the colors and densities of the prints were calibrated correctly, Kodak sent a kit with color prints and original unexposed negatives 'so that when they processed their negative, they could match their print with our print,' DeMoulin says. 'It was almost a foolproof operation.'

Each color print was an original shot of Shirley Page, who worked as a studio model for Kodak's new products.

'They would take hundreds of pictures. And, of course, she had to have her eyes open and be smiling,' DeMoulin recalls. 'It was days in the studio, and sometimes we'd have to take a day off to give the model an eye rest.'

The Shirley cards were used all over the world, wherever the Kodak printers were used. 'It didn't make any difference which model came in later to do it,' he says. 'It was still called "The Shirley."'

... over the years, subsequent 'Shirleys' have been equally as anonymous – sometimes wearing pearls, gloves, hats and even swimming suits for beach scenes. In the early days, all of them were white and often tagged with the word 'normal.'

'The people who were producing the cards had a particular image of beauty, captured in the Shirley card,' says Lorna Roth, a media professor at Canada's Concordia University who has researched the history of Kodak's Shirley cards.

'At the time, in the '50s, the people who were buying cameras were mostly Caucasian people,' she says. 'And so I guess they didn't see the need for the market to expand to a broader range of skin tones.'

According to Roth, the dynamic range of the film – both still photo stock and motion picture – was biased toward white skin. In 1978, the filmmaker Jean-Luc Godard famously refused to use Kodak film to shoot in Mozambique because he declared the film was racist. People also complained that photos of blacks and whites in the same shot would turn out partially under- or over-exposed.

(Del Barco, 2014)

Identifying the personal trouble and public issue

■   What can you identify as the personal trouble in this piece about the Shirley card? Similarly, can you identify the public issue?

Through this example, it is hoped that you can see how examples of pre-digital technology have a part to play in the sociological imagination. Technology can be used to try to rectify personal troubles, such as women cycling, or it can contribute to personal troubles, such as people of colour being misrepresented in photography. Similarly, technology can be used in attempts to rectify public issues, but it can also be implicated in public issues.

5 The digital sociological imagination

In this section we will consider what the sociological imagination might look like in the digital age.

How might we see and identify personal troubles (or biographies) and public issues (or history)? What are the sources available to us? In the previous examples you saw how Kat Jungnickel used archives to find examples of personal troubles. In the food bank example you saw reports and articles used to describe personal troubles.

Emerging digital spaces and technologies have allowed for more personal troubles to be articulated. However, as you will examine further in Chapters 10 and 11, digital spaces and technologies may also be implicated in public issues such as misinformation and political interference. It could be easy to say that the digital age presents just as many technological solutions as it presents societal problems. Throughout the course of this book you will use the sociological imagination among many other sociological theories to better understand digital societies.

When considering the digital sociological imagination we need to think about the sources available for us to identify personal troubles in the digital age. Is social media a reliable source of personal troubles? Perhaps a thread on Twitter could tell the story of the personal troubles facing an EU citizen living in Brexit Britain. So too, a YouTube video from a vlogger discussing body positivity could describe a public issue around societal expectations of women's body shapes and sizes.

These are examples of how public issues and personal troubles are discussed and described in digital settings such as on social media platforms.

But are there any personal troubles or public issues that are unique to digital technologies? When describing digital research methods, new media academic Richard Rogers talks about 'natively digital' data as data that has been created by digital transactions or events, rather than existing data that has been copied into digital settings (Rogers, 2013). For example, your street address is data that you make digital when you enter it into an online form, however a website address (URL) or email address is natively digital data because it first existed in a digital setting.

Thinking back to the example of the Shirley card, you saw a situation where a technological object (the Shirley card) highlighted a personal trouble (disappointing photographs for people of colour) and a public issue (racial bias from a manufacturer). By thinking about digital objects and artefacts as part of personal troubles and public issues, we see a digital sociological imagination beginning to emerge.

6 Conclusion

In this chapter, you have been introduced to one of the core sociological ideas, the sociological imagination, and C. Wright Mills's description of the relations between *individuals and society*, biography and history, and personal troubles and societal issues has been brought to life. This was done by giving examples of how you might view historical events, such as the adoption of cycling and the development of photographic film, and highlighting how personal troubles act as symptoms of broader social issues, such as racism and sexism. Similarly, you examined the increase of food bank use in the UK in the 2010s. By doing this, you have identified the personal troubles and social policies that lead to individuals and households making use of food bank services. You have also seen how prolonged periods of poverty and reliance on food with poor nutritional value could lead to a broader social issue of chronic health problems.

The chapter has also introduced the concepts of technological determinism and technological optimism. As sociologists, we see these concepts as binary opposites, sitting on either side of a spectrum. It is important to pay attention to who benefits from the introduction of new technologies and how those benefits exclude others.

This chapter has deliberately steered clear of using examples of recent technologies such as the internet or social media. This was done to broaden your view of technology and reiterate that the introduction of technology in society has impacted individuals over the course of millennia.

And, finally, you have been encouraged to consider what a digital sociological imagination might look like and how you might develop it for yourself throughout the course of reading this book. Where might you find examples of the personal troubles and public issues in digital settings? What might be some of the difficulties or opportunities in finding these examples?

In the next chapter you will venture into digital settings, such as social media platforms, to consider how people interact online. To do this, you will be introduced to the sociological concepts of the 'presentation of self' and 'capital'. Both of these concepts will help you explore what people are displaying to one another online and how they go about it.

References

Del Barco, M. (2014) *How Kodak's Shirley cards set photography's skin-tone standard*. Available at: https://www.npr.org/2014/11/13/363517842/for-decades-kodak-s-shirley-cards-set-photography-s-skin-tone-standard (Accessed: 27 February 2018).

Franklin, U.M. (2004) *The real world of technology*, Rev. edn. Toronto: House of Anansi Press Inc./Berkeley, CA: Publishers Group West.

Garthwaite, K.A., Collins, P.J. and Bambra, C. (2015) 'Food for thought: an ethnographic study of negotiating ill health and food insecurity in a UK foodbank', *Social Science & Medicine*, 132 (May), pp. 38–44. doi: 10.1016/j.socscimed.2015.03.019.

Jungnickel, K. (2018) *Bikes and bloomers – Victorian women inventors and their extraordinary cycle wear*. Cambridge, MA: Goldsmiths Press.

Mills, C.W. (2000) *The sociological imagination*. New York, NY: Oxford University Press.

Chapter 2

The presentation of self in digital spaces

Jessamy Perriam

Contents

1 Introduction

Imagine you are sitting on a bus or on public transport. You find yourself with a few minutes to spare so you pull out your smartphone to scroll through social media and kill some time before you get to your destination. Have a think about the people you follow and the posts you are reading or watching. Do you know these people you're following? You might pause as you think what you gain from following them, or conversely, what they gain from you following them.

How people present themselves in digital spaces is a common question that is asked by sociologists, anthropologists, social psychologists and media and communication studies scholars. Is it any different to how people present themselves in face-to-face situations?

Another common question that sociologists might ask is: what are people presenting to one another and how does that matter to others around them? In this chapter we cover some key ideas used by sociologists to explore these questions further.

1.1 Teaching aims

The aims of this chapter are for you to:

- examine two sociological ideas to help explain some online behaviours: Erving Goffman's concept of 'the presentation of self in everyday life', presented in his book of that name (1959), and Pierre Bourdieu's idea of 'capital', presented in 'The forms of capital' (2011), originally published in 1986

- explore key terms around the presentation of self in everyday life, such as dramaturgical, front stage, backstage and audience

- consider how the presentation of self in everyday life can be applied to social life in digital settings

- describe various types of capital, such as economic, social and cultural capital

- critically evaluate how these types of capital might be understood in digital settings such as social media and among influencers and internet celebrities.

2 Goffman and the presentation of self

Erving Goffman wrote his book, *The Presentation of Self in Everyday Life* in 1959. In his book, he talks about social interactions and often uses the analogy of a theatre to help us understand the ideas he is putting forward.

Who was Erving Goffman?

Erving Goffman was a Canadian sociologist and **ethnographer** who studied and worked in the UK and North America.

Goffman was born in Alberta, Canada in 1922 and was the son of Ukrainian immigrants. He began to study sociology in his twenties and later went on to do his PhD at the University of Chicago, which was famous for pioneering the field of sociology. As part of his doctoral research in the 1950s, Goffman spent more than a year living in the Shetland Islands, observing how Shetlanders lived in their community. This research formed the basis of his most famous publication, *The Presentation of Self in Everyday Life*, where he describes how people perform different versions of self depending on who they are interacting with and where the interaction is taking place.

Goffman also went on to research social identities and change in mental hospitals, which lead to the publication of *Asylum* (1991), a book that shaped reform in mental health institutions. His further publications throughout the 1960s and 1970s focused on behaviour in everyday life and social interactions.

2.1 Unpacking performance

The idea that we want to focus on from this book is around 'performance'. Goffman asserts that in many of our social interactions, we are performing a version of ourselves to match the situation that we are taking part in. Further, he describes that version of ourselves that we portray as the 'front stage' version of ourselves. This is in contrast to our 'backstage' version of self that is relaxed, or perhaps preparing for the next performance. Goffman deliberately uses words associated with theatre and drama to ask us to be reflexive about our own interactions with others. He suggests that when we are interacting with people, we are actors within a certain setting; we act according to what our fellow actors are doing, how we want to be perceived and what else is happening in that setting.

To help you understand this in practice, think about the last time you were at a party and received a gift from a friend who is not the best at choosing gifts. Imagine they are really excited about the gift they have given you and are eagerly waiting for you to unwrap it. As you unwrap it, you realise that they have given you a shirt that does not really fit with your style. You really like and appreciate your friend and you prefer not to disappoint them by complaining about the gift, so you pretend that you are excited about it. When your friend leaves the party, you turn to another friend and tell them you do not really like the gift.

Now look at the scenario through Goffman's eyes. Think about the setting: it is a party, so is probably in a public space or someone's home. The other actors in this situation are friends; people you get along with and probably want to continue getting along with. When you receive the gift, you and your friend are the main actors on the stage. Because you do not want to hurt your friend's feelings, you need to perform the version of yourself that is absolutely delighted with the gift. You will do this through what you say and perhaps through your body language. When your friend leaves the party, you feel as though you no longer need to keep up this performance and, as a result, you are frank about your dislike for the gift.

Goffman would consider the gift-giving performance to be a front stage performance, while he would consider you to be backstage when you are discussing the gift behind your friend's back after their departure.

Goffman himself describes this in *The Presentation of Self in Everyday Life* through the example of staff serving customers in a hotel restaurant. In this example, he describes how these workers perform courteously while serving customers fine food. Goffman explains that workers perform in this way so that customers believe they are in an exceptional setting and are having an authentic hotel experience. But behind closed doors in the restaurant kitchen, these same workers may misbehave, mock customers or eat local food rather than that served to diners. Can you identify the performances going on and what might be considered to be front stage or backstage in this scenario?

2.2   Receiving the performances of others

The presentation of self isn't only about how we present ourselves to others in social situations. It is also about how others perceive our performances at any given time. As Goffman writes:

> When an individual enters the presence of others, they commonly seek to acquire information about him or to bring into play information about him already possessed. They will be interested in his general socio-economic status, his conception of self, his attitude towards them, his competence, his trustworthiness, etc. Although some of this information seems to be sought almost as an end in itself, there are usually quite practical reasons for acquiring it. Information about the individual helps to define the situation, enabling others to know in advance what he will expect of them and what they may expect of him. Informed in these ways, the others will know how best to act in order to call forth a desired response from him.
>
> (Goffman, 1959, p. 13)

In this extract, Goffman explains the general concept or phenomenon that he is describing. If we had to simplify this using one phrase, we could call this 'first impressions'. Goffman is interested in knowing how we show and tell others about our standing in society. He describes this interaction as a two-way street: the people we meet want to know how they should 'read' us or respond to us and we want to portray a version of ourselves that best fits the situation at hand. However, this two-way street is based on our ability to take these first impressions at face value. As Goffman explains:

> [T]he 'true' or 'real' attitudes, beliefs, and emotions of the individual can be ascertained only indirectly, through his avowals or through what appears to be involuntary expressive behavior. Similarly, if the individual offers the others a product or service, they will often find that during the interaction there will be no time and place immediately available for eating the pudding that the proof can be found in.
>
> (Goffman, 1959, pp. 13–14)

What Goffman is saying here is that we need to pay attention to how people present themselves and the settings that shape these presentations. Consider how you might interact with someone who is working at a supermarket, in comparison to how you might interact with them if you met them in a context outside of their workplace.

But what exactly does Goffman describe as the presentation of self in everyday life? And how has it become so relevant to social scientists? In the rest of the chapter, you will read more about how social scientists and other scholars apply Goffman's work to life in the 21st century.

2.3 Goffman and understanding digital societies

If you attempt to apply Goffman's theory to digital social interactions, you should begin to have some questions. How do concepts such as front stage and backstage look online? Where could we locate these two stages within digital life?

Consider your own interactions in digital settings. Is there a front stage version of yourself that you display on social media? You might have very strong ideas about who your audience is or should be, so much so that you may be surprised or disconcerted when someone you didn't expect likes or comments on a post. And then consider online celebrities and influencers – those who make a career from presenting their everyday life across a range of digital platforms. What do you think their impressions of what front stage and backstage might be?

These questions are worth asking and it is why many sociologists are returning to Goffman's work after 60 years to understand and perhaps challenge commonly held beliefs about how we relate to one another online. Sociology, like any other academic discipline, has certain ideas that fall in and out of fashion over time.

When we are looking at theories that were written in a pre-digital age we need to consider whether the ideas match up to what we observe and experience today. With that in mind, read the work of pre-digital era theorists such as Goffman, Mills and Bourdieu with an open, yet critical mind. If some of their mid-20th century writing does not make sense to the social situations you observe today, then it is an opportunity to question it and suggest other theories that might apply better. Social scientists call this a gap in knowledge, and it is generally a good indication that there is a phenomenon worth investigating through further research.

2.4 Contradictions of the presentation of self in everyday life

When reading about the presentation of self you may have started to wonder what happens when two performances collide and how actors manage those situations on the front stage. As an example, what if you were walking down the street with a work colleague and you bumped into a friend from secondary school? Depending on the kind of work you did, your colleague might have certain expectations of how you might act or express yourself. Similarly, your friend knows you very well and might inadvertently say or do something that undermines your respectability in front of your colleague. How would you manage the performance of your 'professional self' while managing the performance of your 'childhood self'?

Goffman calls this practice of acting in different ways in different situations, 'audience segregation'. He writes:

[B]y audience segregation the individual ensures that those before whom he plays one of his parts will not be the same individuals before whom he plays a different part in another setting.

(Goffman, 1959, p. 57)

If Goffman were around today to see how we interact with one another in digital settings, he may very well have written a whole new book to expand his thoughts on audience segregation. On social media, contexts can clash easily; perhaps you have encountered situations where your friends or followers from vastly different social contexts disagreed over something you have shared? Or imagine if a friend of yours tags you in a photo where you are shown to be doing something an older family member who follows you might disapprove of. Quite often these situations can be quite humorous, but in other circumstances they can be socially awkward or disagreements can spill over into face-to-face settings. How then can we present ourselves online while navigating the many and varied audiences we might encounter?

Figure 2.1 A band performing for their fans

Communication and media studies academic Nancy Baym discusses this problem of navigating multiple online audiences in her work about musicians and their relationship with fans. Specifically, she details the difficulties famous musicians face when negotiating their various audiences on social media platforms:

> Audiences on social media include some of the people who show up at concerts, but also many others. A social media account may reach fans, friends, family, peers, other music professionals, people who don't know the artist or like the music but like the tweets, as well as people who hate the music or artist and take pleasure in being mean to them online. These platforms thus complicate the notion that musicians have a singular audience and raises questions about what counts as an "audience" in the first place. ...
>
> Goffman describes conversationalists as sorting one another into different categories of listeners through their microactions, creating "participation frameworks" that orient participants toward one another and toward what is being said [Goffman (1981) cited in original]. Some listeners—like those at a live concert or facing you at the merchandise table, are "ratified," meant to hear the message. "Addressed" recipients are ratified listeners who have the right, and may be expected, to respond. Bystanders, like venue staff and other people waiting in the merchandise line, are ratified. Speakers know they are there, but it is socially inappropriate for them to reply to what's said. On social media, anyone following an account is ratified, although specific recipients can be addressed by name, making the others into bystanders. Nonratified recipients—those who listen while pretending they don't—are what Goffman calls eavesdroppers.

(Baym, 2018, pp. 158–159)

In the excerpt above, Baym describes three types of audience that may need to be negotiated in social situations: addressed recipients, bystanders and eavesdroppers. Reflect on a social situation you may have encountered recently where you have had to navigate your interactions with multiple audiences at the same time. This could be on social media or in another social setting. Try to identify who is an addressed recipient, who is a bystander and who is an eavesdropper. From there, consider the attributes each of these people has that have made you place them into those audiences. Or alternatively, you might want to jot down some examples where you're felt like an addressed participant, a bystander or, an eavesdropper. Try to think about why you might have felt that way in each of those situations and make a note of it.

3 Bourdieu and capital

While Goffman's work on presentation of self in everyday life is helpful in grappling with how people interact with others, it tends not to address what we present to one another and what we think people will make of us. To help us think through those questions, we will look at the work of French sociologist Pierre Bourdieu and his ideas around capital.

Who was Pierre Bourdieu?

Pierre Bourdieu (1930–2002) was a French social scientist. He was interested in the power dynamics at play in society and culture.

Bourdieu's work focuses on class and taste, in particular, what people demonstrate to one another to show they belong to a certain class group. He calls this 'capital'. According to Bourdieu, capital demonstrates our values in and to society in ways that go beyond our bank balance (or economic capital).

In addition to economic capital, Bourdieu describes other forms in play such as:

- social capital – who you know
- cultural capital – what you know and understand

- technical capital – the skills you have.

Bourdieu considered the role of the sociologist in public and political life to be of utmost importance, at one point describing sociology as a martial art.

His seminal work, *Distinction* (1984), which looks at the symbolic ways that people distinguish themselves from others, was listed as one of the top ten most influential pieces of sociological writing in the 20th century.

3.1 Observing values and capital

Where might you observe examples of these values or capital in your everyday encounters? You could identify examples of economic capital on the street: is someone conspicuously driving an expensive car, or wearing expensive-looking clothing or jewellery? Despite whether the jewellery is genuine or not, these people are displaying their economic capital, whether genuine or desired. Or perhaps someone demonstrates their cultural capital by attending art galleries, or travelling to places off the beaten track. Someone who is regularly seen with a large group of friends could be said to be demonstrating social capital.

Another way of looking at capital is through education: what do children need to have in order to do well at school? Families need the 'economic capital' to purchase the necessary books, stationery and technology for their children to be able to fully participate in classroom activities. But then consider 'cultural capital'; it would be considered beneficial to a child's education to have been to museums or experienced music or theatre productions. These cultural experiences would mean that child would have prior knowledge of historical events before encountering them in the classroom. However, in some areas, access to cultural capital requires economic capital to afford tickets and entrance fees (at the time of writing, entry to a special art exhibition costs approximately £18 for an adult ticket).

And then let's think about 'social capital'. If a student's family knows the head teacher outside of the context of the school, they are likely to have a better understanding of how the school works and how to make the most of the opportunities, exams and tests that happen there. When a student completes their education, they are awarded a qualification. Bourdieu calls this 'symbolic capital', as it symbolises the skills and achievements that a person has. However, it's important to note that in many cases symbolic capital is the culmination of having enough economic, cultural and social capital to be able to attain that symbolic capital.

When considering capital through this example it becomes evident that those with less economic capital are put at a disadvantage in gaining symbolic capital from a very early stage. Having less economic or social capital to access quality education impacts a student's ability to gain the symbolic capital to access educational opportunities in elite institutions such as Oxbridge or Ivy League universities. In recent years, there has been a rise in families paying for after-school tuition in the hopes of advancing their child's opportunities in education and beyond:

Reading 2.1

Sally Weale, '"An education arms race": inside the ultra-competitive world of private tutoring'

Geoff Clayton, a retired garage worker, has been bringing his 10-year-old grandson, Brooklyn, to Explore Learning for about nine months. Brooklyn lives with his grandparents and likes football, Minecraft and maths. "He's done really well," says Clayton. "His reading has got a lot better, everything's got better." The membership takes a significant chunk out of his pension, but he is happy to pay it to give Brooklyn "a bit of a leg up".

"Nowadays, it's all about exams and certificates and what you know," he says. "When I left school, it was more: 'Can you do the job?' Brooklyn has done a heck of a lot better since coming here. Sometimes he moans, but he's OK once he's here. It does work if you're prepared to put the time and effort in."

The Sutton Trust, a charity that seeks to improve social mobility through education, has documented a huge rise in private tuition in recent years. Its annual survey of secondary students in England and Wales revealed in July that 27% have had home or private tuition, a figure that rises to 41% in London.

With tutoring commanding a fee of about £24 an hour, rising to £27 in London (although many tutors charge £60 or more), the trust is concerned that the private tuition market is putting children from poorer backgrounds at even greater disadvantage. ...

"We are in an education arms race," says Peter Lampl, the founder of the trust. "Parents are looking to get an edge for their kids and having private tuition gives them that edge. But if we are serious about social mobility, we need to make sure that the academic playing field is levelled outside the school gate."

...

Nevertheless, huge inequities in education persist. Nowhere is this more evident than in children's battle to pass the 11-plus to get into grammar school. Research published earlier this year revealed that private tutoring means pupils from high-income families are much more likely to get into grammar schools than equally bright pupils from poorer families. John Jerrim and Sam Sims from the Institute of Education at University College London looked at more than 1,800 children in areas where the grammar school system is in operation. They found that those from families in the bottom quarter of household incomes in England have less than a 10% chance of attending a grammar school, compared with a 40% chance for children in the top quarter.

(Weale, 2018)

In the newspaper excerpt above, we can see that although parents and carers spend a lot of economic capital on after-school tutoring to try to give their child an educational advantage, it is often not enough to get them as much of a social advantage as they hoped. In order to understand this more, we need to take a closer look at Bourdieu's ideas around cultural capital.

3.2 Class, capital and generational divides

In many countries, economic capital is best gauged by property ownership. If you have a mortgage or own your own home, this asset is considered to be a key indicator of your economic capital. Sociologists throughout the decades have been concerned with studying class: how it is measured, what indicates membership to a certain class group. The way sociologists have measured class over time has differed across cultural contexts, economic climates and the theoretical influences of researchers. Mike Savage and his colleagues conducted the Great British Class Survey in the early 2010s as one way of measuring class in early 21st-century Britain. They chose to include home ownership, savings (including pensions and money in savings accounts) and household income as the key indicators of having acquired economic capital – and therefore belonging to a higher class. But to place someone into a class solely based on their economic capital would be questionable. Unless you have inherited wealth, economic capital is something that you accumulate over a long period of time. This is why age is linked to increased economic capital.

However, it is increasingly difficult to gather economic capital. In the UK, the combination of wage stagnation along with an increase in buy-to-let property purchases has caused an affordable housing shortage, especially in London and the South East. This problem, however, is not unique to the UK, with other major cities in the US, Canada and Australia facing similar problems, albeit due to a range of factors such as foreign investment, short-term lets such as Airbnb and influxes of wealthy employees from technology companies such as Facebook, Google and Amazon.

What are some of the problems that you can identify with housing being inextricably linked to economic capital?

3.3 Unpacking cultural capital

Bourdieu wrote a brief introduction to the forms of capital in 1986 and he makes cultural capital his starting point. He describes three forms of cultural capital:

- embodied state

- objectified state

- institutionalised state.

The 'embodied state' of cultural capital is knowledge, ideas and practices that you gather over time until they become what Bourdieu describes as 'long-lasting dispositions of the mind'. You could consider it as being similar to becoming fluent in another language; it takes time to learn the basic words and phrases until you are able to one day hold a conversation with someone in that language. But crucially, nobody can acquire an embodied state of cultural capital on your behalf and hand it over to you in an instant; it takes time and involvement on your behalf. Bourdieu likens an embodied state of cultural capital to gaining a muscular physique or getting a suntan; you have to do the work yourself, no one can do that for you.

In comparison, the 'objectified state' of cultural capital can be gained through purchasing books, paintings or perhaps even a musical instrument. However, you need a certain amount of economic capital to take part in the objectified state, and also the knowledge that comes with an embodied state of cultural capital to be informed about the objects you end up purchasing. At this stage it can seem as though cultural capital is a chicken and egg scenario on a societal scale, you cannot achieve one state of cultural capital without the other.

Bourdieu also writes that the embodied state of cultural capital is gained through 'the best hidden and socially most detrimental' method, by domestic transmission. Put simply, Bourdieu observes that people gain – or miss out on – an embodied state of cultural capital due to their home environment and upbringing.

Bourdieu also describes the 'institutionalised state', which is a formal certification of your cultural capital. A university degree or a professional accreditation is an example of the institutionalised state of cultural capital. These hold power, because they are objects that symbolise to others your ability to think and respond in certain ways based on the embodied state that you have gained over the course of your studies or work experience. This can often be translated into opportunities to gain economic capital through work. As you read in the previous excerpt, the institutionalised state of cultural capital is considered so vital to social mobility that lower-income families are willing to spend as much money as necessary to help their children attain it to the highest standard.

Take a moment to consider your own relation to cultural capital, thinking about each of the states at play. How has your embodied state of cultural capital been developed throughout your life? How has this been demonstrated through objectified or institutionalised states of capital? Compare this to someone who may come from a low-income background or someone who comes from long-standing wealth.

By unpacking Bourdieu's work a bit further, we have seen his suggestion that economic capital and cultural capital are linked. However, we see a slightly different story when compared to Mike Savage's work from the Great British Class Survey. Savage and his team suggest that in the 21st century, cultural capital is no longer restricted to highbrow pursuits such as going to the theatre, listening to classical music or attending art exhibitions featuring famous artists. To be sure, these are still markers of a certain type of cultural capital, but Savage and his team suggest that there is a form of emerging cultural capital that is linked less to the high arts. Mike Savage explains:

Reading 2.2

Mike Savage, *Social class in the 21st century*

To put this in another way, culture becomes a wider social currency in which people differentiate between those with it, and those without it – and who could do with more of it. Rather like money …

Yet, though it seems clear that cultural tastes carry with them a loaded set of signifiers, we also need to be cautious about relying on Bourdieu's concept too closely today. This is for four reasons. Firstly, Bourdieu's criticisms of 'elitist' culture hit home, to the extent that it has generated worries among those working in the arts themselves in relation to their role as cultural policy-makers. Cultural institutions have themselves become much more aware of their own elitism and snobbery and have taken steps to counteract these things. Museums and galleries are now full of interactive devices to facilitate more accessible forms of visitor engagement and to encourage children to enjoy museums even if they are not used to them. Entry to the major national museums is free. There is more effort to show off a wider diversity of cultural works, rather than just those of the 'great old men'. There are now, for instance, museums of football, sex and rock music. The National Trust does not only look after grand aristocratic homes, but also displays Glasgow tenement houses, the family homes of John Lennon and Paul McCartney and old industrial factories.

Secondly, we now live in a much more intensely 'cultural' world. When Bourdieu conducted his surveys for *Distinction* only half of French households had television sets, and certainly no computers, smartphones or iPads. Just as we have seen the absolute increase in economic capital, so the sheer volume and availability of art, literature, music, film and television has risen sharply. Perhaps the proliferation of media devices over the past four decades has made all cultural forms more accessible? Do we still live in an age of such marked cultural divisions compared to the era when you could only hear opera by actually going to an opera house? Is it still elitist to like opera when people can now freely download opera music on Spotify even if they can't afford to go to Covent Garden?

Thirdly, we have also seen the rise of a whole series of cultural activities which don't seem 'highbrow'. A good example would be stand-up comedy, which has moved from being a marginal and largely disparaged taste, to being a mainstream of entertainment, via the Edinburgh Festival or primetime TV. Aren't there key style icons who have little or no cultural capital in the way that Bourdieu talks about it? What about David Beckham, the upwardly mobile lad from Essex, who has defined new standards of masculine style over the past twenty years, but hardly on the basis of highbrow cultural capital?

Fourthly, in recent decades cultural appreciation has been massively transformed by globalization and flows of immigration which have eroded the appeal and significance of older classical forms of culture which used to be held up as the markers of national excellence. We are no longer so much in thrall to specifically national beacons defining the boundaries of legitimate taste, ranging from the Royal Opera House to the National Theatre. It has become 'cool' – up to a point – to be interested in black culture. Where, if at all, do world music, jazz, bhangra and reggae fit in the hierarchies of today? Isn't it rather old fashioned to just be interested in Shakespeare, Austen and Britten these days?

(Savage, 2015, pp. 100–102; notes omitted.)

From this reading, Savage shows that cultural capital is not as easy to define in the 21st century as it was when Bourdieu was discussing it in the 20th century. Those in charge of cultural institutions have recognised their own bias towards more highbrow expression of culture and have sought to fix that. Savage also suggests that the introduction of digital technologies has allowed many cultural expressions to be distributed much more easily – people are able to access more music, films and books than ever before. And yet despite all of this, there are people with the 'cultural capital' to determine what counts as culture.

3.4 Social capital

In its most basic terms, Bourdieu describes social capital as membership of a group, which then entitles its members to credit in society. But what Bourdieu also reiterates is that it is not only being part of a group that matters, but the network of connections within that group matters too. To expand the well-known cliché; it isn't just what you know but who you know and who they know that will increase your capital.

Because groups are solidified by occasions, places or practices, social capital is never independent of economic or cultural capital. Even in informal friendship groups, your social capital rests on whether you can afford to participate in activities or provide something of interest to other group members.

Finally, each member is a custodian of the limits of membership within a group in that they decide who has the necessary capital to join a social group and benefit from its capital.

A common example of this can be seen with exclusive membership organisations such as the Freemasons, or fraternities or sororities in North American universities. New members are often invited by existing members and once a part of the organisation, they gain social capital. In organisations such as the Freemasons, members may use their social capital to benefit from increased economic capital based on professional connections and advantages gained through their membership.

A similar example of social capital can be seen in politics. In the television drama series, *The Crown*, there is a scene set in the 1950s where the then British Prime Minister Anthony Eden gives a lecture at his alma mater, the prestigious boys' school, Eton. When addressing the audience of students he says:

> Now there's has been a lot of talk recently about how much the world has changed since the war and how much society in Britain has changed. Or how much it jolly well ought to change. And that

places like Eton should no longer be seen as the birthplace of Britain's leaders. To which I, as a fully paid up egalitarian and progressive member of the Conservative Party say what an absolute lot of nonsense. If Britain's leaders aren't coming from Eton, then where should they be coming from? You see before you the 16th Etonian Prime Minister. Sixteen … out of 40. Not a bad percentage. Harrow, incidentally, only accounts for seven. Yes, you might well argue that as a social pool, it is a bit narrow. But narrowness at the top is not necessarily a bad thing. For as any serviceman will tell you, in battle, when the heat is on, one needs a shorthand, a shared language and understanding. A clarity. Eton has for many years provided Britain with that clarity. That code. That shared language.

('Misadventure', 2017)

Although this is a fictional depiction of historical events, we are able to examine social and cultural capital at play. In his speech, Prime Minister Eden describes the social capital needed (in his view) to lead a nation as connections to an elite boys' school such as Eton or Harrow. But he also tries to justify this by saying that this type of education provides a cultural capital or "a shared language" that is compatible with leading the country. He asserts that this form of cultural capital is not readily available to the general public. Nowadays, politics has opened up to people from a broader range of backgrounds and expertise. The fact that Britain has since had two female prime ministers seems to suggest that an exclusive boys' school background is not necessarily a prerequisite for the role. But there is still a long way to go, with inequalities in positions of leadership still having close ties to inequalities in social and economic capital. In later chapters, we will return to this theme, paying specific attention to how some technologies create inequalities in social and economic capital.

4 Capital and internet celebrity

Now let's frame Bourdieu's ideas of capital and transpose them onto social media. This will be done with the help of Crystal Abidin's work *Internet Celebrity: Understanding Fame Online* (2018). In her research, Abidin updates Bourdieu's four types of capital and describes them as values. Abidin asserts that these values – exclusivity, exoticism, exceptionalism and everydayness – contain some of the reasons why we find internet celebrities so compelling. However, Abidin is quick to remind us that these values 'arouse interest and attention, whether positive (i.e., out of admiration or love) or negative (i.e., out of disgust or judgement)' (2018, p. 19). Let's look at these values in more detail.

1   Exclusivity (economic capital)

    Internet celebrities displaying exclusivity tend be those who show their wealth or material possessions that are usually out of reach for others.

2   Exoticism (cultural capital)

    This value deals with people who demonstrate practices using objects that are foreign or novel to the person watching.

3   Exceptionalism (technical capital)

    We often see this value demonstrated by people who possess a particular skill or knowledge. Some sociologists argue that outside of a social media setting, this might form part of cultural capital. Nevertheless, it is helpful to think of it as distinct from exoticism (cultural capital) when examining what people present of themselves online.

4   Everydayness (social capital)

    People who have this value are often described as relatable, ordinary or mundane. They usually have a reputation for consistently posting about their everyday experiences and gaining trust from their audience.

Figure 2.2 Food and travel bloggers often demonstrate their cultural and social capital by posting pictures online or on social media

4.1 Internet celebrity and inequalities

How might we connect the dots between the presentation of self and capital? Let's take a look at online influencers – people who have many followers on social media platforms. Influencers make a living from sponsored posts and online content. But in order to attract the attention of the companies, sponsors and management agencies that make up the influencer industry, aspiring influencers need to gather an audience. Once an influencer can demonstrate that they have a large enough audience of followers, subscribers or views, they will be approached by companies to mention a product in their videos in return for payment. Looking at this through Bourdieu's eyes, aspiring influencers need to demonstrate that they have enough social capital to warrant a sponsorship deal. They might gather this social capitalism by demonstrating what Abidin describes as exceptionalism, exoticism or exclusivity in their videos or posts.

But how would Goffman view influencers and their relationship with their audience? By gaining sponsorships, influencers gather and demonstrate economic capital in ways that they may not otherwise have been able to afford. Once an influencer gains sponsorship, the stage differs. Because sponsors pay influencers to use or talk about the product in pre-scripted ways, they are presenting an advertisement to their audience. In response, the audience begins to perceive their videos more as front-stage advertisements, rather than backstage confessional and frank videos.

5 Conclusion

This chapter has familiarised you with the concept of the presentation of self in everyday life. While the original text deals with observing and analysing face-to-face interactions, it is also useful to keep in mind when observing interactions happening on social media. Not all social interactions – or 'performances' – are equal, nor are the levels of access that audience have to performances. The extract from Nancy Baym's work with musicians on social media platforms highlights the challenges that can arise when we need to manage the expectations of different audiences at the same time.

In this chapter, you have also read an introduction to the concept of capital and how people accumulate or display various forms of capital online. What is important to note about capital is that it is not distributed equally, whether that be our social capital online or the economic capital we may or may not have in our bank balance. Using Crystal Abidin's example, we saw how online influencers display various forms of capital.

In the next chapters of this book, we will be examining technology and its uses in relation to cities and migration. You will be introduced to some new sociological ideas around migration, diaspora and transnational theories. But do keep in mind the ideas discussed in these first two chapters as you progress through the book.

References

Abidin, C. (2018) *Internet celebrity: understanding fame online*. Bingley: Emerald Publishing Limited.

Baym, N.K. (2018) *Playing to the crowd: musicians, audiences, and the intimate work of connection*. New York: NYU Press.

Bourdieu, P. (1984) *Distinction: a social critique of the judgement of taste*. Cambridge, MA: Harvard University Press.

Bourdieu, P. (2011) 'The forms of capital', in Szeman, I. and Kaposy, T. (eds) *Cultural theory: an anthology*. Chichester: Wiley-Blackwell, pp. 81–93.

Goffman, E. (1959) *The presentation of self in everyday life*. New York, NY: Anchor Books.

Goffman, E. (1991) *Asylums: essays on the social situation of mental patients and other inmates*. Harmondsworth: Penguin.

'Misadventure' (2017) *The Crown*, Season 2, episode 1. Netflix. Available at: https://www.netflix.com/watch/80149005 (Accessed: 16 August 2019).

Savage, M. (2015) *Social class in the 21st century*. London: Pelican.

Weale, S. (2018) '"An education arms race": inside the ultra-competitive world of private tutoring', *The Guardian*, 5 December. Available at: https://www.theguardian.com/education/2018/dec/05/an-education-arms-race-inside-the-ultra-competitive-world-of-private-tutoring (Accessed: 4 December 2019).

Section 2

Society, technology, citizens and cities

Introduction to Section 2

Umut Erel, Liz McFall and Sophie Watson

Welcome to Section 2. In this section you will explore how we live together as citizens, and in particular how digital technologies interrelate with people's sense of belonging and the ways in which they participate in society. This will be guided by the question, 'How do the social and the technical shape each other?'. You will look at how living together as citizens is affected by changes in technology in three different sites: cities, migration and transnational networks of families and religion.

Citizenship has been interpreted in different ways. T. H. Marshall (1958) pointed out that full membership of the community is what defines citizenship. As sociologists, we are particularly interested in two aspects of citizenship: participation and belonging. We will particularly look at how participation and belonging shape and are shaped by the digital. For example, we will look at how people use information technologies in order to engage in society.

Citizenship and cities

In Chapter 3, we will use the very different examples of Milton Keynes and Edinburgh to explore how technologies are used to plan for 'smart' futures and those of their citizens. At the heart of such plans are ideas and predictions about how people will live, work and travel in the city. This includes modelling what sorts of people their future citizens will be. How will age, ethnicity, nationality, spoken languages, disabilities, gender, skills, income level, family size etc. be distributed across the population? This chapter asks what difference digital technologies make to how people take part in the life of the city.

There are many different ways in which these issues could be approached. But as sociologists we will look in particular at the ways in which *individuals and society* interrelate, how *power and inequality* shape our living together, and how *people and things* relate to each other. Guiding these explorations will be the question of how the social and the technical shape one another in the planning and imagining of a city. We will also look at how technical developments have shaped the ways in which different citizens have been included or excluded from city life.

Figure 1   Self-driving pod car in Milton Keynes.

Migration

Migration is considered to be a phenomenon which affects us all. Whether we have ourselves moved to another place within the same country or transnationally, we are all affected by the mobility of people, goods and services. This mobility has changed the way we eat, what movies we watch and who our neighbours, school friends and work colleagues are. That is why in Chapters 4 and 5 you will look at a range of sites in which migration and the digital intersect.

In doing this, you will explore how different theories of **diaspora**, **transnationalism** and digital migration can help us to better understand the relationships between *individuals and society*, *power and inequality*, *people and things* in these different sites of citizenship.

Chapter 4 introduces you to different concepts and theories for understanding migration. Theories of transnationalism help us understand the movement of people as affecting both the *societies* from which *individuals* migrate, as well as the *societies* to which they move. The concept of diaspora highlights that people who have origins in one place but live in another may have many different reasons for migrating. While many continue to uphold a sense of belonging to their shared homeland, the concept of diaspora also draws attention to how the cultural identities of different ethnic groups mix and develop into new forms beyond the idea of essential ethnic differences. Diasporas and transnational migration have always been closely bound up with technical developments enabling people, things, ideas and cultural products to move in a two-way process which shapes both technology and society.

Chapter 4 looks specifically at how refugees make use of digital technologies for their journeys, exploring the relationship between *people* and *things* through the example of refugees' use of smartphones. It also looks at *power* and *inequality* in terms of the way people can choose or may be forced to migrate. Chapter 4 asks how these social processes are shaped by the opportunities and limitations technical developments offer and vice versa. How do digital technologies help to create and secure borders on the one hand, while also contributing to the ability of refugees to cross these borders?

Figure 2 Migration is a contested aspect of citizenship.

In Chapter 5 we explore the relationship between technology and society by looking at the examples of transnational social networks of families and religion. The chapter looks at how family members living in different countries create and maintain a sense of belonging together as a family. Migrant workers face the challenge of reconciling their participation in the societies in which they live because of their work, with participating in the lives of their families and communities back home. *Individuals* participate in both the *societies* they come from and those they currently live in by communicating, sending back parcels and money, and also travelling back for holidays. How do digital technologies make a difference in the ways these migrant workers conduct their work and family lives? For example, many people use webcams to be (virtually) part of family occasions in real time. Yet, *power and inequalities* make a difference to how families can use digital technologies for staying in touch. Consider the family members of migrants who are affected by unequal access to technology, both globally and regionally: think of family members living in regions with poor digital infrastructure, where accessing the internet is not always possible.

The example of religious networks shows that religion has long been mobile, for example, Christianity as a 'world religion' has historically been characterised by global interconnections, becoming increasingly driven by international missions and imperial expansion in the 19th century. This demonstrates wider global *inequalities* of *power*, with European religious authority, alongside political and social influence, dominating other parts of the world. Yet, as these global power relations between countries changed through decolonisation, in the mid 20th century in particular, Pentecostal Christianity is an example of how migration has influenced the development of new ways of belonging and participating in transnational religion. You will look at the example of how new migrants from Brazil or Nigeria to the United Kingdom bring with them practices of Christianity. Their churches work transnationally, with the country of origin still playing a central role. Technology – satellite TV, mobile phones, internet, social media – therefore plays a vital 'everyday' role in the religious lives of many migrants. The digital is contributing to forming religious identities and communities. *Things* such as mobile phones and computers connect *people* in the countries they come from and their new countries. These technologies and the strong communities of faith that migrants form in the UK, also contribute to shift the centre of religious authority and power from Europe to countries such as Nigeria or Brazil.

Throughout this section we will be asking how the social and the technical shape each other in terms of how we practice citizenship. Does the technical reinforce relations between *individuals and society*, *people and things* and *power* relations and *inequalities* that have existed for a long time or does it challenge and change these? Perhaps the technical can make a difference in reinforcing some social relationships, while challenging others?

Identity, technology and the sociological imagination

Who are you? You have probably played a few games that try to answer this question. There are plenty of personality quizzes around, some serious and some playful, that respond to the fascination with understanding and describing ourselves and others. Throughout this section, you will use what C. Wright Mills called a 'sociological imagination' to explore identity.

Figure 3 Digital technologies are part of our personal lives, but they also link us to society, for example allowing companies to gain insights into our habits.

Writing in the 1950s, Mills wanted to explain why private lives were often experienced as a 'series of traps' full of problems that individuals struggled to escape from. People often understand these struggles as their own responsibility or in Mills's words as 'private troubles'. They are much less likely to understand their troubles 'sociologically'; as connected to, and part of, much broader 'public issues.' (Mills, 2000, p. 8). People tend not to see the connections between their lives and historical or political events; or how this shapes the kind of futures they might have. The job of sociology is to expose these connections. Human individuals are never wild things, they never live outside of the social world. A sociological imagination means discovering how this social world shapes individual lives.

References

Marshall, T.H. (1958) *Citizenship and social class and other essays*. Cambridge: University of Cambridge Press.

Mills, C.W. (2000) *The sociological imagination*. New York, NY: Oxford University Press.

Chapter 3

Planning the cities of the future

Liz McFall and Darren Umney

Contents

1   Introduction

This chapter considers how two cities, Edinburgh and Milton Keynes, understand and plan for their digital futures and those of their citizens. The cities are very different and they face distinct challenges. Milton Keynes is known as a post-war new town, the home of The Open University, many roundabouts and some concrete cows. Edinburgh is a capital city, famous for its heritage, its castle, and its festivals. It is also known for a unique smell composed of hops mixed with leaves and greenery coming from Princes Street Gardens mingled with the tidal River Forth, stone buildings, traffic and shifting with the prevailing south-westerly winds. Nonetheless, Edinburgh and Milton Keynes share the ambitions of many cities internationally to be marked out as future-facing and technologically 'smart'. They have both published visions for 2050 and made strategic investments in material infrastructure, embracing the role digital technologies will play in making the cities, communities and societies of the future. At the heart of such plans are ideas, predictions and projections about how people will live, work, travel, and spend time and money in the city. This includes modelling what sorts of people their future citizens will be. How will age, ethnicity, nationality, spoken languages, disabilities, gender, skills, income level, family size etc. be distributed across the population?

Planning city futures means thinking about how to incorporate and take advantage of new technologies. High speed broadband, autonomous vehicles, contactless payment, real-time public transport apps and street sensors might come to mind as technologies for the 'smart cities' of 2020. But what about the cities of 2050? What kinds of futures and what kinds of technologies will they need to plan for? Demographers and climate scientists can point to general trends in population numbers and the catastrophic consequences of failure to take action to address the climate emergency, but the specific new technologies that will be adopted are notoriously difficult to predict. There are plenty of inventions – see roof-shoes below – that never make it into production and technologies like flying cars that are long imagined but have not come to be. The path to adoption is more crooked than straight.

Edinburgh, for example, abandoned its tram network in 1956. Fifty years later, in a bid to reduce carbon emissions and provide a more sustainable transport network, the Scottish Parliament voted to recover it. Electric cars and buses did not become common until after 2008 but the first versions were actually produced 150 years ago. The first planners of Milton Keynes imagined a city of cars free-flowing through roundabouts. They also carefully planned and built a leafy network, the redways, exclusively for pedestrians and cyclists. The redways were designed to weave up, around and under the road network. This means they have certain features – sharp slopes ending abruptly on blind right-angled corners are a particular favourite among cyclists – that have limited their appeal.

Figure 3.1 1970 *Tomorrow's World* prediction: roof-shoes.

The best laid plans fail for many reasons. One major one is that what people will do, even in the immediate future, is notoriously hard to predict. City planning is prediction on a vast scale. It concerns the relationship between people and technologies and, more fundamentally, the relationship between people and objects, including those not generally defined as technologies. Pavements and roads, street lighting and public toilets, traffic lights and road signs, trees and parklands, pigeons and foxes, disused buildings and notable landmarks, are among the many city objects that planners have to think about.

Planning requires a huge range of skills and people. There are national and local government officials, architects, financiers, industry leaders, builders and lawyers but there are also artists, landscape gardeners, environmentalists, designers, demographers, data scientists, geographers, programmers, historians, sociologists and of course the people who live there. This chapter explores how the interactions between these people, the technologies they use, and a diverse array of other, sometimes unexpected, objects make the city.

RyanMcGovernePhoto @RyanMcGoverne · 15 Jul 2019
Another pic. Hopefully this should shame @forthports and @Edinburgh_CC into clean up action. (Pic credit Jim Jarvie on I Love Leith FB)

♡ 3   ↺ 3   ♡ 2

Show this thread

Figure 3.2 A complaint tweeted to Edinburgh City Council showing storm damage in the Water of Leith.

1.1   Teaching aims

The aims of this chapter are for you to:

- be able to define and explain what 'digital' and 'technology' mean in the context of the city

- explore how the technologies used in the city shape society – and how society shapes the technologies

- be introduced to the concepts of digital divide and digital inequalities

- use the cases of two very different UK cities to explore how history, place and technology interact in planning city futures.

2   Digital technologies and the city

'For, taking the ten horns o' the beast, ye may easily estimate by
your digitals'

(Scott, 2004)

Most of us think the word 'technologies' means new, future oriented
tools. A couple of decades ago the term Information and
Communications Technology, or ICT, was often used. More recently
the phrase 'digital technologies' started to dominate. Before going any
further it's worth thinking more closely about these words and phrases.
Where did they come from? What do we really mean when we use
them?

'Digital' is particularly opaque. The online 2019 *Oxford English
Dictionary* (OED) lists five main definitions for the noun digital and
eight main definitions, with six sub-definitions, for the verb digital.
Amongst these, 12 definitions are connected to digital technologies.
The remainder are about mathematics and fingers. 'Digitals' or more
commonly 'digits', once meant, quite simply, human fingers. This might
seem bizarre, but as the quote from Scott above, originally published
in 1822, implies there is an ancient link between fingers, counting and
mathematics – fingers across history and cultures are the first counting
tools. Fingers and computers then are both digital tools – albeit of
different species.

All forms of digital technology involve numbers, measurement,
counting and value. More precisely they depend upon 'signals,
information, or data: represented by a series of discrete values
(commonly the numbers 0 and 1), typically for electronic storage or
processing' (OED, 2010). In everyday language this technical definition
blurs and the digital often just describes a type of object. In the 1970s
some watches and clocks were called digital, in the early 2000s it was
cameras, scales and photo-frames. These are not the only objects built
around digital technologies. Strangely, while watches and cameras are
often labelled as digital, computers, tablets and mobile phones seldom
are. Similarly, digital is often used as an adjective to describe files
containing sound, video or audio. Computer software, on the other
hand, is almost never described as digital.

Figure 3.3 From mobile to smartphones, 2007.

The pace of recent technological change has meant names change fast. The convergence of telecommunication and computing that produced ICT in the early 1990s was soon overtaken by the internet. The internet was still ICT, but super accelerated – as one of its first names, the 'information superhighway', suggests. Music, games, photography and film were soon available on the internet. The smartphone followed and within a few years a vast range of connected devices – wearable fitness trackers, smart thermostats and smart speakers – became known as the internet of things (IoT) or sometimes the internet of everything (IoE).

The world, in other words, changed fundamentally after the release of the first iPhone in 2007. Social media, mobile technology, cloud-based storage and data analytics came together and with them, a new set of what C. Wright Mills described, writing in 1959, as the 'private troubles' and 'public issues' that sociologists confront (Mills, 2000). These changes are so profound that digital became a historical moment; not just a technology, but a type of world. Whether the focus is on cities, offices, schools or homes, a new social world has emerged – one where humans and machines, media and politics, cities and citizens, mix in new ways.

All this innovation, disruption and upheaval is mystifying for many people. Expensive machines and complex, technical expertise are needed just to take part. A gap has opened up between those who have access to the data, information and physical resources that characterise digital societies and those who do not. This gap has been described as a 'digital divide'. The Netherlands-based sociologist, Jan A.G.M. van Dijk, has conducted extensive research into the forms digital inequalities take. He concludes that the metaphor of a 'digital divide' is an oversimplification. Inequalities of access to digital technologies take many different forms and arise for many different reasons (van Dijk, 1999). Government and policymakers have responded to digital inequalities by trying to improve access to physical resources, notably, computers and network connections. Access to these resources is essential of course, but it does not, in and of itself, solve the problem. Meaningful access is not just about device and internet connections. It is about training, skills, the opportunities and confidence to put them to use. People have to see in the internet a way of solving the immediate problems they encounter in life. Would they be able, for instance, to pay local taxes, apply for jobs, find a school or a bus route on the internet? Would it be any easier to do things that way?

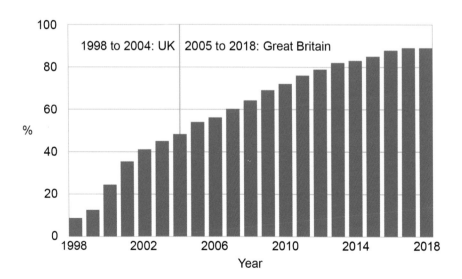

Figure 3.4 Internet access in the UK, 2018 (Office for National Statistics, 2018).

This is what van Dijk and Hacker call the problem of 'mental access'. By this they mean the absence of 'elementary digital experience caused by lack of interest, computer anxiety, and unattractiveness of the new technology' (2003, p. 315). This basic problem has been confirmed by numerous research studies since the term digital divide first appeared. How it affects people has changed with the increasing popularity of using mobile technologies, smartphones and tablets to access the internet. In 2018 almost 9/10 UK households (see Figure 3.4) had internet access but digital inequalities persist. The reasons for this are explored further in Reading 3.1. Van Deursen and van Dijk's argument is based on the distinction they draw between physical access and material access. Physical access means access to networked computers. Material access is just as important and a lot more complicated. In the simplest terms, those who own fewer devices have fewer opportunities to become adept at using them. Those who benefit most are 'males, majorities, and the employed, well-educated, and married people', while digital disadvantage disproportionately falls on those outside these groups.

Reading 3.1

Alexander J.A.M. van Deursen and Jan A.G.M. van Dijk, 'The first-level digital divide shifts from inequalities in physical access to inequalities in material access' [extracted]

A common opinion among policy-makers is that the digital divide problem is solved when a country's Internet connection rate reaches saturation. However, scholars ... have concluded that the divides in Internet skills and type of use continue to expand even after physical access is universal. ....

[A]ge, gender, majority status, employment, education level, and household composition, as well as material resources (income), social resources (quantity and quality of support), and Internet attitudes are all related to unequal ownership of devices and peripherals. Furthermore, there are systematic differences in the material access dimensions, as these are strongly associated with Internet attitude, income, support quantity, and support quality. Furthermore, males, majorities, and the employed, well-educated, and married people benefit most in terms of material access. In most cases, this is also true for younger people. However, we also found that younger people are more likely to only use a tablet or smartphone (while the overall percentage is low), confirming the existence of an age-related "mobile underclass" (Napoli and Obar, 2014) in the Netherlands. While mobile devices rapidly increase in functionality, they should not be considered equal to desktop and laptop computers. Both offer their own specific advantages, suggesting that using only mobile or nonmobile devices limits the potential range of Internet activities and outcomes. ...

The findings show that device opportunity is related to Internet skills and Internet-use frequency and diversity. Using a higher diversity of devices is related to a higher diversity of Internet use and more Internet outcomes. Furthermore, having more maintenance expenses contributes to Internet skills, and Internet-use frequency and diversity. ... By extending basic physical access combined with material access, the study finds that the opportunities these devices offer, diversity in the access to devices and peripherals, and ongoing expenses required to maintain the hardware, software, and subscriptions all relate to inequalities in Internet skills, uses, and outcomes.

Reference

Napoli PM and Obar JA (2014) The emerging mobile Internet underclass: a critique of mobile internet access. *The Information Society* 30(5): 323–334.

(van Deursen and van Dijk, 2019, pp. 369–371)

What all this points to is that taking part in cities, in communities, in countries, means having the opportunity to use a range of connected devices. Computers, phones, TVs and game consoles all connect to the internet but they don't do quite the same jobs. Objects have different **'affordances'**, that is they permit – or afford – different sorts of uses. Not all of these are intentional design features – anyone who has hung a cardigan on the back of a chair or stood on a chair to change a lightbulb, is using the object's affordances. Chairs may have been designed to be sat upon but they also work fairly well as coat-hangers and ladders.

Discovering affordances is also typical of how people relate to digital objects. Mobile payment is a wonderful example of this. The first large scale and best known example, M-Pesa, was established in Kenya. The M-Pesa scheme allowed people to transfer airtime to relatives and friends, as a proxy for money. The practice is now well-established but it began with people exploiting an affordance of two connected digital objects: the prepaid scratch-card and the mobile phone. Pre-paid cards were an innovation that transformed mobile phones from devices that had been accessible only to the affluent into objects that, at a cost of around a dollar a day, became accessible to many.

As van Deursen and van Dijk show in Reading 3.1, digital inequalities do not arise only because of poverty. There are other factors at play that act in some surprising ways. It is often assumed, for example, that a generational pattern separates those who grew up with the internet from those who did not. Generational cohorts are a way of describing how populations are made up and is known more formally as the study of demography. These cohorts are invoked in commonly used terms including 'baby boomer', 'Generation X' and 'millennial'. The youngest demographic cohort to have earned its own nickname is 'Generation Z'. Generation Zs, or Gen-Zs, are those born after the mid-1990s. This group are sometimes described as 'digital natives'. This is a description that implies a generation with digital skills at their fingertips – or maybe their thumbtips, since those born before 1990 are far less likely to be able to use a smartphone with two thumbs!

But terms like 'digital native' can disguise grave digital inequalities within younger demographics (Bayne and Ross, 2011). High penetrations of internet access and smartphone ownership among marginalised populations, including the young, homeless and refugees (Faith, 2016; Gillespie et al., 2016; Rhoades et al., 2017; Rice et al., 2011), does not protect these groups from digital disadvantage. This will also be dealt with in the next chapter of this book. In Reading 3.2, Rebecca Faith, who studied mobile phone use among marginalised young women in Brighton for her PhD research at The Open University, describes how these women depend on their phones but are – at the same time – disadvantaged by their dependence.

Reading 3.2

Rebecca Faith, *How does the use of mobile phones by 16-24 year old socially excluded women affect their capabilities?*

Do you have access to a computer at home?

I do not... BUT, Phone. It does everything.

Is there anything you can't do on it?

There's nothing I can't do on my phone.

Courtney [...] had a small baby and was homeless: 'sofa-surfing' at friends and relatives' houses. She was managing her day-to-day life, appointments and communications on her phone. This quote reflects her feelings about her mobile phone: that it was a multifunction device which she could use for a wide range of activities: to manage appointments, look up information she did not know and maintain vital social connections as she did not have a permanent place to live. ... mobile phones are now a dominant technology in the lives of young people in the UK and 80% of respondents in this study used a Smartphone.

This chapter looks at how the women in this study used the possibilities for action – or instrumental affordances – offered by mobile phones to address issues in four areas of their lives: employment, education, housing and health. These aspects correspond to indicators of social exclusion that are adopted in policy contexts and also relate to elements of the Central Human Capabilities that were identified by Nussbaum (2003).[...]

[...] the young women interviewed for this study were predominantly unemployed, pregnant or stay at home mums. Those women that were looking for work were asked whether they used their phone for job hunting. A youth employment advisor from Brighton's Youth Employment Service, that has pioneered the use of social media to reach out to young people, was also interviewed. They use Facebook to advertise job vacancies and apprenticeships that are suitable for 16–24-year-olds and have developed their own Smartphone app. The particular affordances of the device that were of use in terms of job seeking were its portability enabling respondents make or receive voice calls away from home. The ability to surf the Internet on a

Smartphone meant that women were able to look for jobs and apprenticeships and fill in application forms.

[...] Work and job-hunting have been transformed by these instrumental affordances of the Smartphone, which enabled young people to make and receive calls away from home and also to search for jobs. Emily, the youth employment advisor who was interviewed reflected on shifts in access in time she had been working with young people between 2009–2014. Her perception was that the majority of young people she works with now have some form of access to the Internet via a Smartphone for job hunting, which was not the case five years previously. For the respondents in this study, mobile phones were playing a role in enabling them to look for work: both by searching online and by ringing up employers. However the affordances of a small screen and challenges with text input meant that they experienced difficulties using them to complete full job applications.

Those that were using the phone as part of a job or apprenticeship search tended to be using the device to search, rather than apply for jobs. The quote below shows how Kayla saw her phone as a way of getting an overview of apprenticeship information by 'skim' reading rather than using it for the full application.

So you're looking for an apprenticeship at the moment... do you use your phone for stuff like that?

Yeah I go on apprenticeships.org.

Is it easy to use on a phone?

Yeah it's not too bad... but the real website *[on a computer]* is better obviously.

And you wouldn't apply for it on your phone you'd just look at the information?

Yeah probably. It's like... you can skim read on your phone.

Reference

Nussbaum, M. 2003. Capabilities as fundamental entitlements. Sen and social justice. *Feminist Economics* , 9.

(Faith, 2016, pp. 127; 131–132)

A young, homeless woman owning a smartphone may seem counter-intuitive, but the type of 'ownership' here is actually part of the problem. Faith's research subjects do not, strictly speaking, own their phones. Buying phones on a credit contract is common across all sectors of the population. For these women, credit contracts place them in a vicious cycle of dependence and debt. The phone is not only their sole means of internet access – it is their address. It is the only way many people who live on the streets can be reached.

Related – but more dangerous – adverse consequences arise for other marginalised populations. The phone is a very poor substitute for a home – but it does at least provides some means of accessing community, civic and social welfare agencies. For the migrants and refugees studied by Gillespie *et al.* (2016) the phone is an essential technology used to map very dangerous journeys. Even if these journeys end well, refugees who make it to the UK encounter difficulties. For example, at the time of writing, refugees arrive in a 'hostile environment' as defined in the immigration policy announced by the Conservative-Liberal Democrat coalition government in 2012 under then home secretary, Theresa May. One affordance of mobile digital technologies is that their locations can be tracked by third parties. Government agencies, the European Union, international aid agencies, Facebook and people traffickers all have this capacity. It does not require advanced technical expertise to work out where a phone is, where it's been, who it belongs to and who it has been used to contact. Related techniques are used in many smartphone features and apps including 'find my phone', WhatsApp and Snapchat, among others.

None of this is as far removed from planning the cities of the future as it might seem. Understanding the way core technologies, like smartphones and meaningful digital access, are distributed across the population, is essential for city planners.

So what is a technology? The answer is surprisingly simple – a technology is just a way of doing something. Smartphones bear a profound family resemblance to smart city technologies. Objects become 'smart' by combining digital, mobile and sensor technologies and this can change the way all sorts of tasks associated with living in a city are done. Local governments provide services to their citizens. This increasingly means using smart technologies to govern the city – while also governing the risks new technologies bring with them. Adopting smart systems to deliver key public services means figuring out whether citizens can use them – and how. This principle affects every aspect of public service delivery, from the procurement of new public transport vehicles, to street lighting, to cashless bus payment. Digital technologies are not universally adopted overnight, some – like the social media platform MySpace – succeed briefly, only to fail quickly. So at what point should innovations that must serve a diverse city be adopted?

The stakes of these decisions are high. Cities are among the major drivers and procurers of new technologies and they have increasing influence over them. The technologies cities adopt are not neutral (Kitchin, 2013; 2016). They are inherently and inescapably social – they reflect and they create social differences and inequalities. Nor are the technological challenges that cities face new. Cities have always had to make decisions about how they will work for their future citizens.

You can see this clearly in a city that was planned out from the start – Milton Keynes.

3   Making a brand new city: Milton Keynes

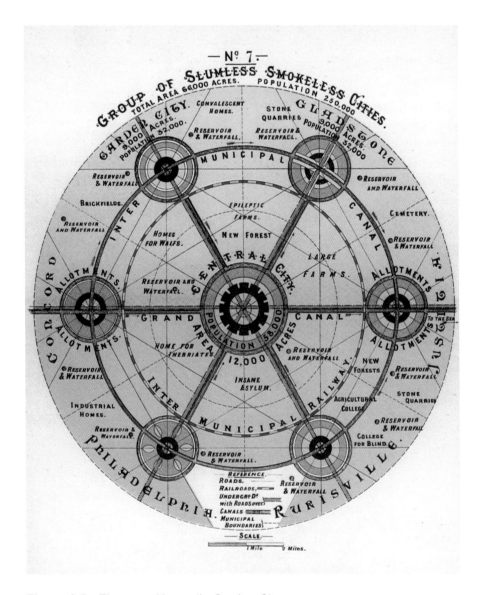

Figure 3.5   Ebenezer Howard's Garden City.

There is a sense that the modern city is more sophisticated, more
technologically advanced, more futuristic and, well, more modern, than
its predecessors. The industrial cities of the 19th century are an
obvious example of this, but it is not too hard to imagine that the

infrastructural advances of, say, the Romans, might also in their time have been seen as futuristic. We don't venture that far back in this chapter, but we do go back half a century. Milton Keynes, a 'city' that is still identified as 'new', was designated in 1967. It was planned around models and assumptions about how its future citizens would live and who they would be. By its fiftieth birthday in 2017, it had already departed from many of the principles of the original plan to expand as a smart city.

Technically, Milton Keyes is not a city, it is one of the last of the post-war new towns. British new towns were a response to well-known problems in the towns and cities that had developed, more organically, around specific features like rivers, ports and industries. The idea of a garden city was developed by Ebenezer Howard in the late 19th century as a solution to the overcrowding, poverty and pollution of the industrial inner cities. With a planned blend of rural and urban spaces, garden cities were meant to enrich the lives of all their residents. Howard's diagrams of a garden city shows how these different elements would work together.

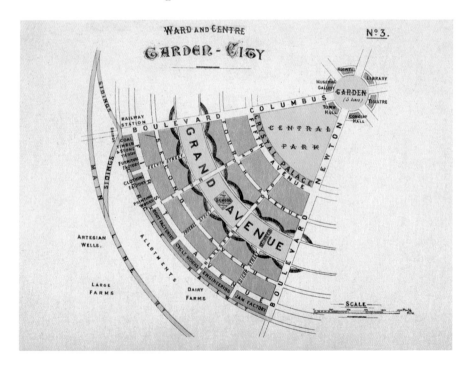

Figure 3.6   Ward and centre of Howard's Garden City.

Howard's ideal of how people should live in the future was utopian. The two garden cities that were developed in the UK – Letchworth and Welwyn – achieved some elements of Howard's ideal, but not all. Garden cities did, however, set a precedent for the post-war new town movement.

The 1946 New Towns Act set out radical plans for towns across the country. As the programme developed, the role of research, statistics, data production and analysis in the planning and promotion of new towns grew. By the 1960s, Milton Keynes planners were using the most recent research methods to predict how people would live, work and move around in the future city. Melvin M. Webber, an American urban planner, who had a major influence on Milton Keynes, captures this:

> In previous eras, when the goals, the beliefs, the behavior, and the roles of city folk were clearly distinguishable from those of their rural brethren, and when urban settlements were spatially discrete and physically bounded, schoolboy common sense was sufficient to identify the marks of "urbanness." Now all Americans are coming to share very similar cultural traits; the physical boundaries of settlements are disappearing; and the networks of interdependence among various groups are becoming functionally intricate and spatially widespread. With it all, the old symbols of order are giving way to the signs of newly emerging systems of organization that, in turn, are sapping the usefulness of our established concepts of order.
>
> (Webber, 1963, p. 24)

Milton Keynes' planners knew they had no crystal ball. They had research data profiling their prospective residents but, since the planning was done before the city existed, there were no residents to consult. The solution of Milton Keynes Development Corporation (MKDC) was to make a plan that was flexible and that left space for change. But MKDC also had to work out how to share their vision, how to draw people to the place. In 1972 Milton Keynes was launched at the Design Centre in London. At the time there was not much to show since little had actually been built, so the design agency used a different approach. They used abstract images – an archery target was one example – to give visual form to a place that didn't exist (see Figure 3.7).

Figure 3.7 Milton Keynes archery target promotional poster.

Later campaigns drew on more concrete images of the parts of the city that were completed (see Figures 3.8a and 3.8b). The Corporation had to make the city look attractive enough to residents and businesses to entice them away from the comfort and familiarity of their existing locations, to somewhere unknown.

Figure 3.8a   Concrete jungle poster promoting Milton Keynes.

Figure 3.8b   Back streets poster promoting Milton Keynes.

One of the first neighbourhoods was Netherfield. Built in a 1 km grid square towards the south of the city, it included generous provision of both private space, in internal layouts and gardens, and public space in parkland, sports fields, and community facilities such as schools, shops and healthcare. One of the more striking aspects of the estate is the external design of the houses. In the 1970s, and particularly after high rise blocks of flats had become unpopular, architects were beginning to explore new forms of lowrise housing solutions. Some had traditional pitched roofs while others, like Netherfield, were more experimental. The long flat-roofed terraced streets were meant to appeal to modernist tastes. The uniform streetscape represented a kind of democratic design; the houses looked equal from the outside but had varied and flexible internal layouts.

Reading 3.3

Robert Maxwell, 'Netherfield'

For this estate is not a model of a community, but of a class: the extended middle class made up of people who feel freer from penury and exploitation than did their grandparents: who feel that now they can look after themselves. Perhaps it is particularly to members of this class that the New Town idea appeals. At any rate it seems to be to these that Netherfield is addressed, to judge by the way the architect has filled out his drawings with tell-tale incidentals. These depict a replica of consumer society, as if to prove that all delights are possible even within the compass of a Parker Morris home. Mother in her fitted kitchen activates a Braun mixer while father polishes the Volkswagen. The make of car, the variety of potted plant, are specified, and it is possible to see from a perusal of the house plans that imaginary tenants have already indicated their preference in pets or in musical instruments.

(Maxwell, 1975, pp. 1258–1259)

Figure 3.9a   Netherfield (original design).

Figure 3.9b   Terraced houses in Netherfield, 2017.

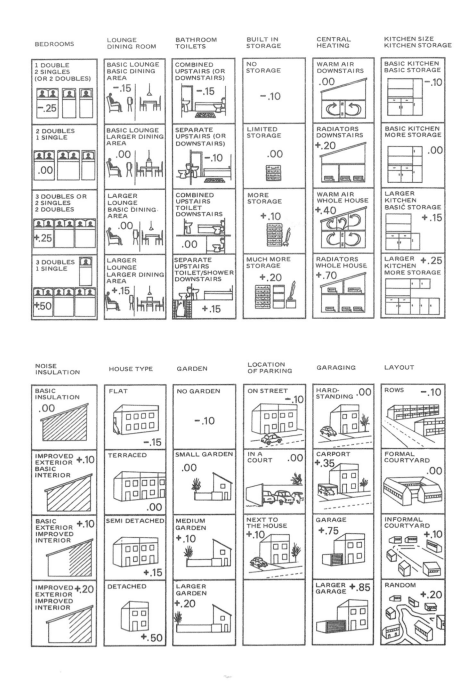

Figure 1 PRIORITY EVALUATOR
example for Greenleys 3B5P house

Figure 3.10 Priority Evaluator example for housing in Milton Keynes.

While Netherfield was being built, the MKDC were beginning to ask residents of the other early estates what they thought of their houses. This kind of data collection, from a randomised sample of households and asking a broad range of questions about their new homes in their new city, can provide insight into living conditions and residents' attitudes towards their environment. It has, however, some noticeable limitations. Such data gathering exercises collect information and feedback only from certain people at certain times and places. Many factors affect the way that people answer the questions put to them including broader public socio-economic issues and personal or individual concerns.

One element of this process was the 'Priority Evaluator', a graphic that summarised various aspects of the houses and asked residents to decide which mattered most to them (Figure 3.10). This was a way of finding out what people needed and expected from their homes and also a way of letting them know the budgetary implications of providing for different needs.

The world of city planning has changed dramatically since 1975. There are now very different technologies available that can collect and process vast quantities of data harvested from people – and from objects. Milton Keynes confronted this new environment by adopting a smart city approach and sponsoring collaborative projects including 'MK:Smart'. In September 2015, the MK Futures 2050 Commission was set up to develop 'a way of thinking about the future of the city, helping to create a long term vision for the way MK should grow and prosper over the coming decades'. The Futures Commission identified two central drivers that would support this objective. The first was to ensure Milton Keynes' citizens had access to the best education and training opportunities in Europe and the second was to offer sustainable mobility for all. Milton Keynes' approach to sustainable mobility is best known through its role as a testbed for self-driving pod cars and delivery robots. Delivery robots use the redways network and managed to navigate during heavy snow storms in 2018 when few other vehicles were on the road. Ryan Tuohy, a senior vice-president at Starship Technologies, the company behind the robots, commented:

> In some locations, like Milton Keynes, some of our most popular customers are parents who struggle to leave the house because of their children. It's a lot easier to get a robot delivery than try and get two young kids in the car, find parking, walk round the

grocery store and then drive back. It's a lot more environmentally friendly as well.

(Albrecht, 2019)

In and of themselves neither driverless cars nor delivery robots will achieve 'sustainable mobility for all'. They are a tiny part of a vast jigsaw and raise difficult questions for national and civic authorities about the costs and benefits of using privately owned companies for delivering public services. Managing how, and when, it is appropriate for private, commercial interests to deliver public services is a challenge that also preoccupies those involved in planning Edinburgh's future.

Figure 3.11   Delivery robot in Milton Keynes.

4   Edinburgh: from Auld Reekie to Data Capital

City Region Deals are agreements between the Scottish Government, the UK Government and local government designed to bring about long-term strategic approaches to improving regional economies. They are implemented by regional partners and overseen by the Scottish City Region Deal Delivery Board. Each deal is tailored to its city region, reflecting its individual economic strengths and weaknesses, and comprises a programme of interventions to support positive, transformative change.

Planning for the future of Edinburgh and its citizens is being driven by the Edinburgh and South East Scotland City Region Deal. Edinburgh is a World Heritage Site and despite having what Robert Louis Stevenson (1903, p.1) described as 'one of the vilest climates under heaven', it has a growing, dynamic and revolving population of permanent residents, students and visitors. This means future planning has to accommodate – and attempt to reconcile – the interests of at least three groups of people: permanent residents, students, many of whom are resident only in term-time, and visitors. Digital technologies, particularly the growth of platforms, have altered how the city looks, feels and works for each of these groups. In the case of housing, platforms like Airbnb have had a negative effect on the supply, quality and costs for many permanent residents. Edinburgh, like Milton Keynes, nevertheless understands that digital and data-driven technologies will play a vital role in future planning. This is evident in national and local governmental policy. The Edinburgh City Region Deal includes a £60 million commitment towards a Data Driven Innovation programme intended to build economic infrastructure across the region.

But where did the idea of planning future cities come from? It sounds like a new strategy, a response to emerging global challenges, platform capitalism, sustainability, the climate emergency, inclusive growth, international migration, the refugee crisis. Future planning is, however, a paradox – the future is unknowable and what we think might happen is as much a function of present and past problems as it is of future projections.

The case of Milton Keynes demonstrates how planners used a range of methods and data to anticipate the city's future, who its citizens would be and how they would live. Still their projections could only be made from the perspective of the known present. The ethnic diversity of present-day Milton Keynes, for example, was not something planners anticipated. The 2011 census classified the ethnic make-up of Milton Keynes Urban Area as 78.4% White, 8.7% South Asian, 7.5% Black, 3.5% Mixed Race and 1.2% Chinese (Office for National Statistics *et al*, 2016). Between 2001 and 2011 the proportion of the population identifying as Black and members of any minority ethnic groups rose from 13.2% to 26.1% in Milton Keynes against a national average of 20.2% in other English cities. In contrast, Edinburgh's Black and minority ethnic population was recorded in the 2011 census as only 8.2% – but the city is ethnically diverse (The City of Edinburgh Council (2013)). The percentage of its population born outside the UK is double the Scottish average at 15.9%, with the largest proportion (47%) coming from other European countries. Of these, 3.1% were born in the Eastern European 'accession countries' who became members of the European Union in 2004. In 2011, the largest number of Edinburgh citizens born overseas were from Poland (2.7%). This figure grew after the 2004 accession but it also built on an existing Polish community formed during the Second World War (marked in the *Wojtek* bear statue in Figure 3.12) that itself has long historical roots. There are historical and political precedents to all patterns of migration but the character of demographic change that has taken place across the UK since the 1960s is not something city planners could have foreseen.

Urban planners face a task that is ghosted as much by the past as visions of the future. In a city like Edinburgh the past weighs heavily on how it envisions the future. The future has to be made out of land, buildings, infrastructure, materials, methods and regulations that already exist. Cities are not blank slates. This is true even in new town projects. Milton Keynes was built around a geography of lakes, canals, rivers and forests as well as the existing settlements of Bletchley, Stony Stratford, Wolverton and the original Milton Keynes Village. Edinburgh's mix of wide new town streets laid out on a geometrical grid, connected by several steep bridges to the layered and knotted streets of the medieval old town, is an artefact of its geography, but only in part. It is also the outcome of civic planning, of the use of methods and data to survey and improve social and economic conditions.

Figure 3.12   *Wojtek* – the Polish 'Soldier Bear' in Princes Street Gardens, Edinburgh.

Until the end of the 18th century Edinburgh was confined by its geography. The Castle sits on a hunk of volcanic rock with a spine that runs eastwards to the larger, volcanic outcrops of Salisbury Crags and Arthur's Seat. To the south and the north of this central spine were deep flooded ravines, the nor loch (now Princes Street Gardens) and the borough loch (now the Meadows). The nor loch was used as a dump for everything, including human waste. The old town was crammed in between these features and grew upwards in a rickety network of medieval sky-scraping tenements. Inside the tenements the floors were ordered socially with the 'high-born' occupying the top, lighter and airier floors. At the bottom of the same buildings the poor were crowded into the darkest and – bearing in mind that sanitary hygiene meant throwing human waste from upper windows onto the streets below – the dirtiest floors.

The tenements were also precarious structures. In 1751 a six-storey building collapsed; it wasn't the first, but it was one of the grandest and the fatalities included members of Edinburgh's richest families (Campbell, 2016). In the aftermath, surveys concluded that many of the city's tenements were equally unstable. A year later the pamphlet *Proposals for carrying on certain public works in the city of Edinburgh* was published. This was the start of a future planning exercise that led directly to the construction of the new town. The proposals made an argument about how the city's problems should be tackled that is not that dissimilar to the approach driving the city-region deal.

> Wealth is only to be obtained by trade and commerce, and these are only carried on to advantage in populous cities. There also we find the chief objects of pleasure and ambition, and there consequently all those will flock whose circumstances can afford it.

> (Elliot, 1752, p. 31)

As the proposals were put into practice, Edinburgh developed as a centre for law, medicine and the social science of civic planning. All of this centred around the growth of the financial industries, particularly insurance, financial investment and retail banking. As the financial historian Ray Perman explains:

> The Darien disaster of 1700 drove Scotland into union with England, but spawned the institutions which transformed Edinburgh into a global financial centre. The crash of 2008 wrecked the city's two largest and oldest banks and its reputation. In the three intervening centuries, Edinburgh became a hothouse of financial innovation, prudent banking, reliable insurance and smart investing. The face of the city changed too as money transformed it from medieval squalor to Georgian elegance.

> (Perman, 2019)

Edinburgh made money and this money built the city. The new town was built on the proceeds of financial innovation but also on the proceeds of slavery. Edinburgh, like Scotland in general, has been slow to acknowledge it, but income derived from slavery, and later from reparations when it was finally abolished, was a substantial driver of growth in its urban economies (Devine, 2015; Palmer, 2007). Many of the new town's grandest properties were built by slave owning families. Dundas Street, a street that commands a view all the way to Fife, together with the massive Melville Monument in St Andrew Square (Figure 3.13), commemorate Henry Dundas, Viscount Melville, who as home secretary resisted the abolition of slavery.

Figure 3.13 Melville Monument,
St Andrew Square, Edinburgh.

There were further projects aimed at planning the future city. In the late 19th century Patrick Geddes' (1911; 1915) new social science of 'civics' aligned with the ideas enshrined in Ebenezer Howard's garden city movement in an attempt to address the crowding, poverty and pollution of the industrial cities. After the Second World War, future planning was conducted on a much grander scale with the enactment of the 'cradle to grave' reforms to health, education, poverty and housing proposed in the Beveridge Report (1942). This was the beginning of the post-war welfare settlement. It was in this environment that a series of comprehensive surveys of the conditions in existing cities and the 1946 New Towns Act took shape.

This mode of centralised, bureaucratic city planning slowly gave way after Margaret Thatcher took office in 1979. What followed was a steady redistribution of civic and social responsibilities – from the state back to the individual. Infrastructures from telecommunications to transport were taken out of public ownership. Beginning with a re-regulation of ownership and financial services, future planning became more privatised. By the 1990s, schools, hospitals and housing were often built through public-private partnerships. One effect of these changes, particularly the failure to replace stock following the tenant's 'right-to-buy' council housing scheme, was a rapid decline in the amount and condition of social housing. Reduced funding for maintenance and repair, combined with industrial decline and poverty throughout the 1980s, resulted in a rapid degeneration of housing that had been carefully designed to accommodate future citizens, a fate suffered by Netherfield.

Figure 3.14   West Granton Crescent, Edinburgh, 1996, immediately prior to demolition.

Patterns of urban change accelerated dramatically in the early 2000s. At the same time as digital and internet-based technologies were becoming established, urban development was booming. The deregulated financial industries permitted unprecedented levels of public and private borrowing. This was part of a broader process of financialisation, whereby profits are made through investment in financial assets and instruments rather than through trade and commodity production (Krippner, 2005). All this had a major impact on how cities were governed and planned. Across the UK, financialisation has been underpinned by a vast sell-off of public land to the private sector, including land formerly occupied by council housing (Christophers, 2019). These factors culminated disastrously in the global financial crisis of 2008. The economic recession that followed gave the justification for the policies of austerity and the hostile environment pursued by the Coalition and Conservative governments since 2010.

At street level this mix of technological, economic and political factors has transformed how cities and towns look and feel. Consolidation and digital technology meant that banks and insurance companies no longer needed numerous high street branches and offices. In cities like Edinburgh many of these buildings have been transformed into hotels, restaurants, bars and coffee shops. This is an example of the slow replacement of visible, material infrastructures by digital infrastructures. Ticket offices, cheque-books, bank counters, cash and taxi ranks for example, have not quite disappeared but they have become much less common. One of the characteristics of digital infrastructures is that we can't quite picture them – but they still shape the city.

The sociologist Karen Gregory (2018) has argued that internet platforms like Airbnb, Uber and Deliveroo have to be rooted in an urban environment to function. There have to be sufficient concentrations of people who want short-term lets, rides and food deliveries to maintain a labour force who are not employees of these companies but workers in the 'gig economy', where labour is freelance or based on short-term contracts. These platforms have had drastic impacts in many urban environments. Airbnb, for instance, may have begun as a platform for informal short-term lets, but it has transformed access to housing in many cities. Investment capital flows in as housing stock is bought up specifically for short-term lets, increasing the cost and reducing access to housing for local residents. Deliveroo, Uber, Airbnb and other platforms represent themselves as service providers or intermediaries – but they are also powerful financial and political actors.

Platform companies are particularly valuable because they attract venture capitalists, not only because of the companies' potential growth, but also because they are data aggregating systems. Everyone has heard the phrase that data is the new oil. What all these platforms are doing, regardless of whether they are delivering your food or helping to clean your house, is not only to aggregate data but also to generate new forms of data that have not existed before. Airbnb, for instance, has one of the world's largest databases of interior photographs. That is valuable to advertisers, architects and city planners (Gregory, personal communication, 2019).

Figuring out how to use these new forms of data for public purposes plays a crucial role in Edinburgh's ambition to become a 'data capital'. The Edinburgh and South East Scotland City Region Deal Document argues that 'the ability to collect, store and analyse data from an array of diverse sources will become increasingly important in driving economic growth, social change and public services' (2018). Data-driven innovation is positioned as the key to improving regional economies and delivering public services from transport to council tax payment.

5   Conclusion

You have covered a lot of ground in this chapter. One of the key points to take away is that cities and their changing infrastructures provide a way of seeing how societies are being transformed by digital technologies. As you have seen, technologies, at core, are ways of doing things. From paying bus fares to ordering garden waste collection, these tasks increasingly depend on digital and data-driven technologies. These changes have not benefited everyone. Some groups, for example, those on low incomes, those dependent on insecure, privately rented housing, and street dwellers who lack the means and opportunity to access digital resources, have been left behind, while males, majorities, the employed, the well-educated, and married people have benefited. Not even city-dwellers who are well-equipped with digital skills, access and resources are unscathed by the platform economy. Younger people in particular are being priced out of the property market in most major cities, partly as a result of the effect of platforms like Airbnb, Deliveroo and Uber on work and housing. Milton Keynes and Edinburgh present two very different cases but they are not exceptional. Cities, regions and nations all face the challenge of reconciling their specific histories and present problems with the promise of technological solutions.

References

Albrecht, C. (2019) *ArticulATE Q&A: why starship's delivery robots are as wide as your shoulders.* Available at: https://thespoon.tech/articulate-qa-why-starships-delivery-robots-are-as-wide-as-your-shoulders/ (Accessed: 11 February 2020).

Bayne S. and Ross J. (2011) '"Digital native" and "digital immigrant" discourses', in Land, R. and Bayne, S. (eds.) *Digital difference: perspectives on online learning.* Rotterdam: Sense Publishers, pp. 159–169.

Beveridge, W. (1942) *Social insurance and allied services (The Beveridge Report).* London: His Majesty's Stationery Office.

Campbell, T. (2016) 'Story of cities #10: how the dirty Old Town became enlightened Edinburgh', *The Guardian*, 29 March. Available at: https://www.theguardian.com/cities/2016/mar/29/story-of-cities-10-edinburgh-new-town-old-town-scottish-enlightenment-james-craig (Accessed: 31 July 2019).

Christophers, B. (2019) *The new enclosure: the appropriation of public land in neoliberal Britain.* London: Verso.

Devine, T.M. (ed.) (2015) *Recovering Scotland's slavery past: the Caribbean connection.* Edinburgh: Edinburgh University Press.

Elliot, G. (1752) *Proposals for carrying on certain public works in the city of Edinburgh.* Available at: http://tinyurl.gale.com/tinyurl/BbDYz5 (Accessed: 28 August 2019).

Faith, R. (2016) *How does the use of mobile phones by 16-24 year old socially excluded women affect their capabilities?.* PhD thesis, The Open University.

Geddes, P. (1911) *The civic survey of Edinburgh.* Edinburgh: University of Edinburgh.

Geddes, P. (1915) *Cities in evolution: an introduction to the town planning movement and to the study of civics.* London: Williams and Norgate.

Gillespie, M., Ampofo, L., Cheesman, M., Faith, B., Iliadou, E., Issa, A., Osseiran, S. and Skleparis, D. (2016) *Mapping refugee media journeys: smartphones and social media networks.* The Open University/France Médias Monde. Available at: https://www.open.ac.uk/ccig/sites/www.open.ac.uk.ccig/files/Mapping%20Refugee%20Media%20Journeys%2016%20May%20FIN%20MG_0.pdf (Accessed: 22 January 2020).

Gregory, K. (2018) *Platform capitalism: when side hustle becomes main business.* Available at: https://fortytwomagazine.com/magazine/digital-transformation-and-employment/ (Accessed: 22 January 2020).

Gregory, K. (2019) Email to Liz McFall, 30 May.

Howard, E. (1902) *Garden cities of tomorrow.* London: Swan Sonnenschein & Co.

Kitchin, R. (2013) 'The real-time city? Big data and smart urbanism', *GeoJournal*, 79(1), pp. 1–14. doi: 10.1007/s10708-013-9516-8.

Kitchin, R. (2016) 'The ethics of smart cities and urban science', *Philosophical Transactions of the Royal Society A: Mathematical, Physical and Engineering Sciences*, 374(2083). doi: 10.1098/rsta.2016.0115.

Krippner, G.R. (2005) 'The financialization of the American economy', *Socio-Economic Review*, 3(2), pp. 173–208. doi: 10.1093/SER/mwi008.

Maxwell, R. (1975) 'Two housing schemes at Milton Keynes', *The Architects' Journal*, 162(50), pp. 1247–1260.

Mills, C.W. (2000) *The sociological imagination*. New York, NY: Oxford University Press.

New Towns Act 1946. Available at: http://www.legislation.gov.uk/ukpga/1946/68/contents/enacted (Accessed: 22 January 2020).

Office for National Statistics (2018) *Internet access – households and individuals, Great Britain: 2018*. Available at: https://www.ons.gov.uk/peoplepopulationandcommunity/householdcharacteristics/homeinternetandsocialmediausage/bulletins/internetaccesshouseholdsandindividuals/2018 (Accessed: 30 June 2019).

Office for National Statistics; National Records of Scotland; Northern Ireland Statistics and Research Agency (2016) *2011 Census aggregate data*. UK Data Service (Edition: June 2016). doi: 10.5257/census/aggregate-2011-1.

Oxford English Dictionary (2010). Oxford: Oxford University Press.

Palmer, G. (2007) *The enlightenment abolished: citizens of Britishness*. Penicuik: Henry Publishing.

Perman, R. (2019) Interviewed by Liz McFall. 7 May.

Rhoades, H., Wenzel, S. L., Rice, E., Winetrobe, H. and Henwood, B. (2017) 'No digital divide? Technology use among homeless adults', *Journal of Social Distress and the Homeless*, 26(1), pp. 73–77. doi: 10.1080/10530789.2017.1305140.

Rice, E., Lee, A. and Taitt, S. (2011) 'Cell phone use among homeless youth: potential for new health interventions and research', *Journal of Urban Health*, 88(6), pp. 1175–1182.

Scott, W. (2004) *The fortunes of Nigel*. Chapter VI. Available at: https://www.gutenberg.org/files/5950/5950-h/5950-h.htm (Accessed: 12 November 2020).

Scottish Government (2018) *City region deals*. Available at: https://www.gov.scot/policies/cities-regions/city-region-deals/ (Accessed: 22 January 2020).

Stevenson, R.L. (1903) *Edinburgh: picturesque notes*. London: Seeley and Co.

The City of Edinburgh Council (2013) *2011 Census topic summary: ethnicity and related themes.* Edinburgh: The City of Edinburgh Council, Planning Information, Planning and Building Standards, Services for Communities. Available at: https://www.edinburgh.gov.uk/downloads/file/24253/ethnicity-and-related-themes-topic-report-for-edinburgh (Accessed: 22 January 2020).

van Deursen, A.J.A.M. and van Dijk, J.A.G.M. (2019) 'The first-level digital divide shifts from inequalities in physical access to inequalities in material access', *New Media & Society,* 21(2), pp. 354–375. doi: 10.1177/1461444818797082.

van Dijk, J.A.G.M. (1999) *The network society: social aspects of new media.* London: Sage Publications.

van Dijk, J.A.G.M. and Hacker, K. (2003) 'The digital divide as a complex and dynamic phenomenon', *The Information Society,* 19(4), pp. 315–326. doi: 10.1080/01972240309487.

Webber, M. (1963) 'Order in diversity: community without propinquity', in Wingo, L. (ed.) *Cities and space: the future use of urban land.* Baltimore: John Hopkins Press.

Chapter 4

Migration, diaspora and transnationalism in the digital age

Rhys Crilley and Marie Gillespie

Contents

1 Introduction

Many of us living in Europe take it for granted that we have a home, belong to a nation, have a passport, and that we can travel legally. For some 65.5 million refugees worldwide who have been forced to migrate due to war, persecution or poverty, this is not the case (Winsor, 2018). But refugees are not the only kinds of migrants. Many Europeans enjoy freedom of movement and migrate to work in different countries. They can exercise choice. The United Nations defines a migrant as 'someone who changes his or her country of usual residence' for a year or more. This is called 'voluntary migration' to differentiate it from 'forced migration' – the experience of refugees who move to another country for fear of persecution (UN, 2016). Worldwide, it is estimated that 257.7 million people – 3.4% of the world's population – are transnational migrants (Migration Data Portal, 2019), which means that they have migrated across international borders, from one country to another. However, many more people migrate within the borders of their country, and these people are called internal migrants or, if forced to migrate due to war or persecution – Internally Displaced People.

This chapter explores how migration and digital technologies together shape societies in ways that transcend national borders. It introduces the concepts of **diaspora** and **transnationalism**. These terms focus our attention on different aspects of migration. The term diaspora refers to people dispersed around the world from the same homeland, so the relationship between people in the homeland and countries of settlement comes to the fore. Transnationalism refers to a much wider set of practices – not all related to migration – and examines the ties and connections that transcend or bypass national belonging, citizenship or identity – especially the new kinds of connectivity afforded in the digital age.

This chapter invites us to think about the relationships between *individuals* and the *societies* they are born into, migrate to and settle in. It will highlight how *power and inequality* are expressed, reproduced but also transformed through the twin forces of migration and technologies. It will also allow us to think about *people and things*; how the smartphone makes a difference both to individuals using them and to the societies they live in. It also asks us how poverty and inequality mean that some people have access to smartphones but not others.

1.1 Teaching aims

The aims of this chapter are for you to:

- understand how concepts of diaspora and transnationalism can be used to analyse migration and the relationship of migrant individuals to different societies

- compare and contrast different kinds of migration – including forced and voluntary migration – and understand how these reflect different relations of *power and inequality*

- evaluate the relationship between *people and things* in the context of migration by considering how migrants and refugees use digital devices, and how technologies have shaped and changed diaspora and transnational social formations

- understand uses of smartphones among refugees and how they affect experiences of forced displacement and migration, and vice versa.

2 Migration, diaspora and transnationalism

Let us reflect for a moment on Ahmad's situation. Ahmad is a 24-year-old Syrian refugee now living in London. He was forced to leave his home in 2015 due to the conflict in Syria. 'We woke up to the sound of bombs nearby. It became impossible to stay – ISIL [The Islamic State of Iraq and the Levant] would either kill us or force us to kill for them. My father said "enough!"'. He gave us whatever money the family had left and told my brother and me to get out quickly and not to say goodbye to our mother for fear that her heart would break' (Ahmad, 2017).

As the fighting came closer to Ahmad's home in Aleppo, he had to move quickly to escape the violence while he still could. 'I grabbed a few items of clothing in a rucksack, some bread, some water and our phones and we headed out of town, ducking to avoid snipers. The rest is history. Food, phones, water – essential for our journey into exile.' Ahmad's phone was as important to his journey as food and water, and he reminds us that digital technologies have become essential for many people in contemporary societies, particularly in the movement of people across national borders. The image below offers a potent reminder of why some people are forced to migrate.

When it comes to migration, we hear different terms that can leave us feeling confused. What do we mean by asylum seekers and refugees? Are they the same as immigrants, migrants, emigrants and expats? These terms are often used interchangeably but they are bound up with *power and inequality*, as they refer to different types of legal status and determine who has the right to move, to remain and to become a citizen. The words we use to describe people matter, because they ascribe them with a status that justifies or denies them rights.

For example, we refer to Ahmad as a refugee because he has been granted that status by the UK's Home Office after seeking asylum due to the war in his home country. His case is one of forced migration – he had no choice. In contrast, when we use the term 'migrant', we might instead think of someone who has chosen to migrate abroad in order to work or find a better way of life. If the British Home Office decides that someone who has applied for asylum is an economic migrant, they are deemed undeserving of the right to protection that is

Figure 4.1   Aleppo, Syria in 2016.

granted to 'deserving' refugees. These distinctions were made stark during Europe's so-called 'refugee crisis' of 2015–16; a period when over one million people made perilous journeys across land and sea to Europe to seek safety and asylum.

The 1951 UN Refugee Convention came after World War II in the aftermath of the murder in the **Holocaust** of six million Jewish people and the forcible displacement of hundreds of thousands of others. 'Never again' was the idea that inspired the Convention as it sought to prevent such death, destruction and devastation from happening again. It defines a refugee as any person seeking sanctuary 'owing to well-founded fear of being persecuted for reasons of race, religion, nationality, membership of a particular social group or political opinion' (UN, 1951). In principle, the Convention should protect refugee rights. In practice it does not always do so because the distinction between forced and voluntary migration is often hard to prove to the political authorities, and legal systems in different countries implement the Convention in different ways.

There are myriad reasons why people migrate – but above all one has to have the capacity and financial means to do so, and global inequalities mean that the poorest people in the world simply cannot move. Regardless of the reasons, the language we use to talk about people who move across borders has important implications. Language influences how we think, talk and act in response to migration. At the height of the 2015–16 migration crisis, popular news media portrayed refugees mainly as dangerous outsiders, and these media affect public opinion, which in turn shapes political decision-making about migration.

Figure 4.2 The Life Jacket Graveyard on the island of Lesvos where nearly a million jackets used by refugees to cross the sea from Izmir in Turkey to Lesvos were discarded by the municipality.

Let us now examine the concepts of diaspora and transnationalism in more detail. They are often used interchangeably and indeed it is hard to imagine a diaspora group which is not transnational, or which does not engage in any transnational activity. But they are different. First, while a diaspora refers to a dispersed population, dispersal is not a determinant for transnationalism. Second, the term diaspora is often used to refer to a globally dispersed ethno-national group and as a product of migration. In contrast, transnationalism tends to be used to refer to processes that go across and beyond national borders, but do not necessarily involve migration.

3 Diaspora

Diaspora derives from ancient Greek, meaning 'dispersal' – originally referring by way of an agricultural analogy to a scattering of seeds. The earliest use of the term diaspora referred to the dispersal of Jews who had been forcibly expelled from their homeland by the Egyptians (in biblical times), and had scattered all over the world. Diasporas are understood to be religiously and ethnically homogenous groups who had been traumatically displaced from an original homeland. This is why the concept of homeland is central in diaspora theory and 'in the collective memory of a forcibly dispersed group' (Cohen, 2008, p. 4).

The sociologist Robin Cohen outlined common features of diaspora, including:

- traumatic dispersal from an original homeland

- migration from a homeland in search of work

- an idealised, collective memory and myths of the homeland

- a return movement to the homeland

- a common history, culture, and/or religion, and a sense of community

- a troubled relationship with societies in countries of settlement, or the possibility of an enriching life in countries of settlement with a tolerance for pluralism.

(Adapted from Cohen, 2008, p. 17)

Whilst diaspora formations are different in many ways, they share a common thread in that they all depend on technologies. Developments in technology have long shaped how people have been able to move and migrate. Sailing ships, navigational technologies and the steamboat enabled European empires to conquer other continents in the 19th century (Headrick, 1979, p. 234). They also enabled people to migrate to these places. More recently, the invention of the aeroplane, and the decreasing costs of air travel have further facilitated migration across the globe for some. Developments in technologies have changed the relationship between *individuals* and the *societies* they live in.

Sociologists expanded the meanings of diaspora in the late 20th century to refer to different categories of migrant and mobile populations such as 'expatriates, expellees, political refugees, alien residents, immigrants and ethnic and racial minorities' (Safran, 1991, p. 83) who had left their homeland to live in 'host' states. Some argued that the notion of trauma associated with a homeland was not always relevant to modern migration. For example, the sociologist Stuart Hall wrote about how diasporas in the UK were created by the history of colonial rule and the post-war, mass migration of Caribbean and South Asian people to Britain. He argued against defining these newcomers exclusively by their race, nationality or ethnicity (1994). Essentialising identities in this way – boiling them down to some core essence – reproduces racist and nationalist frames of thinking and acting, and exacerbates inequalities of power, income, education and opportunity.

Diaspora and transformation

Hall noted that diasporas should not be seen as 'scattered tribes whose identity can only be secured in relation to some sacred homeland to which they must at all costs return' but instead are best 'defined, not by essence or purity, but by... hybridity. Diaspora identities are those which are constantly producing and reproducing themselves anew, through transformation and difference' (Hall, 1994, p. 235). For Hall then, modern diasporas are complex formations in which people sharing the same language, cultural and ethno-national ties can remain connected through communications technologies.

The social historian, Benedict Anderson, in his work on the formation of the modern nation, also stressed the importance of communications technologies in forging communities. He argued that the advent of print technologies and the creation of newspapers and the novel played a critical role in the formation of the modern nation as an 'imagined community' (1983). Anderson was puzzled by the fact that while most members of a nation will never actually meet or know one another as a community, some are willing to die for their nation in wars. The modern imagining of the nation was enabled, he argued, by the shared consumption of news, for example, allowing people to experience events simultaneously, to forge a sense of shared time and a shared narrative of national culture. As such, the nation is an **'imagined community'**.

Globalisation and technologies have allowed for what the sociologist Anthony Giddens refers to as the 'connection of presence and absence' (Giddens, 1990, p. 14). Today's global communications technologies allow the imagination to travel with unprecedented speed, collapsing distances and creating greater simultaneity (shared time) between people and places – what Giddens refers to as 'time-space compression'. Anthropologist, Arjun Appadurai, argued that 'electronic mediation and mass migration mark the world of the present not as technically new forces but as ones that seem to impel (and sometimes compel) the work of the imagination' (1996, p. 4). The global dissemination of media, culture, news and information, he suggests, plays a crucial role in imagining communities and forging identities. As such, things like the television and the smartphone give meaning to people's identities by making them feel as if they are part of a community. In this way, they shape the relationship between *individuals and society*.

Scholars such as Stuart Hall (2017) and Paul Gilroy (1993) reflected on how their own identities were hybrid – both 'British' and 'Black'. They drew attention to how national identities like 'Britishness' can marginalise the diaspora groups and the way in which British society has been profoundly shaped by transnationalism. Populist accounts of British history ignore how modern Britain was built on colonialism and slavery, the appropriation of things (i.e. art and artefacts such as can be found in the British Museum) and the enslavement of people. Right-wing British nationalist groups depict British identity in exclusionary terms as white, Christian, and under threat from 'foreigners' or outsiders within the nation. At the same time, these nationalist groups seek to defend 'British' values. This ignores how Britain, due to its historical diversity, has thrived and how we are transnationally interconnected and influenced by other places and people. 'Britishness' is by its very nature transnational, as captured by West Yorkshire poet Matt Abbott:

Matt Abbott, 'Nazis on the Doorstep'

The most British thing in the world is a British night out,
And what exactly do you do on a British night out?
You go up the road to an Irish pub

Sup some Belgian beer, nip out for some grub

You find the nearest takeout, and eat a Turkish kebab

Get driven home by an Asian, in the back of a German cab

You fall asleep in an armchair that you bought in a Swedish shop

Watching American shows on a Japanese telly

Just tell me when to stop.

(Abbott, 2014)

The poem, written in response to the rise of the British National Party and the far right, highlights how integral transnationalism and migration are to 'Britishness'. The poem provides a good introduction to further reflect on how, in today's global world, all nations are fluid, heterogenous societies – constituted by individuals who share certain things in common, such as a language and religion – but they are also mutually dependent on and intimately connected to people, places, businesses, products and societies beyond the nation state. That's why we need the wider, more versatile conception of transnationalism to characterise today's world in which migration and technologies are characteristic features.

4 Migrant transnationalism and digital technologies

Scholars of transnationalism recognised that 'migrants are embedded in networks stretching across multiple states, and migrants' identities and cultural production reflect their multiple locations' (Chaloyan, 2017, p. 31). Transnationalism refers to:

> sustained cross-border relationships, patterns of exchange, affiliations and social formations spanning nation-states.... Facilitated, but not caused, by improved transportation, technology and telecommunications, [entailing] the increasing extent, intensity, velocity and impact of global interconnectedness across a broad range of human domains.
>
> (Vertovec, 2009, p. 2)

Communication technologies help 'migrants to maintain transnationally – effectively both 'here' and 'there' – their originally home-based relationships and interests' (Vertovec, 2001, pp. 574–575). The mix of political, cultural, economic and social practices are no longer confined to one place or time (Chaloyan, 2017). The notion of 'simultaneity' – central to Benedict Anderson's conception of the nation as an imagined community – is also key. The regular simultaneous sharing of media and cultural artefacts through things, that is, objects of digital communication (such as smartphones) with family and friends contribute to the formation of transnational communities as they give meaning to people's identities, and create notions of what it means to belong to one society or another. These developments have led to a new body of scholarship that places the digital at the heart of diaspora and transnational formations. The extract below is from the introduction to a special collection of studies on digital migration published in *Social Media + Society*. As you read it, think about how *power and inequality* shape the relationship between diasporas and digital media.

Reading 4.1

Koen Leurs and Kevin Smets, 'Five questions for digital migration studies: Learning from digital connectivity and forced migration in(to) Europe'

A rich body of scholarship exists that has charted how media and communication technologies have historically played an essential role in the everyday lives of migrants across the world. Migrants have maintained networks and relationships across distance and borders through exchanging letters and audio-cassettes, setting up diaspora newspapers, transnational radio stations, accessing satellite television, engaging in transnational telephone conversations and sending **remittances**. Scholars have also documented how satellite dishes, Internet cafés and more recently migrant smart phone usage and refugee selfies have been projected in populist, right-wing and anti-immigrant discourse as symbols of threat, exclusion, and the supposed failure of integration and multiculturalism. Over the course of the last decade, the scale, intensity, and types of migration and digital mediation have drastically changed and accelerated. Notwithstanding persisting digital divides, the international proliferation of information and communication technologies (ICTs) has greatly impacted upon a variety of migration dynamics, most notably for forced migrants. The transformation of migration toward an always already digitally mediatized migration is a twofold process. The context of forced migrants coming in (to) Europe is the specifically situated example explored in this special section, however it is only one of the possible entry-points to begin to understand the contemporary global conjuncture of migration and digital mediation.

...

[T]here is a sense in which we are all migrants now, whether or not we move physically from one part of the world to another. Via digital technology, most of us are in touch on an everyday basis with a diversity of cultures and opinions. Distance is no longer any barrier to instantaneous communication, driven by a vast expansion in computer power—Anthony Giddens (in Kunushevci, 2017, n.p.).

Anthony Giddens draws on the figure of the connected migrant to reflect on the global contemporary human condition, which is increasingly shaped by transnational communication, mobility, and potentially cosmopolitan encounters. … The barriers [to mobility and connectivity] Giddens speaks of are more easily surmountable by certain mobile populations, rather than others. Particular forms of human mobility (forced migration) are problematized and undesired, while others are championed and welcomed (highly skilled expatriate migrants from the Global North). …

Migration, and particularly forced migration, can be considered one of the most pressing contemporary political issues of our age. … Means of digital communication have spurred new ways for imagined communities to exist on a more global scale.

Thinking about the political in digital migration opens up ways to conceive migrants and migration not merely as the outcomes of political push factors or the objects of law-making and political instrumentalization. Instead, attention for the political in digital migration highlights the agency of diasporic communities and their roles as powerful political actors. …

While to some extent, the potential of media and communication technologies as tools for diasporic engagement with 'homeland politics' has been demonstrated even before digitization … the digital era has equipped diaspora communities with new political opportunities and mobilizing structures. As Kumar (2018) argues, different online platforms and digital tactics are 'transnational springboards for new and more public forms of diaspora identity politics.' Diasporic communities gain voice, visibility, and effective political impact by making use of the opportunities provided by digital technologies ….

We should be wary, however, not to fall into the trap of blind techno-optimism when it comes to the political empowerment of migrants and diasporic communities. The flip side of the digital migration coin presents an image that is much grimmer. The digital is of course also profoundly political in its abilities to provide different actors with possibilities to oppose migration or impede on the rights of migrants. Syrian activists have shared how anti-regime diasporas face 'digitally enabled transnational repression' and anti-Assad protests have been deterred through the reach of 'networked authoritarianism' (Moss, 2016, p. 1).

References

Kumar, P. (2018). Rerouting the narrative: Mapping the online identity politics of the Tamil and Palestinian diaspora. *Social Media + Society*. Advance Online Publication: 10.1177/2056305118764429.

Kunushevci, L. (2017). Anthony Giddens: We are suffering from "cosmopolitan overload" and a huge task lies before us—to create responsible capitalism. *Economy, Sociology and Political Economy*. Retrieved from https://economicsociology.org/2017/11/15/giddens-we-are-suffering-from-cosmopolitanoverload-and-a-huge-task-lies-before-us-to-create-responsible-capitalism/.

Moss, D. M. (2016). The ties that bind: Internet communication technologies, networked author- itarianism, and voice in the Syrian diaspora. *Globalizations*, 1–18. online ahead of print. doi:10.1080/14747731.2016.1263079.

(Leurs and Smets, 2018, pp. 2, 9 and 11; bold added for glossary term)

Transnational communities are now digital in several ways. First, digital technologies make national and local forms of culture global. An individual living in the UK can watch news broadcasts from Moscow, listen to music from the Caribbean, or watch a Bollywood film (Gillespie, 1995), and digital technologies are central to maintaining transnational identities (Nedelcu, 2018). Second, digital technologies provide 'a new territory for diasporas in the virtual space' (Nedelcu, 2018, p. 244), and have become 'more relevant for identity and belonging' than physical spaces (Georgiou, 2010, p. 32). Communities can now communicate, protest, organise and come together entirely online. Third, digital technologies allow communities to become 'transnational agents of change in the homeland' (Nedelcu, 2018, p. 245). Diaspora communities that mobilise online – such as Afghan, Somali, Nepalese and Egyptian diaspora in the USA – have had an impact on the local and national politics of their 'home' nations (Brinkerhoff, 2009). In such cases, civil society struggled to develop on the ground, yet evolved online, and had an impact on debates about human rights and democracy (Nedelcu, 2018). For example, since 2011, the Syrian diaspora in the USA and UK has played an important role in attempting to spread awareness about the war crimes and human rights abuses of the Assad regime (Crilley, 2017). In 2015 as the war in Syria unfolded, the smartphone became a vital tool in the journey to safety of individual refugees. But it was also a threat in some cases – an issue we explore next.

5 The digital passage to Europe for Syrian refugees

We the exiled ones,
who live on anti-depressants,
Facebook has become our Homeland,
it opens the sky
they close in our faces
at the frontiers.

Maram al-Masri, Syrian poet living in Paris (al-Masri, 2018, p. 35)

Since 2011, the civil war in Syria has had a devastating toll on lives and homes. Ahmad's story, which we mentioned above, is but one among millions of lives torn apart by violent conflict. About one-third of all homes and schools, and about half of all medical facilities, have been damaged or destroyed in the conflict. Half the country's pre-war population have fled, and more than six million people are displaced inside Syria. Another five million are refugees in neighbouring countries. Over a million people have fled to Europe. It is sometimes hard to imagine that each number represents an individual life and journey to safety (Reliefweb, 2019).

Amidst this monumental human devastation and suffering, digital technologies have come to the fore as both an essential tool but also a threat. The poet Maram al-Masri reflects on how Syrian refugees suffer from the absence and loss of family, friends and home. In exile, Facebook becomes a kind of virtual homeland, a space that connects them to family and friends. It opens up the world for those who feel trapped within it. This part of the chapter is based on collaborative research led by Marie Gillespie with Syrian and Iraqi refugees about their journeys to Europe and the role of smartphones. We situate smartphone use in the context of the digital infrastructure that either enables or obstructs its use during what we can now refer to as the 'digital passage to Europe' (Latonero, 2015). This is because smartphones have become an essential feature of the refugee journey.

137

The quotations of Syrian refugees and examples of their uses of smartphones referred to in this chapter are taken from research reported in two publications: Gillespie *et al* (2016) and Gillespie *et al* (2018).

5.1 The digital infrastructure

Infrastructures are fixed or stable 'things' that provide us with, for example, water, oil, gas and electricity (Star and Ruhleder, 1996). They are usually invisible to us and only become visible when they break down. The same is true of the digital infrastructure. Nowadays the digital infrastructure is just as important for refugees as the physical infrastructures of roads and railways, boats and planes that get them to safety – to navigate, to communicate and to document their lives. It includes technical systems such as Wi-Fi, SIM cards, charging docks and plugs. In turn, these rely on other material infrastructures, such as energy systems for electricity and power, and are embedded in and entangled with a range of other power structures (such as the economy, national and international laws). Smartphones, as things, must 'plug into' these infrastructures, but access is unequally distributed among different people. This creates certain vulnerabilities.

5.2 Infrastructural vulnerabilities

Accessing Wi-Fi and battery charging points are a constant worry for refugees on their journey, especially when they have limited access to financial or technical resources. Most Syrians crossed the Mediterranean Sea from Izmir in Turkey to Greece in small dinghies. Faced with dangers at sea, informing loved ones of their safe arrival is a very important goal. But during the crossing, alerting coastguards when boats capsize or the sea gets too rough is crucial to survival. Most refugees who die at sea do so because they cannot call coast guards for help. Without battery life, refugees risk being cut off. Even if disconnected for a short time this can mean failing to meet a smuggler, getting lost or separated from companions. This life or death reliance on certain objects, things and connectivity poses a huge risk and makes refugees vulnerable to exploitation.

It is very easy for refugees to fall victim to fraud on their journeys. Abu Islam, who fled Syria, for example, bought a SIM card in Greece which he thought would work across Europe. He needed the phone to navigate his way to Germany, but it didn't work once he crossed the Greek border into Macedonia. In the end, he had to buy '13 SIM cards. That's how I got to Europe' (Gillespie *et al*, 2018, p. 5). Abu Islam also commented on the difficulties he and others faced with regard to smartphone batteries: 'Everyone had 2 to 3 batteries with him, and a charger. We constantly swap and exchange batteries' (Gillespie *et al*, 2018, p. 5). Charging services can be expensive. Nader was 15 years old when we interviewed him in 2016, and he was a school student in Syria before he fled. He explained that he paid five Euros in Macedonia to charge his iPhone's battery.

One central problem refugees – and other vulnerable people, such as homeless people – face is that without the necessary identity documentation (such as evidence of fixed address on a utility bill) it is not possible to register with a mobile network (Faith, 2016). Abdel Rahman explained that refugees often ask someone who speaks the local language and is of fixed abode to accompany them to the supermarket with the necessary documents to register with a network. This is risky and unreliable – and not to mention illegal. It renders individuals vulnerable to blackmail or exploitation. Nabil, from Mosul, recounted his own experience with SIM cards in Paris:

> I was advised to buy an Orange line, I bought it for 20 Euros and I added 20 Euros for credits … but each 2-3 days the company calls me to tell me they'd stop my number as I'm not registered. I went back to the shop and he told me the problem is the company's. Then the number stopped working … I went to the company; they told me they needed a residence permit or a passport. I don't have a passport; I have a copy of it on my phone!
>
> (Gillespie *et al.*, 2018, pp. 5–6)

Even when the passage to Europe is broken up by lengthy spells of time in camps, refugees still face problems maintaining stable Internet access. In such circumstances, smartphones can become a kind of currency. They are bought and sold, exchanged and bartered, fought over and gifted, personalised and loved. They are very important things for people. They may be co-used by entire families or social groups travelling together – albeit accompanied by gender and generational inequalities.

Hassan, for example, was forced to leave Syria, hoping to reach Sweden. He passed through Turkey, Greece, Macedonia, Serbia, Albania, Romania, Hungary and Italy before arriving in France. He did not want to apply for asylum in France, so he avoided biometric registration. The Dublin Regulation of 2003 defines which European state is responsible for assessing an asylum claim. It requires that refugees apply for asylum in the first European country where they arrive and can register. In reality, many asylum seekers, like Hassan avoid having their fingerprints taken in order to continue their journeys to a country where they can reunite with family. So while biometric technologies can be beneficial in that they enable a permanent digital identity, they can also make refugees vulnerable to state surveillance.

Refugees have to negotiate the potential of biometric and other technologies for surveillance and control alongside their potential for enabling choice and **agency**. For example, border guards or hostile forces can confiscate phones and this can pose a threat to a refugee if the data or images on the phone incriminate the hostile forces from whom they may be fleeing. The loss of a functioning phone also means a loss of agency, as it makes it harder to migrate and travel. When asked what he felt like when without a phone, Hassan said, 'Without my phone, I feel completely lost, stripped, naked, like missing a limb' (Gillespie *et al.*, 2018, p. 6). While for many of us the loss of our phone or of connectivity can be frustrating, Hassan highlights the much deeper insecurity refugees can feel upon losing or damaging their smartphones, or, indeed, their 'communication rights' (Leurs, 2017).

Access to the affordances of smartphones (what they allow an individual to do) is dependent not only on refugees' abilities to connect with Wi-Fi or mobile networks en route but also on their family's access in their home countries of Syria, Iraq, or elsewhere. Transnational families rely on transnational connectivity. As Samir explained, 'I wasn't able to communicate with my family because Internet access is cut there, and the phone is cut. I haven't spoken with them since I left' (Gillespie *et al*, 2016, p. 48). Cutting the internet is another tool of state control and a way of depriving people of their communication rights, and their means of staying in touch with family far away.

We cannot do justice here to the heartbreak so many expressed about their communicative separation from loved ones. Abdel Rahman could connect with home but in a restricted way: 'I barely talk to my parents,

after 2 am, because ISIL prohibited the Internet and the satellite then'
(Gillespie *et al*, 2016, p. 50). Refugees' ability to maintain their kinship
network and connection to friends in their countries of origin relies on
contingent sociotechnical contexts on the ground in Syria and Iraq,
and on the journey.

Figure 4.3 A refugee's phone featuring a selfie of their journey.

Syrians faced not only prohibitions on internet use from violent
extremist groups such as ISIL, but also genuine fear about the Syrian
regime and other hostile forces accessing and surveilling conversations,
profiles, and other online activities, especially for political activists and
dissenters on, for example, Facebook pages (Moss, 2016). Online
suppression is transnational and extends beyond people living in Syria
to include political activists living abroad – many are forced to
reconsider their participation in online activism or to rely on avatars or
pseudonyms. Even in Europe, the extent of transnational surveillance
can mean refugees live in fear. When refugees flee, their political
opponents can also flee. Refugees may avoid socialising with other
Syrians they don't know in case communication back home means their
family might be affected by hostile forces.

The multimedia affordances of smartphones have made them a tool
for producing and circulating material in resistance to the Syrian
regime and violent extremist groups like ISIL. Saleem, who is called

the 'Hacker' by his friends, said that he did not travel with his smartphone in Syria, as he would have been identified as a political opponent to the regime. Fighters at government, ISIL, and border checkpoints commonly demand Facebook passwords in order to access Facebook profiles to determine individuals' allegiances in the war. As Kenan said,

> When I got to the border in Turkey, the guard took my phone and asked me for my Facebook password. At first I wouldn't give it to him because I was so scared, but they threw me in prison for 15 days and they beat me, they stole my phone and I was stuck.
>
> (Gillespie *et al.*, 2018, p. 6)

Online surveillance practices render refugee journeys even more dangerous and precarious, and surveillance may continue after arrival as European authorities ask asylum applicants for information about their Facebook profiles, prompting refugees to 'clean' their profiles (Latonero and Kift, 2018, pp. 691–692). The digital traces refugees leave behind in Syrian regime-controlled or ISIL-controlled areas are grounds to be detained, tortured and even killed (Weise, 2016). These examples demonstrate the many forms of 'infrastructural violence' (Rodgers and O'Neill, 2012). This might involve those exercising power depriving people of things – such as destroying or confiscating refugees' smartphones, or debilitating their connectivity. At the extreme, it might involve killing them for their online activities that expose war crimes or protest at contraventions of human rights.

The contradictory dynamics of smartphone use becomes apparent as, simultaneously, they can become a threat to life and a means for survival. This demonstrates how the relationship between *people and things* is complex. People can use things to their advantage, e.g. when travelling, but things, in this case smartphones, may also pose a risk to refugees that use them.

Infrastructures too have contradictory potential. They are unstable and can be simultaneously occupied by regimes of control as well as care. Inclusive, participatory spaces can be fostered by refugee solidarity groups, and powerful 'digital solidarities' emerge among refugees, volunteers and NGO refugee support groups. They can produce new kinds of shared inclusive spaces. Critical interventions and transformations in the practice and circulation of news and information for migrants and refugees are proliferating – from grassroots WhatsApp groups that enable volunteers to mobilise rescue missions, to more top-down interventions such as the European Commission-funded platform InfoMigrants.net.

Refugees often referred to their smartphones as a place of comfort and connection, solace and sociality – a 'mobile home' where they could escape to listen to music, watch films, and nurture social and kinship networks (Smets, 2017). During the journey, families may be separated by loss or death but also the everyday pressures of survival can be intense. Anxiety and depression, marital conflicts, divorce, death, and kinship disputes – all common enough under ordinary circumstances – are exacerbated by the stress of the journey. At the same time, smartphones offer access to communicative channels which provide sustenance – from daily conversations with loved ones, to sharing images, or even participating in wedding ceremonies digitally (Khoury, 2015). The powerful, emotional dimensions of smartphones, captured so beautifully by Maram al-Masri in her poem quoted at the beginning of this article, crystallize how Facebook, for example, can blur frontiers and open up imaginative horizons that make the loss and separation of exile just about bearable. As al-Masri suggests, for many people forced to migrate, 'Facebook has become our homeland', and this highlights how digital technology shapes the relationship between *individuals* and the *societies* they are born into, migrate to, and settle in.

5.3 Smartphone affordances

Having outlined the fragile, contingent infrastructural contexts of smartphone use by refugees, we now look more closely at particular affordances – or possibilities for action. The communicative affordances of smartphones for most of us include:

(a) portability – they can be easily carried anywhere

(b) locatability – they allow people to navigate and find places and people

(c) multi-media – they can capture images and sound, as well as text – they are multi-sensory devices that allow creative production and cultural consumption.

Affordances – what people can do with smartphones – are not static or fixed but emerge. We may all use smartphones in similar ways, but for particular groups like refugees on their journeys they have very specific uses at different moments in Syria, en route, and upon arrival. These uses are best traced across time and place to illuminate the fluid nature of affordances, and the agency which users can exercise, even in contexts of exile. As with Ahmad, refugees flee their homes suddenly, without planning, and often with only their mobile phones and some money – just enough for them to make their way to Europe.

Refugees we spoke to mentioned three central things about their smartphones: mobility, locatability and safety. Navigation and communication platforms are essential. Abu Islam, like many other refugees, travelled in a small group. His group elected him as the leader because of his 'cultural capital' (see Section 1), in particular his competence in the English language, and technical proficiency in using smartphone applications. The group depended on him to guide them using Google Maps. Aktham too spoke about his experience crossing by sea from Turkey to Greece and how he relied on remote advice:

> We were in the rubber boat, all the phones were in those little plastic bags we all buy, he [the leader of the group] was the only one not to put his phone in a bag so he could stay in touch with coastguards and send our location to his brother in the Netherlands. Every few minutes, he used to tell his brother where we were. His brother was able to help guide us from a distance as he has already made the journey.
>
> (Gillespie *et al.*, 2018, p.7)

Refugees actively sought to be, and depended on being, locatable and visible to ensure their survival at sea. This desire for traceability contrasts with the imperative to hide online activities while in Syria or ISIL-controlled parts of Iraq. For refugees on the move, commuting between online visibility and invisibility is essential. Digital practices change based on which border they are crossing or which actors they expect to encounter. Negotiating the smartphone infrastructure for refugees involves much learning to avoid detection, arrest, detention and deportation.

Refugees' journeys required versatility and agility in digital skills, as they had to jump between various smartphone applications to communicate and navigate. Pioneer refugees inform others about legal-political differences between countries – for example, where best to claim asylum or how to avoid biometric registration processes in a country like Greece. Some respondents received tips about routes and how to prepare in dealing with state actors: 'wear hair gel and dress smartly at borders.' Many access information on their smartphones before leaving, and so are knowledgeable about claiming asylum in Europe.

Figure 4.4 'The road to Germany' – a map shared on Facebook to help refugees reach Germany from Izmir, Turkey.

Nabil explained that he received information from other refugees he met on the road. He spoke about a Facebook group where refugees shared information between themselves. These digital solidarity networks often endure well beyond the journey: 'Where are you going? I'm going to Finland, you can have this, this and this [referring to shelter, food and financial support].' Another refugee stated that their digital discussions explored 'Where are you going? I'm going to Germany. I can have my fingerprints taken there and claim asylum and family reunification is easier there', and these statements remind us how technology plays a prominent role in the lived experiences of migration, transnationalism and diaspora in the digital age. These technologies shape the relationship between *individuals and society*, are bound up with *power and inequality*, and things such as smartphones subsequently have important meanings for the lives of migrants, refugees and diaspora across the world.

6 Conclusion

This chapter has outlined the concepts of diaspora and transnationalism, and how they have been used by sociologists to analyse the twin experiences of migration and digital technologies. We have examined how the capacity to migrate is linked to the power of the state to define citizens and non-citizens, and how through accidents of history, war and birthplace, inequalities prevail. This can mean unequal access to resources, opportunities or the power to choose where to live or how or when to migrate. We saw how the decision to migrate and a refugee's journey is now reliant on the relationship between 'things' like the smartphone device and infrastructure, and the different societies that refugees travel through, and the different state regimes that must be encountered at borders. We saw how there is a deep tension between the possibilities for benefits but also for harm when refugees use smartphones.

The same affordances that allow refugees to 'keep on moving on' and communicate with families and friends are also used by immigration control, hostile regimes and extremist forces to target activists and political opponents. The locatability affordances which provide orientation – and are navigation and survival tools for refugees – also involve geo-locatable data that enable state and non-state actors to monitor and exclude, capture and detain, repatriate and return refugees. Furthermore, while the multimedia affordances of smartphones enable refugees to document and share their personal stories, and open up new possibilities for information gathering and the co-production of knowledge and representation, they also run the risk of promoting the circulation of misinformation and personal exposure as, for example, when recorded images of torture or abuse on refugees' phones fall into the hands of the perpetrators, causing untold harm and even death. Thinking about *people and things* offers a way in to a deeper understanding of these tensions: invisibility and exposure, mobility and immobility, risk and opportunity. A smartphone makes users visible, connected and networked, but this can also expose them to risks.

References

Abbott, M. (2014) *Nazis on the doorstep*. Available at: https://youtu.be/j6hb-x4Pk6U (Accessed: 3 October 2019).

Ahmad (2017) Interview with Ahmad. Interviewed by Marie Gillespie, 23 January (surname withheld to protect identity).

al-Masri, M. (2018) *Liberty walks naked: poems*. Translated by T. Dorgan. Cork: Southword Editions.

Anderson, B. (1983) *Imagined communities: reflections on the origin and spread of nationalism*. London: Verso.

Appadurai, A. (1996) *Modernity at large: cultural dimensions of globalization*. Minneapolis, MN: University of Minnesota Press.

Brinkerhoff, J.M. (2009) *Digital diasporas: identity and transnational engagement*. Cambridge: Cambridge University Press.

Chaloyan, A. (2017) *Fluctuating transnationalism: social formation and reproduction among Armenians in Germany*. Wiesbaden: Springer VS.

Cohen, R. (2008) *Global diasporas: an introduction*. Abingdon: Routledge.

Crilley, R. (2017) 'Seeing Syria: the visual politics of the National Coalition of Syrian Revolution and Opposition Forces on Facebook', *Middle East Journal of Culture and Communication*, 10(2), pp. 133–158.

Faith, R. (2016) *How does the use of mobile phones by 16–24 year old socially excluded women affect their capabilities?*. PhD Thesis, The Open University.

Georgiou, M. (2010) 'Identity, space and the media: thinking through diaspora', *Revue Européenne des Migrations Internationales*, 26(1), pp. 17–35. doi: 10.4000/remi.5028.

Giddens, A. (1990) *The consequences of modernity*. Cambridge: Polity Press.

Gillespie, M. (1995) *Television, ethnicity and cultural change*. Abingdon: Routledge.

Gillespie, M., Ampofo, L., Cheesman, M., Faith, B., Illiou, E., Issa, A. and Skleparis, D. (2016) 'Mapping refugee media journeys: smartphones and social media networks'. The Open University/France Médias Monde. Available at: http://www.open.ac.uk/ccig/sites/www.open.ac.uk.ccig/files/Mapping%20Refugee%20Media%20Journeys%2016%20May%20FIN%20MG_0.pdf (Accessed: 1 November 2020).

Gillespie, M., Osseiran, S. and Cheesman, M. (2018) 'Syrian refugees and the digital passage to Europe: smartphone infrastructures and affordances', *Social Media + Society*. 4(1), pp. 1–12, doi: 10.1177/2056305118764440.

Gilroy, P. (1993) *The black atlantic: modernity and double consciousness*. Harvard: Harvard University Press.

Hall, S. (1994) 'Cultural identity and diaspora', in Williams, P. and Chrisman, L. (eds) *Colonial discourse and post-colonial theory: a reader*. 1st edn. New York: Columbia University Press, pp. 227–237.

Hall, S. (2017) *Familiar stranger: a life between two islands*. London: Allen Lane.

Headrick, D.R. (1979) 'The tools of imperialism: technology and the expansion of European colonial empires in the nineteenth century', *The Journal of Modern History*, 51(2), pp. 231–263.

Khoury, R.B. (2015) 'Sweet tea and cigarettes: a taste of refugee life in Jordan', *Forced Migration Review*, 49, pp. 93–94.

Kumar, P. (2018) 'Rerouting the narrative: mapping the online identity politics of the Tamil and Palestinian diaspora', *Social Media + Society*, 4(1), pp. 1–18. doi: 10.1177/2056305118764429.

Latonero, M. (2015) 'For refugees, a digital passage to Europe. Thomson Reuters News', *Thomson Reuters Foundation*. Available at: http://news.trust.org/item/20151227124555-blem7/ (Accessed: 1 November 2020).

Latonero, M. and Kift, P. (2018) 'On the digital passageways and borders: refugees and the new infrastructure for movement and control', *Social Media + Society*, 4(1), pp. 1–11. doi: 10.1177/2056305118764432.

Leurs, K. and Smets, P. (2018) 'Five questions for digital migration studies: learning from digital connectivity and forced migration in(to) Europe', *Social Media + Society*, 4(1), pp. 1–16. doi: 10.1177/2056305118764425.

Migration Data Portal (2019) *2017 migration data*. Available at: https://migrationdataportal.org/data (Accessed: 1 April 2019).

Nedelcu, M. (2018) 'Digital diasporas' in Cohen, R. and Fischer, C. (eds) *Routledge handbook of diaspora studies*. Abingdon: Routledge, pp. 241–250.

Reliefweb (2019) *UNHCR – Syria Factsheet (January 2019)*. Available at: https://reliefweb.int/report/syrian-arab-republic/unhcr-syria-factsheet-january-2019 (Accessed: 1 December 2020).

Rodgers, D. and O'Neill, B. (2012) 'Infrastructural violence: Introduction to the special issue', *Ethnography*, 13, pp. 401–412.

Safran, W. (1991) 'Diasporas in modern societies: myths of homeland and return', *Diaspora: A Journal of Transnational Studies*, 1(1), pp. 83–99. doi: 10.1353/dsp.1991.0004.

Smets, K. (2017) 'The way Syrian refugees in Turkey use media: understanding "connected refugees" through a non-media-centric and local approach', *Communications*, 43, pp. 113–123. doi:10.1515/commun-2017-0041.

Star, S.L. and Ruhleder, K. (1996) 'Steps toward an ecology of infrastructure: design and access for large information spaces', *Information Systems Research*, 7(1), pp. 111–134, doi:10.1287/ISRE.7.1.111.

UN (1951) *The 1951 Refugee Convention*. Available at: https://www.unhcr.org/1951-refugee-convention.html (Accessed: 4 April 2019).

UN (2016) *Definitions*. Available at: https://refugeesmigrants.un.org/definitions (Accessed: 1 April 2019).

Vertovec, S. (2001) 'Transnationalism and identity', *Journal of Ethnic and Migration Studies*, 27(4), pp. 573–582. doi: 10.1080/13691830120090386.

Vertovec, S. (2009) *Transnationalism*. Abingdon: Routledge.

Weise, Z. (2016) 'Isil murders five media activists for exposing Syria atrocities', *The Telegraph*, 26 June. Available at: http://www.telegraph.co.uk/news/2016/06/26/isil-murders-five-media-activists-for-exposing-syria-atrocities/ (Accessed: 1 November 2020).

Winsor, M. (2018) *On World Refugee Day 2018, a record 68.5 million forcibly displaced last year.* Available at: https://abcnews.go.com/International/world-refugee-day-2018-record-685-million-forcibly/story?id=56026315 (Accessed: 1 April 2019).

Chapter 5

Transnational digital networks: families and religion

Umut Erel and John Maiden

Contents

1 Introduction

In the previous chapter you have learned about how refugees use digital technologies on their journeys. In this chapter, which addresses the broader area of migration and digital technology, you will explore how migrants engage with digital technologies in ways which foster transnational networks. 'Transnationalism' is defined by Vertovec as 'sustained cross-border relationships, patterns of exchange, affiliations and social formations spanning nation-states' (Vertovec, 2009, p. 2). This chapter will help you gain a better understanding of the concept of transnationalism through the study of families and religion. It will demonstrate how concepts such as connected presence, ambient co-presence and the social 'capital' of religion can help us understand the social world, and the role played by digital technologies.

To begin with, you might like to consider how you use digital technologies to stay in touch with home when either you or your family members travel. How, for example, do you/they keep in touch with family? Perhaps you use text messages to let them know you arrived safely or take selfies or use webcam. How do you/they keep in touch with 'home' society more broadly? Do you/they use online news media, for example, or websites or forums for particular groups, clubs or societies? You might also want to imagine the challenges of maintaining close relations with home if, instead of going on a short trip, you are absent for several years, or even permanently, as is the case for many migrants.

1.1 Teaching aims

The aims of this chapter are for you to:

- examine the role of digital technologies for transnational families and religion

- explore how digital technologies in migration, both in the case of families and religion, are part of the relationship between individual and society and between power and inequality

- consider how digital technologies help migrants to maintain their family relationships through connected presence, ambient co-presence and **always-on lifestyles**
- compare and contrast key theoretical concepts concerning global religion and migration.

2 Transnational families and care

In 2011, Donna, a Filipina had lived and worked for two years in a care home in the UK. She video-called her husband and two sons aged 10 and 12 every evening at 10 pm when it is 6 am in the Philippines. Her sons were getting ready for school and having breakfast, while Donna was proud to see them in their neat school uniforms, asked them about school and homework. Once they had left for school, she video-called her mother who looked after Donna's eight-month-old daughter. Donna found out whether the baby had eaten and slept well and sang songs to her and played peek-a-boo until Donna herself had to go to sleep in preparation for her early morning shift. When she woke the next morning, the first thing was to check for her sons' texts, and to remind her son to take his medication. She then briefly video-called her husband and mother to find out about their day, and briefly called again during her break just to say hello. On Sundays, when she was not working, the family used webcam to talk to each other, often leaving the camera on for eight hours.

(Adapted from Madianou, 2012, pp. 287–288)

This vignette shows how digital technologies can be used to create a feeling of closeness in the lives of transnational families, overcoming some of the challenges that geographical distance poses. These 'transnational families' use the possibilities of digital communication in their family practices. By connecting with each other through digital media, as well as offline, these people integrate the digital into the everyday ways of 'doing family'. The concept of family practices employed by sociologists (Morgan, 2011) emphasises the ways in which people create meaning for their intimate relations with each other through their everyday activities. In the vignette above, you can see that the use of digital media has become an important part of transnational family practices. The remainder of this case study will explore how this influences family relationships and roles, and what benefits and challenges the use of digital media offers transnational families in caring about each other.

Figure 5.1 Family talking on webcam.

Since the late 20th century, we have seen increased migration and an increase in transnational family forms. Transnational family forms are part of the lives of professional global elites, middle class skilled migrants, but also poor migrant workers, refugees and undocumented migrants; that is, those who migrate without the paperwork required by the countries of destination and therefore do not have the right to live or work in the country. Oftentimes, those who have more resources, such as money, education or citizenship of a country in the **Global North**, have more rights and opportunities to migrate. Bryceson and Vuorela (2002, p. 3) define transnational families as 'families that live some or most of the time separated from each other, yet hold together and create something that can be seen as a feeling of collective welfare and unity, namely "familyhood", even across national borders'.

One particular concern for social researchers has been the experience of women from poor countries who migrate to the Global North. These migrations are often motivated by the desire to earn enough money to raise their children and provide them with a good education. While there are no available data on the total number of children left behind globally, we know that it is a significant issue, in some regions of the world affecting between a tenth to a third of children (Jan *et al.*, 2017).

In order to economically provide for their children, women migrate, leaving their children behind in their countries of origin, and therefore are unable to provide the day-to-day, hands-on care that is often expected of mothers. Feminist sociologists have argued that this is not simply a paradox for the *individual* families involved, but a problem for *society*: They argue that migrant women who leave behind their own children create a care deficit in the countries they come from. This care deficit has to be filled by grandparents, older siblings, aunties and paid nannies and domestic workers who look after the children left behind. This is particularly poignant, as many women from poor countries migrate in order to work as care givers to the elderly, sick or children in countries of the Global North. These migrant families' experiences show that care and economic resources are not distributed equally. Instead, migrant women can create an 'emotional surplus' in the countries in which they work, while at the same time their own families may suffer from a care deficit, in particular the children (Hochschild, 2000). Thinking back to C. W. Mills, whose work you encountered in Chapter 1, the global distribution of resources to care is an important example of private troubles becoming public issues. This, then, highlights that the *individual* experiences of migrant families are part of a wider *social* issue of *power* and *inequality*. Individual mothers are motivated to migrate because of the global inequalities in opportunities to earn sufficient money to support their families. In the **Global South** these mothers cannot earn enough, therefore they migrate to the Global North to earn more money and regularly send money, called financial remittances, back home to support their families. Yet this migration can lead to new *inequalities* of access to care, with their own children in the Global South having to miss the hands-on care of their own mothers, while these very mothers are engaged in caring for people in the Global North who benefit from an emotional surplus value.

We also know, however, that not all transnational family forms are characterised by deeply entrenched global inequalities. For example, Baldassar, Baldock and Wilding (2006) used qualitative **ethnographic research** to find out how migrants to Australia organised and cared for their elderly parents in their home countries. This was a large study including families from a range of countries: Ireland, Italy, the Netherlands, Singapore, New Zealand and Iran. While they also found that it can be challenging to organise family life across long distances, particularly in situations of a health crisis, they highlight that the care among these transnational family members is not one-way from the adult migrant children to their aging parents. Instead, they found that family relationships were fluid and dynamic, changing over time and according to life-cycle events such as births, deaths and migration. So over time, they found that the same members of the family network can be receivers and providers of care, emotional and financial support. Therefore, they suggest thinking of care as 'circulating'. This finding may be because their research included migrants who had a more secure, long-term migration status and were also financially more secure. In contrast to the idea of a care deficit on one hand and emotional surplus on the other, the idea of care circulation is a different way to think of how care shapes transnational family relationships.

2.1 Technologies for caring

Now let us think about how transnational families use technologies for staying in touch and caring for each other. In their qualitative research with Filipina migrant workers in the UK, Mirca Madianou and Danny Miller found that when they started their research in 2007, not all family members in the Philippines had access to the internet, as those in remote areas were not able to access telephone landlines. These families instead used dedicated international telephone cards to make the cost of calling cheaper, yet on average spent £150 to £200 per month on phone calls, which was a significant proportion of their incomes as low paid workers. This contrasts with the mobile phone packages that many employed and local people have access to at a far smaller cost. Yet, even families with internet access had to navigate a number of issues in order to communicate on the internet, such as learning to use the technology, sometimes attending classes to do so – that is, they needed to gain the necessary skills or cultural capital to use digital technologies. In particular migrants, such as domestic workers or carers, who lived in their employers' homes needed to get permission from their employers to connect to the internet. In addition they needed the financial capital to buy the equipment (computers, smartphones) and afford the cost of connecting to the internet. All of these factors are shaped by *power and inequalities*, for example, a migrant domestic worker whose permission to stay in the country depends on her employer may find it difficult to persuade the employer to grant her access to the internet or even permit her to own and use a smartphone. On the other hand, the lack of internet infrastructure in migrants' home regions is part of regional inequalities in the countries of origin, where some regions do not receive the same level of provision of infrastructure by the government and technology companies as others.

2.2 How do transnational families use digital technologies to 'do family'?

Earlier in the chapter we looked at how migrating, and in particular leaving children behind, reflects the contradiction between being a breadwinner for one's children at the same time as feeling the obligation and wish to emotionally care for them. This contradiction is both *individually* experienced by mothers, but it also refers to the *societal* expectations that mothers should be closely involved in the hands-on care and upbringing of their children. This expectation on mothers is widespread in many cultural contexts and countries.

Opportunities for intensive mothering

Digital media's affordances have enabled many migrant mothers to be more intensively involved in caring for their children at a distance. Think back to Donna who was introduced earlier in the chapter, and how she uses webcams and digital telephony, as well as text messaging, to be closely involved in her family's life in the Philippines. She closely monitors what her children eat and wear, plays games with the youngest child on webcam, and helps her older children with their homework over Skype or email. She is also involved in organising and managing their lives by discussing details of their care and schooling with her mother and husband. Moreover, she has a say over how household money is spent, as she can discuss any major and regular expenses with the carers back home. Before the advent of digital media, many migrant mothers were concerned that the regular money they sent back home might not be used as they would wish. Nowadays, digital technology offers them more power to monitor how this money is spent, for example some demand that the carers who look after their children (often family members, sometimes paid domestic workers) send them scanned receipts for their expenses. Furthermore, Donna can see through the webcam that money has been spent on neat and clean school uniform for her children – she does not need to rely on the children's carers to verbally assure her of this. In this sense, the smartphone and webcam give *power* to Donna and other mothers to be closely involved in and have a say over how their children are raised.

Connected presence

Digital media afford these families the opportunity to create a sense of 'connected presence' (Licoppe, 2004), an ongoing 'dialogue' that helps to 'maintain the feeling of a permanent connection ... that the link can be activated at any time' (Licoppe, 2004, p. 141). This helps migrant women to negotiate their relationship to societal norms of what a good mother should do, and whether migrating to earn money for their children should be part of these norms.

Juozeliūnienė and Budginaitė have studied the experiences of transnational families from Lithuania, through an analysis of media texts and qualitative interviews with migrant mothers and their children. They find that media and politicians in Lithuania strongly criticise women for leaving children behind to become breadwinners abroad. They label them as 'bad', 'selfish' mothers who 'abandon' their children. Against the backdrop of these very negative presentations of migrant mothers, the researchers found that when they interviewed migrant mothers themselves, they developed a different presentation of self. Like the Filipina mothers, they argue that digital technologies enable their connected presence with their children. These digital technologies enabled them to resist the label of bad mother and instead assert their own, positive presentation of mothering through digital connected presence as 'modern mothering' (2018, p. 273). This speaks to the theme of *individuals and society* through Goffman's idea of presentation of self that you encountered in Chapter 2. We can see that in this case, digital technologies allow individual migrant mothers and their families to challenge the ways in which society, in the form of media and politicians, present them as problematic. Instead of accepting societies' negative views, the individual mothers develop a different, more positive presentation of self, as successfully fulfilling social expectations of mothers through technology.

Ambient co-presence

Thinking back to Donna's example, we can see that migrant families use a range of different media for different purposes. Madianou and Miller (2011) coin the term polymedia, to describe this: migrants can make up for the disadvantages of a particular type of media by using another form of media to connect with family members. However, for a number of migrants, social networking sites like Facebook have begun to take the place of a range of other digital media. One consequence of this is that migrants and their family members experience a new sense of community through 'ambient co-presence' – that is the feeling of awareness of what friends and family are doing, even when they are far away, because you can get an idea of their activities at any one time, through social media. When using social networking sites, such as Facebook, migrants connect to a network of family and friends, which also includes the friends of their contacts. The newsfeed provides them with updates of their network, so that they are constantly updated on the activities of their family members by 'status updates, photographs, videos, links to other sites, records of usage of applications (such as games) and "likes"' (Madianou, 2016, p. 218).

Figure 5.2 Woman on her mobile phone.

While these newsfeeds allow users to find out what their family members are doing at a particular moment in real time, the information is also retrievable (unless it has been intentionally deleted) and therefore also functions as an asynchronous reminder of the others' activities and presence. These newsfeeds offer a large amount of visual information, and through the rise of smartphones, which enable family members to access the social network sites wherever they are, they have fed into an 'always on' lifestyle (boyd, 2012), where people can receive continual updates on their family members. In addition, many migrant families also use the locative functionality, which informs the newsfeed of their loved ones' geographical location. These affordances 'enable a peripheral awareness of distant others' (Madianou, 2016, p. 189). The Filipina migrant mothers in Madianou's research are usually constantly on social networking sites and check them several times an hour, which means that these newsfeeds are woven into their everyday lives.

What follows is an extract from an article that explains the concept of ambient co-presence in more detail and why it is an aspect of connecting and reassuring transnational family members.

Reading 5.1

Mirca Madianou, 'Ambient co-presence: transnational family practices in polymedia environments'

Ambient co-presence extends the possibilities of co-presence at a distance. Even though it rests on indirect communication, ambient co-presence can have powerful emotional consequences.

The reassuring nature of ambient co-presence can be understood when considering the anxiety that often emerges in its absence. When Donna noticed that her sons had been inactive online for several days, she became worried. She even called her teenage son on his mobile phone – something she has rarely done since she started using social media and Skype quite heavily. Similarly, several participants became worried when their significant others did not appear 'online' at a usual time. If one expects one's partner or child to come home at a regular time and to switch on his or her laptop and automatically log on to Skype, then this establishes a pattern. When an established pattern is disrupted, it becomes a source of concern or anxiety, which may be accentuated by physical distance as it is difficult to check on a relative to find out what is going on.

A metaphor that can shed light on the reassuring nature of ambient co-presence in the context of deterritorialized relationships comes from physical, geographical co-presence. Ambient co-presence can provide a comforting background awareness of others appearing and disappearing online, waking up or returning from work, announcing their visit to a shopping mall or sharing pictures of their dinner. It is comparable to the familiar sounds of family members going about their parallel activities in one's home without necessarily interacting with each other but being profoundly aware of the others' presence, such as the soothing sounds of someone cooking in the kitchen, or of a child playing in her room. Although indirect, ambient co-presence allows for the regular presence of distant others in the lives of migrants. Compared with the pre-Web 2.0 era participants now have access to a plethora of details about their families' whereabouts, activities, food, clothes and other possessions. ... However, this was not so a few years ago when the only visual cues afforded to migrants were photographs, whether attached to an email and sent and received via an internet café, or posted through a letter, which might take weeks to arrive.

This does not imply that intense emotions have no place in transnational communication in polymedia environments. ... [C]onflict is clearly present in transnational families. The ambient awareness of domestic rhythms can only be reassuring when family members enjoy good relationships. When there are tensions, frequent or constant communication can reveal problems that make situations fraught and difficult. The difference with the past situation is that conditions of 'always on' reveal connectivity problems more easily. ... Furthermore, once problems surface, the constant communication afforded by polymedia provides opportunities, at least potentially, to discuss and negotiate. So, although conflict and arguments continue to be part of transnational family life, as in every family, the intensity of the arguments is potentially assuaged because there are more opportunities to address their causes and, indeed, more opportunities to have arguments. Some participants reported that arguments may be more frequent, but less intense.

(Madianou, 2016, pp. 196–197)

This extract explains the concept of ambient co-presence, that is the feeling of awareness of what transnational friends and family are doing, as you have an awareness of their activities at any one time, through social media. The reading highlights the emotional consequences of ambient co-presence. On one hand, the concept emphasises how family and friends can be sensed as engaged in comforting routine activities through their social media presence. This helps families maintain a feeling of belonging. On the other hand, if these routines are disrupted, migrant family members may become anxious and feel the need to check on their family members' well-being. So, the disruption of a routine of ambient co-presence can be cause for concern or show a conflict or difficult situation between family members. This contrasts with previous forms of communication, where family members found it easier to conceal difficult situations from far away migrants. So far, we have looked at how different digital media platforms afford transnational families ways of connecting with each other. Migrant families choose particular forms of media to communicate with each other, caring for each other across the distance. However, these digital technologies can also have their challenges. For example, while migrant mothers appreciate the opportunity to connect with their families on webcam – sometimes virtually spending the whole day with their families back home, having lunch, chatting, helping with homework – the moment of having to say goodbye to loved ones and disconnect the webcam can also be an occasion where the physical distance is acutely felt, and can be a moment of great sadness. Another challenge of digital technologies can be that while it can be reassuring to know through a social media newsfeed what, for example, a distant boyfriend is doing at any given moment of the day, this can be very difficult when the relationship breaks down. Digital technologies have the potential to maintain close family relationships through allowing migrant mothers to know the everyday detailed movements of their children, yet this can be seen as both an advantage and a disadvantage, depending on the perspective.

Madianou reports an example where a mother found out that her son had dropped out of school because his social network site status showed him as available at a time when he should have been at school. This example shows the possibility of digital technology for greater control by migrant parents. So, from the point of view of the mother, technology had a positive effect, as her son could not mislead her. The son on the other hand might think that his mother's ability to find out about his dropping out of school, despite his efforts to conceal it, is something negative. As you may remember in the previous chapter, refugees also experienced both positive and negative effects of digital technology, with a negative effect being that it could be used by border guards and militant groups to gain information and control over their social connections and their movements.

2.3 Summary: transnational families

Globally, we see an increase in mobility, and this in turn creates a larger number of transnational families. For these transnational families, digital communication has become an important part of doing family. Digital communication has helped them to overcome some constraints, it has enabled them to show care and in particular has enabled migrant women to intensively mother children left behind. This has allowed some women to forge a more positive self-presentation as mothers, against the backdrop of negative presentations in media and political discourses of migrant mothers as 'selfish' or uncaring. On the other hand, digital communication has also created new opportunities for a wider pool of family members, such as cousins, nephews, nieces, aunts and uncles, who live at a distance to create and maintain family relationships, an activity that used to be largely undertaken by women. In this sense, digital communication has contributed to sharing the care for a range of family members more equally among genders and generations. Webcams, and always-on lifestyles, have enabled transnational families to practise a connected presence, while social networking sites have helped families to develop an ambient co-presence. Yet, these family practices are embedded in a range of other ways of showing care for each other, such as telephone calls, text messages, letters, or through family visits. While digital media can compensate for long distances by enabling emotional support and advice giving, they fall short of some aspects of face to face relationships, such as hands-on care, and cannot enable other sensual forms of bonding, such as touch and smell.

The next section of this chapter will look at another example of how migrants' religious lives are enabled by digital technologies.

3 Transnational religion

'All over the world, the Spirit has been moving, and today he is online.'

(African pentecostal pastor, quoted in Asamoah-Gyadu, 2015, p. 161)

We now turn to transnational religion. We are going to look at a specific variety of Christianity called Pentecostalism. Pentecostalism is a highly influential type of Christianity worldwide, with many different churches and millions of followers in the Global South. Here cities such as Lagos, Nigeria, and Sao Paulo, Brazil, are now global centres of Christianity. Although Christianity in previous centuries came to many places in the Global South through missionaries from the Global North – sometimes working in tandem with imperial expansion – migration and mission from the Global South are increasingly bringing Christianity back to places such as Western Europe and North America.

Church denominations often have a central headquarters, and many local churches (sometimes known as parishes) worldwide. In this chapter we will use the Redeemed Christian Church of God (RCCG), a large Pentecostal denomination, which has its headquarters in Lagos, Nigeria (see Figure 5.3), as a case study. This is transnational, having established congregations all over the world, in fact almost wherever migration from West Africa has occurred (see Figure 5.4). Pentecostal churches such as the RCCG can form their members – who may be migrants or their descendants who have settled in a new country – into transnational religious communities (or 'societies'), often utilising digital technologies to achieve this. Before we consider this further, however, we might ask why the study of religion should be taken seriously by social scientists in the contemporary world?

3.1 Religion in a globalising world

During the 1960s, it became common for social scientists to argue that religion and modernisation were incompatible. This was 'secularisation' theory, defined by the sociologist Bryan Wilson as 'that process by which religious institutions, actions, and consciousness, lose their social significance' (1982, p. 149). The guiding idea behind this theory was that *individuals'* sense of belonging to *society* would be changed in modernising societies. The classical version of this was that secularisation was the inevitable consequence of three 'core' processes said to be basic to modernisation:

Differentiation: new social systems provide services once offered by religious organisations, such as healthcare and education

Rationalisation: science provides explanations and answers to problems which religions previously defined and claimed to solve supernaturally

Societalisation: rural-urban migration and industrialisation break up traditional local communities which religious organisations bound together.

Figure 5.3 'Redemption Camp', the headquarters of the Redeemed Christian Church of God, Nigeria.

This theory assumed that as modernisation was global, so the social influence of religion would decline globally. In one famous statement, sociologist Peter Berger argued: '[By] the twenty-first century, religious believers are likely to be found only in small sects, huddled together to resist a worldwide secular culture' (1968, p. 3).

Figure 5.4   The Redeemed Christian Church of God in Sheffield, United Kingdom.

However, many scholars have since challenged classical secularisation theory, suggesting the evidence points to a far more complex reality. Berger himself wrote in 1996: 'The world today, with some exceptions … is as furiously religious as it ever was, and in some places more so than ever' (1996, p. 3). Some critiques of secularisation theory are based on observations of global developments. Since the 1960s, religions have appeared resurgent in the Global South. In some Muslim majority nations, for example Iran and Egypt, religious organisations – often encouraged by the state – have increased their role in civil society (Herbert, 2003). In many Global South contexts, religious expressions with an emphasis on embodied practices and experience of the 'supernatural' in everyday life, flourish, often utilising new technological developments to assemble communities and share experiences. The fact that such expressions of 'spirit' are frequently combined with, and transmitted through, digital technologies seems to blur ordinary Western distinctions between religious and secular.

In the case of Christianity, while broadly speaking the social significance of the historic churches has declined in the Global North, the Global South situation is very different. The American historian of global Christianity, Philip Jenkins, argues: 'Over the past five centuries, the story of Christianity has been inextricably bound up with that of

Europe and European-derived civilizations overseas, above all in North America … Over the past century, however, the center of gravity in the Christian world has shifted inexorably … southward, to Africa, Asia, and Latin America' (2003, p. 2). This shift represents a shift in the global relations of *power and inequality*: once missionaries brought Christianity to the Global South, often facilitating the translation of the Bible and other literatures, indigenous peoples became instrumental in making the religion their own. In the 20th century this included the emergence of new churches from the colonial and/or missionary encounter, based in local theologies and traditions of doing religion.

Global North and South are not separate stories. In the case of Western Europe, since the mid 20th century, migration has brought individuals and families from the Global South. Migrants, and their subsequent generations of family, have tended to be more 'religious' than others in the European societies. Indeed Kaufmann, Goujon and Skirbekk argue that as a result of migration 'we may begin to see "de-secularization" in Western Europe in the coming decades' (2012, p. 86). Christian migrants, supported by missionaries and church 'planters' from the Global South contexts, engage in religious 'place-making', establishing local churches, often linked with denominations in places of origin. African Christianity in London is one example of this; a study of the Borough of Southwark identified at least 240 individual 'Black Majority Churches' – probably 'the greatest concentration of African Christianity in the world outside of Africa' (Rogers, 2016).

How does this relate to this chapter's theme of transnationalism? We can think of transnationalism in terms of global flows – including of *people and things*. The anthropologist Arjun Appadurai describes transnationalism using this metaphor of 'flows'; of technology, finance, ideas, media and people (Appadurai, 1996). Transnational religion involves such flows: for example, of people who transport religious beliefs and practices, and religious organisation; of money to support religious work; of media and technologies, as various as magazines, phone calls, emails and the internet, to build religious networks. As one scholar asserts: religion is a 'powerful, under-explored site of transnational belonging' (Levitt, 2004, p. 14).

3.2 Transnational Pentecostalism and digital technology

Secularisation theory, broadly speaking, posits that scientific and technological advances mean religion will play less of an important role in modernising societies. Why, then, has Pentecostalism flourished? Pentecostalism emerged in Global South contexts partly due to missionary enterprise from North America and Europe. A report by the Pew Foundation in 2006 found that in Brazil, 49%, and in Nigeria, 26% of the total population was Pentecostal (the Pew report uses the term 'charismatic', which is a label of which you might be aware, to denote a particular brand of Pentecostalism). Pentecostalism looks set to become 'the predominant global form of Christianity of the 21st century' (Casanova, 2001, p. 435). The most distinctive aspect of Pentecostalism is emphasis on embodied spiritual experience. The encounter with the Spirit of God provides individual believers with extraordinary gifts, particularly healing, speaking in tongues and prophecy. Pentecostalism also tends to be 'this-worldly'; for example, divine victory over evil forces at work in the world; or divine blessing resulting in health and prosperity. Pentecostal worship tends to involve exuberant physical actions such as raising hands or clapping, and spontaneity rather than formality.

Pentecostal churches based in the Global South utilise digital technology to build transnational networks and support expansion resulting from migration and mission. Websites and social media link believers and congregations in the Global North with denominations in the Global South, often projecting the authority and teaching of key (usually male) authority figures. Social media platforms can convey the authority of religious leaderships by allowing followers to testify to the power of their ministry, perhaps with 'likes' or written messages (Asamoah-Gyadu, 2015, pp. 166–167).

3.3 The Redeemed Christian Church of God: transnational Pentecostalism

RCCG has its roots in Nigeria in the 1950s. The epicentre of the denomination is 'Redemption Camp', a complex near Lagos which includes an auditorium for half a million people as well as a university, shops, schools, banks and housing (see Figure 5.3). Leadership of the RCCG is focused on the General Overseer, at the time of writing, in

2019, Dr Enoch Adeboye. He is a globally influential person, included in the *Newsweek* 'Top 50 Global Power Elite' list of 2008–09. He oversees an organisation which by 2009 had 14,000 branches worldwide, 440 parishes in Britain alone by 2019 (Burgess, 2012, pp. 127–130).

The RCCG is organised through centralised power along with local churches being able to act and take decisions flexibly. The Church 'is a network of units weaved together under a paramount leader who exercises absolutely authority and power in matter of doctrines, administration, liturgy and finance but allows each unit sufficient scope to develop according to where it is located' (Ukah, 2003, p. 273). Alongside a strong centre, regional and local leadership is encouraged in ways which allow for a flexibility of leadership and practice depending on the context. Although there are major efforts also to evangelise beyond the core constituency, RCCG parishes overseas tend to attract persons of Nigerian or West African heritage.

In early 2019, John Maiden spent time researching the online presence of RCCG in order to explore its religious transnationalism. This is evident in its 'vision' statement:

> To make heaven.
>
> To take as many people with us.
>
> To have a member of RCCG in every family of all nations.
>
> To accomplish No. 1 above, holiness will be our lifestyle.
>
> To accomplish No. 2 and 3 above, we will plant churches within five minutes walking distance in every city and town of developing countries and within five minutes driving distance in every city and town of developed countries.
>
> We will pursue these objectives until every Nation in the world is reached for the Lord Jesus Christ.
>
> (RCCG, 2017a)

Transnational networks are supported in various ways. The international website of the RCCG includes a parish locator ('Locate a parish near you!') which contains details of local congregations worldwide (RCCG, 2017b). The website displays its global appeal by including a page of links – displayed as images of flags – of national and regional 'units'. Through such mechanisms, a Nigerian migrant, for example, could move to a city elsewhere in the world and rapidly locate a familiar church.

Individuals and parishes worldwide are connected with 'central' teaching and resources. The website claims the arrival, with digital technologies, of a 'knowledge age' prophesied thousands of years ago by a biblical prophet. It claims that Mobile App products enable believers to 'key into the knowledge age' and 'bring you closer to the word of God and/or bring the word of God closer to you' (RCCG, 2017c). The latest sermons from Redemption Camp are available on the website, and the Church has a presence on Twitter, YouTube (where services are live-streamed), Facebook and Instagram (RCCG, 2017d). These platforms disseminate the authority of the church leadership and particularly of the General Overseer, affectionately nicknamed 'Daddy GO'. Other online presences do the same. A website eaadeboye.com is devoted to the General Overseer and, as of May 2019, Adeboye's combined social media followers on Facebook, Twitter and Instagram were claimed to number nearly 4.5 million. Posts by Adeboye quickly receive many comments, often affirming the 'power' of his ministry with messages such as 'Amen' or 'Amen in Jesus Mighty name'.

The online presence of RCCG can shape the religious practices, or spirituality, of members worldwide. A devotional website, 'Open Heavens' (Adeboye, 2019), is 'a daily companion for your everyday life'. Subscribers receive daily newsletters to their electronic devices, and devotional resources are accessed, often relevant to 'this-worldly' issues. One devotional text reminded readers 'In the Redeemed Christian Church of God, our help comes from above, and I am happy to announce to you today that Jesus has never failed us.' It urges readers, 'Beloved, I want you to look up to God for that miracle you are expecting – be it provision, victory, healing or whatever' (Adeboye, 2019). Open Heavens and the various other websites and platforms mentioned connect believers worldwide under the leadership of Adeboye.

Digital technology allows two-way transnational participation. Both Open Heavens and eaadeboye.com enable believers to submit prayer requests; the RCCG website includes a digital 'altar call' allowing someone who wishes to convert to Christianity to submit a form to inform the Church (RCCG, 2017e). Various platforms also enable financial transactions, in order that believers can give to ministries. The

Church has a scheme called 'Partners 75' (RCCG, 2017f). The website explains: 'The General Overseer of the Redeemed Christian Church of God (Worldwide), Pastor E. A. Adeboye has requested that His Children (Those that call him Daddy) become members of "Partners 75".' Participants were asked to pray for 75 minutes ('or more') every month. They could also give '75', joining one of eight 'groups'; for example, group one could donate per month 75 Kobo, 75 US cents or 75 pence sterling; group seven, 750,000 Naira, US Dollars, Pounds sterling or Euros (group 8 could donate a higher amount monthly). Through such spiritual and financial exchanges RCCG members worldwide participate in a transnational spiritual society.

3.4 Transnational religion as social 'capital'?

Pierre Bourdieu distinguishes between different forms of capital – economic, cultural and social – and various scholars suggest religious groups specifically produce social capital, which includes social contacts with people that can be used for social mobility (Smidt, 2003; Adogame, 2013). Can Pentecostalism generate social capital, and what is the role of digital technology in this?

In their new Global North settings, churches may produce social capital in various ways, simultaneously providing continuity with religious and ethnic identities and practices from 'home' while also helping migrants adapt to their new social contexts, perhaps helping them to negotiate legal processes or providing practical support. One pastor quoted in a study of the RCCG in Britain said: 'Its almost like a home away from home, like a community away from home. Because once you find yourself here you don't have the support network that you once knew back at home. Therefore the church becomes a form of support network' (quoted in Burgess, 2012, p. 130). Digital technologies are often utilised to build and maintain congregations. Such congregations dovetail the 'embodied' and the digital. In the case of African migrant churches, the individualism of Global North contexts can make it even more necessary to resort to digital modes of communication rather than traditional 'personal' modes (Adogame, 2013, p. 134). Research on Brazilian Pentecostal churches in Europe has shown how they reach out to newly arrived migrants and publicise church events through social networking platforms (Oosterbaan, 2010). While these churches have taken advantage of digital technology, they have not compromised their supernaturalism. Afe Adogame has observed a sign outside an RCCG congregation reading: 'Please switch off your mobile phones. The only urgent call expected here is the voice of God'. He suggests this is 'an indication of how the RCCG negotiates modernity' (Adogame, 2013, p. 122).

In the following reading, an academic discusses the generation of 'capital' in the RCCG in London:

Reading 5.2

Richard Burgess, 'African Pentecostal growth: the Redeemed Christian Church of God in Britain'

One way the RCCG contributes to 'faithful capital' is through its congregational welfare departments which assist members in financial difficulty. Churches also organize seminars on such topics as business management, investment, immigration issues, marriage and health awareness. RCCG's Royal Connection parish, located in the ethnically-diverse London borough of Newham, has an 'integration team', run by volunteers, to assist migrants to settle. Above all, churches provide access to social and spiritual resources for new migrants by providing contexts for communal worship, prayer and Christian fellowship, thus contributing to the stocks of social capital necessary for successful integration. Prayer in particular is considered an important resource for dealing with obstacles to successful integration. Every parish has a regular prayer meeting and most worship services provide opportunities for people to receive prayer for particular needs, whether these are immigration issues, financial and health problems or family relationships. Many congregations have house fellowships to provide pastoral care for members. They also have a variety of single interest groups to support different categories of people, including youth, women, men, lone parents, childless couples and business people.

(Burgess, 2012, p. 132)

It can be argued, then, that Pentecostal churches, like those described here, may have an important role to play in supporting and resourcing individuals and communities. However, while religious groups, such as Pentecostal churches may generate social capital, they may also have negative impacts. Afe Adogame argues, in the case of African migrant churches in the Global North, that while they can generate significant social capital, they 'both empower and disempower their members' (2013, p. 109). Pentecostal churches such as the RCCG, for example, can be very critical of aspects of modern liberal understandings of Lesbian, Gay, Bisexual, Queer and Transgender rights. It may therefore be argued that Pentecostal churches can disempower some members of their own communities.

4 Conclusion

You have looked at the relationship between digital technology and both transnational families and religion. In each case you have explored the themes of *individuals and society* and *power and inequality*. Transnational families can use digital technologies to maintain close relationships with each other despite the geographical distance. For migrant mothers, leaving behind their family members to support them economically is one way in which, as *individuals*, they deal with the unequal opportunities to earn a livelihood in different *societies*. Yet, as mothers are often expected to also provide the hands-on care for their children, these mothers are sometimes faced with negative societal views of them. Digital technologies allow migrant mothers' connected presence with their families, and through ambient co-presence, families can maintain a sense of everyday closeness. For many migrant mothers, this is an important way to challenge negative presentations of themselves, by presenting themselves as mothers who are intensely involved in caring for their children. In this sense, transnational migrant families use digital technologies not only to create closeness, but also to challenge the social stigma of migrant mothers as selfish or uncaring. Migrant mothers then use the digital technology to empower themselves to care for their children from a distance, even when they are faced with the unequal distribution of care between the Global South and the Global North: While many women migrate to the Global North to make a living, they leave behind a 'care deficit' in their own families, while producing an 'emotional surplus' in the Global North. Yet, by building and maintaining close emotional ties with their children and family members back home, the migrant mothers shift this inequality to some extent.

The study of transnational religion, which began with a discussion of theories of global religion, addressed the *individual and society*, showing how Pentecostalism, through its utilising of digital technology, can both engage the individual with churches in lands of origin or heritage and help migrants settle in new social contexts. It also looked at issues of *power and inequality* through a discussion of the contested area of religion – Pentecostalism – and social capital. Certainly, it appears that religious organisations such as Pentecostal churches, while perhaps in some ways in tension with modernity, are far from 'anti-modern' in their use of digital technologies. Such churches, like transnational families, can use digital technology to support, enhance and substitute their physical, face-to-face manifestations and intimacies.

References

Adogame, A. (2013) *The African Christian diaspora: new currents and emerging trends in world Christianity*. London: Bloomsbury.

Adeboye, E.A. (2019) 'From above or from abroad?', *Open Heavens*. 29 January. Available at: https://iopenheavens.com/2019/01/28/open-heavens-daily-devotional-january-29-2019-from-above-or-from-abroad/ (Accessed: 24 May 2019).

Appadurai, A. (1996) *Modernity at large: cultural dimensions of globalisation*. Minneapolis, MN: University of Minnesota Press.

Asamoah-Gyadu, J.K. (2015). '"We are on the Internet": contemporary Pentecostalism in Africa and the new culture of online religion', in Hackett, R.I.J. and Soares, B.F. *New media and religious transformations in Africa*. Bloomington, IN: Indiana University Press.

Baldassar, L., Baldock, C.V. and Wilding, R., 2006. *Families caring across borders: migration, ageing and transnational caregiving*. New York, NY: Springer.

Berger, P. (1968) 'A bleak outlook is seen for religion', *New York Times*, 25 February, p. 3.

Berger, P. (1996) 'Secularism in retreat', *The National Interest*, 46 (Winter 1996), p. 3.

boyd, d. (2012) 'Participating in the always-on lifestyle', in Mandiberg, M. (ed.) *The social media reader*. New York, NY: New York University, pp. 71–76.

Bryceson, D.F. and Vuorela, U. (2002) 'Transnational families in the twenty-first century', in Bryceson, D.F. and Vuorela, U. (eds) *The transnational family: new European frontiers and global networks*. London: Bloomsbury, pp. 3–30.

Burgess, R. (2012) 'African Pentecostal growth: the Redeemed Christian Church of God in Britain', in Goodhew, D. (ed.) *Church growth in Britain*. Farnham: Ashgate.

Casanova, J. (2001) 'Religion, the new millennium and globalization', *Sociology of Religion*, 62(4), pp. 415–441. doi: 10.2307/3712434.

Herbert, D. (2003) *Religion and civil society: rethinking public religion in the contemporary world*. London: Routledge.

Hochschild, A.R. (2000) 'Global care chains and emotional surplus value', in Hutton, W. and Giddens, A. (eds) *On the edge: living with global capitalism*. London: Jonathan Cape, pp. 130–146.

Jan, C., Zhou, X. and Stafford, R. S. (2017) 'Improving the health and well-being of children of migrant workers', *Bulletin of the World Health Organization*, 95(12), p. 850.

Jenkins, P. (2003) *The next Christendom: the coming of global Christianity*. Oxford: Oxford University Press.

Juozeliūnienė, I. and Budginaitė, I. (2018). 'How transnational mothering is seen to be "troubling": contesting and reframing mothering', *Sociological Research Online*, 23(1), pp. 26–281.

Kaufmann, E.P.; Goujon, A. and Skirbekk, V. (2012) 'The end of secularization in Europe? A socio-demographic perspective', *Sociology of Religion*, 73(1), pp. 69–91.

Levitt, P. (2004) 'Redefining the boundaries of belonging: the institutional character of transnational religious life', *Sociology of Religion*, 65(1), pp. 1–18.

Licoppe, C. (2004) '"Connected" presence: the emergence of a new repertoire for managing social relationships in a changing communication technoscape', *Environment and Planning D: Society and Space*, 22(1), pp. 135–156.

Madianou, M. and Miller, D. (2011) 'Mobile phone parenting: reconfiguring relationships between Filipina migrant mothers and their left-behind children', *New media and society*, 13(3), pp. 457–470.

Madianou, M. (2012) 'Migration and the accentuated ambivalence of motherhood: the role of ICTs in Filipino transnational families', *Global Networks*, 12(3), pp. 277–295.

Madianou, M. (2016) 'Ambient co-presence: transnational family practices in polymedia environments', *Global Networks*, 16(2), pp. 183–201.

Morgan, D.H. (2011) 'Locating "family practices"', *Sociological Research Online*, 16(4), pp. 1–9.

Oosterbaan, M. (2010) 'Virtual re-evangelization: Brazilian churches, media and the postsecular city', in Beaumont, J., Molendijk, A. and Jedan, C. (eds) *Exploring the postsecular: the religious, the political, the urban*. Leiden: Brill.

Pew Foundation (2006) *Spirit and power: a 10-country survey of Pentecostals*. Washington DC: The Pew Forum on Religion and Public Life.

RCCG (Redeemed Christian Church of God) (2017a) *Mission and vision*. Available at: http://rccg.org/who-we-are/mission-and-vision/ (Accessed: 29 January 2019).

RCCG (Redeemed Christian Church of God) (2017b) *Locate a parish near you*. Available at: http://rccg.org/rccg-parishes/ (Accessed: 29 January 2019).

RCCG (Redeemed Christian Church of God) (2017c) *Tools and resources*. Available at: http://rccg.org/rccg-mobile-products/ (Accessed: 1 February 2019).

RCCG (Redeemed Christian Church of God) (2017d) *Latest sermons*. Available at: http://rccg.org/rccg-media/ (Accessed: 1 February 2019).

RCCG (Redeemed Christian Church of God) (2017e) *Altar call form*. Available at: https://rccgpayments.trccg.org/holyGhost/trccg.org/altar.php (Accessed: 24 May 2019).

RCCG (Redeemed Christian Church of God) (2017f) *Partner 75*. Available at: http://rccg.org/partners-75/ (Accessed: 25 May 2019).

Rogers, A. (2016) *How are black majority churches growing in the UK? A London Borough case study*. Available at: http://blogs.lse.ac.uk/religionglobalsociety/2016/12/how-are-black-majority-churches-growing-in-the-uk-a-london-borough-case-study/ (Accessed: 22 January 2019).

Smidt, C.E. (ed.) (2003) *Religion as social capital: producing the common good*. Waco, TX: Baylor University Press.

Ukah, A. (2003) *The Redeemed Christian Church of God (RCCG), Nigeria. Local identities and global processes in African Pentecostalism*. PhD dissertation. University of Bayreuth.

Wilson, B. (1982) *Religion in sociological perspective*. Oxford: Oxford University Press.

Section 3

Humans and machines

Introduction to Section 3

Simon Carter

Welcome to Section 3. In this section, we will be examining some of the different relationships between humans and machines. The main sociological thread explored in this block is that of *people and things*; however, there will be a chance to also consider the *individuals and society* and *power and inequality* threads in various places.

Humans and machines

People and things are normally thought of as separate categories. People do things, take action and think; whereas things are passive, they are the objects of action. The advent of sophisticated digital computers has, however, begun to challenge this distinction. For example, over the last four decades, computers have become so commonplace that many of us, at times, imagine that our brains might work similarly. Are our minds anything more than highly complex computing devices? In the digital age, it would be reasonable to imagine that our minds may be no more than sophisticated computers. However, a mirror to this question would be to ask, 'will computers ever possess human qualities?' Will a thing ever be like a person?

The Turing Test

When viewed from this standpoint, the question could be reminiscent of one of the most famous computer/human interactions, the Turing Test. The Turing Test is named after Alan Turing, who is widely regarded as having a significant role in pioneering the development of theoretical computer science and artificial intelligence (AI). During the Second World War, Turing and his colleagues created an automated machine for breaking secret codes known as the Bombe (Figure 1). This machine could find the solution to code-breaking problems in minutes – tasks that would have taken humans weeks to complete. The Bombe could effectively do something that no human could. The Bombe was a moment when it became possible to speculate on the limits of what machines could do.

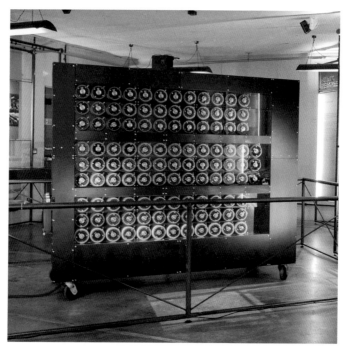

Figure 1 Replica of the original Bletchley Park Bombe.

Turing's work on the Bombe no doubt influenced his thinking on the possibilities that computing may have for the future. In 1947, during a public lecture, Turing gave what is thought to be the first mention of computer intelligence, saying 'what we want is a machine that can learn from experience ... the possibility of letting the machine alter its own instructions provides the mechanism for this' (quoted in Copeland, 2003, p. 2). In 1950 Turing wrote a paper entitled 'Computing Machinery and Intelligence' (Turing, 1950) where he began by posing the question, 'Can machines think?' It is from this paper that the Turing Test derives.

Turing begins by speculating that the question, 'Can machines think?', is difficult to answer because it is very tricky to define thinking or even how it should be measured. Instead of attempting a definition, he chose to 'replace the question by another, which is closely related to it and is expressed in relatively unambiguous words' (Turing, 1950, p. 433). What he proposed was something he called the Imitation Game.

Turing's original version of the Imitation Game involved a thought experiment in which a man (A) and woman (B) are asked questions by an interrogator (C) whose gender is not important for the game. The interrogator sits in a separate room from A and B and asks them questions via an electronic terminal connection. The male respondent A can give misleading answers, while the female B must help the interrogator by being truthful. The object of the game is for the interrogator to determine which one is the woman.

Next, a machine replaces the male respondent A. This is the crux of Turing's thought experiment. 'What will happen when a machine takes the part of (A) in this game?', Turing asks. 'Will the interrogator decide wrongly as often when the game is played like this as he does when the game is played between a man and a woman?' (Turing, 1950, p. 434). In other words, will the fact that male respondent (A) – who is allowed to give misleading answers – has been replaced by a machine make it easier for the interrogator to work out who out of (A) or (B) is the woman or will the task remain as difficult?

The expression, 'Turing Test' was coined much later, and subsequent discussions about it have tended to focus on the question, can a machine pass for a 'thinking human'. In fact, what is now commonly called the Turing Test describes a game played between a machine (A), a human (B) and an interrogator (C), the aim of which is to determine whether (A) or (B) is the machine. Since the early 1990s, there have even been regular competitions to see if a machine can pass the Turing Test. Questions of gender no longer play any significant role in the Turing Test. However, the question of gender in Turing's original Imitation Game will be returned to later, because it raises important, and often overlooked, issues.

Turing realised that his ideas might be controversial and much of his paper on 'Computing Machinery and Intelligence' anticipates potential opposition to the notion that a machine could successfully imitate human thinking. He dismisses various objections including those that grant special status to humans, mathematical limits and theological objections. Perhaps his most important objection is what he describes as an 'argument from consciousness'. Here Turing argues against the belief that a machine could only imitate human thinking if it were truly conscious:

> In short then, I think that most of those who support the
> argument from consciousness could be persuaded to abandon it

rather than be forced into the solipsist position. They will then probably be willing to accept our test.

(Turing, 1950, p. 447)

The objection that a machine can only imitate a human if it is conscious is dismissed as a form of solipsism by Turing. Solipsism is the idea that the self is the only thing that can be known to exist – everything else could be a creation of the mind. Thus, the only way to know if a machine is thinking is to be that machine. As a rule, we do not practice this against other humans, so Turing argues that machines should not be held to a higher standard. In other words, when we talk or converse with a fellow human, we normally accept that we are talking to a thinking and conscious person. Turing concludes that it is not necessary to solve the mysteries of consciousness, rather that the Imitation Game can be used to determine if a machine understands a conversation.

Gender and the Turing Test

In the years since Turing proposed his Imitation Game, there has not been much attention paid to the potential questions his game raised about the nature of gender and sexuality. His original game involved an interrogator trying to determine if they could tell the gender of either: a man pretending to be a woman, compared to a woman being truthful; or a machine pretending to be a woman (or even a machine pretending to be a man pretending to be a woman), compared to a woman being truthful.

There may be serval reasons why Turing chose to incorporate an element of gender determination in the Imitation Game. Some have suggested that Turing simply wanted to stage a fair basis for comparison between machine and human – 'the woman (either as a participant in the game or as a concept) acts as a neutral point so that the two imposters can be assessed in how well they "fake"' (Saygin, Cicekli and Akman, 2000, p. 467) – the gender of the 'faker' was irrelevant. There have also been suggestions that the gender determination could hint at underlying sexism because it implies that a machine would find it easy to imitate a woman but difficult to imitate a man.

The philosopher Judith Genova has provided a feminist analysis of the Imitation Game, that argues the importance of Turing's biography in understanding the unusual design of the game. Turing was gay in a time and place when homosexuality was still a criminal offence. He was charged with gross indecency in 1952 (and pardoned for this in 2013), and to avoid prison he had to undergo hormonal treatment designed to reduce libido (often referred to as chemical 'castration'). Shortly after this, he committed suicide at the age of 42. Genova regards Turing as a significant figure in late 20th-century thought, and his Imitation Game was part of a more general philosophy of 'transgressive boundaries':

> The connection that Turing makes in his 'sexual guessing game' between thinking and gender becomes less surprising the more one learns about his personal life. His homosexuality is particularly important for my purposes. As a homosexual, he was involved in gay life's daily imitation game in which most of the time, especially in Turing's day, one pretended to be straight; at other times, one vogues stereotypical masculinities or femininities.
>
> (Genova, 1994, p. 316)

Genova here is also raising the issue of *power and inequality*. When Turing wrote his 1950 paper, he did not have the power to define his sexuality. Like many other individuals in this period, he suffered an unequal position in society, where he could be subjected to the power of the criminal justice system for expressing a sexual identity. Genova argues that Turing designed his Imitation Game to playfully challenge the idea of discrete categories such as male and female. According to Genova, Turing's Imitation Game was based on the idea that a major part of gender identity was itself a performed role. Gender is not a stable category; rather, social expectations and gender performances construct it. Part of being a 'man' or 'woman' is reproducing roles which we have been socialised into to conform to social norms. If a machine were going to pass for a human, it would have to imitate a gender role – it would have to play the role of being male or female. Turing, as a gay man, by using gender imitation in his game, is trying to hint that gender is a socially imposed concept. Seen from this perspective, Turing's text is not only a manifesto for artificial intelligence, but it is also a 'plea for artificial beings with new gender and sexual opportunities' (Genova, 1994, p. 313).

In recent years there have been several events reported in the press that give the impression that a machine may have passed the Turing Test. On Saturday the 7 of June 2014, it was reported that a program named 'Eugene Goostman' had passed the Turing Test (Sample and Hern, 2014). Eugene Goostman is a Russian chatterbot (Figure 2). Chatterbots are natural-language based programs that can be used to simulate conversation by using simple pattern matching of keywords to generate replies to questions. Such programs analyse a question for keywords and then comb a 'knowledge base' for a possible answer.

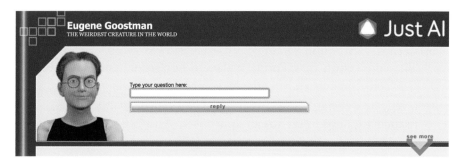

Figure 2 Eugene Goostman chatterbot.

Eugene Goostman took part in a competition held at the Royal Society in London, together with four other computerised contestants. Each had to take part in a five-minute, text-based conversation with a panel of judges. Eugene managed to convince a third of the judges that it was a real person to win the competition. One of the problems with the Turing Test, as currently passed by Eugene, is that it encourages trickery and deception. Eugene uses techniques of distraction and misdirection, practices commonly associated with magicians, to pass the Turing Test. For example, Eugene in the test used various 'tricks' to give the impression that he was a non-English speaking boy of 13. Often 'he' made spelling or grammatical mistakes to give the impression of a careless teenager who was not used to speaking English. When 'he' faced a question that could not be convincingly answered, 'he' simply changed the subject or asked the judge a question to distract from 'his' lack of an answer.

Turing ends his paper with the hope that in the future machines will compete with humans in all purely intellectual fields, which returns us to his original question of whether 'machines can think'. At the time of Turing writing his original paper, it may have seemed reasonable to suppose that imitations of a human in conversation would be a good test to apply. However, now this test may be considered far too narrow in scope and does not test whether machines will be able to compete with humans in intellectual endeavours. Turing posed his 'imitation game' in the context of what he thought would be the emergence of machine intelligence and what he believed would be a reasonable test of intelligence, given the problems with defining something as nebulous as 'intelligence'.

Partly, the problem is that ideas of what counts as intelligent performance have changed considerably over the last half-century. Once, having an aptitude for solving mathematical problems would have been seen as evidence of intelligence; nevertheless computers, ever since the invention of the Bombe, far exceed the mathematical abilities of humans. It was also once thought that playing chess was a mark of human intelligence and that a computer would never be able to win against a human world champion. And then in 1996, IBM's Deep Blue beat Garry Kasparov, then the world chess champion, at chess. Being good at maths and playing chess well are markers of intelligence, but only as very narrowly defined. Imitating a human in conversation is also a marker of intelligence, although again only in a very narrow sense of the word.

Critics of the Turing Test have complained that the test fails to measure important indicators of intelligence, namely cognitive abilities, self-awareness and sentience (Dvorsky, 2014). Indeed many non-human things that do show evidence of these abilities would fail the Turing Test. For example, great apes have abilities to solve complex problems; have a sense of self; can plan for the future; express empathy and have an awareness of other minds (Cavalieri and Singer, 1996), yet would not pass the Turing Test.

Reading this section

In the rest of this section, we will be examining various aspects of how humans and machines interact. In Chapters 6 and 7, we will explore ideas of agency and **autonomy**. In particular, about the extent to which machines can be thought to possess aspects of agency and how this may challenge the idea that only people possess agency. Thus in Chapter 6, we will consider some commonplace digital objects, such as apps and devices, which help people navigate in unfamiliar locations and how these can alter our idea of autonomy and agency. We will then go on to consider how agency may be distributed by looking at a fairly advanced automated system, a commercial flight to Barcelona on a modern aircraft. In Chapter 7, we will discuss several competing sociological frameworks for understanding the relationships between *people and things*. These will be illustrated with examples drawn from contemporary workplace, educational and therapeutic contexts, including workplace monitoring and surveillance, robot co-workers and the use of therapy robots. In Chapter 8, you will be learning about medicalisation and biomedicalisation by looking at the various digital devices that people use to monitor and quantify their mobility and the implications of these for health.

References

Cavalieri, P. and Singer, P. (eds) (1996) *The great ape project: equality beyond humanity*. New York: St Martin's Press.

Copeland, J. (2003) 'The Turing Test', in J.H. Moor (ed.), *The Turing Test: The Elusive Standard of Artificial Intelligence* (pp. 2–23). Dordrecht: Springer.

Dvorsky, G. (2014) 'Why the Turing Test is bullshit', *io9*. Available at: https://io9.gizmodo.com/why-the-turing-test-is-bullshit-1588051412 (Accessed 25 February 2019).

Genova, J. (1994) 'Turing's sexual guessing game. Social epistemology: a journal of knowledge', *Culture and Policy*, 8(4), pp. 313–326.

Sample, I. and Hern, A. (2014) 'Scientists dispute whether computer "Eugene Goostman" passed Turing test | Technology' *The Guardian*. February 6. Available at: https://www.theguardian.com/technology/2014/jun/09/scientists-disagree-over-whether-turing-test-has-been-passed (Accessed 20 February 2020).

Saygin, A.P., Cicekli, I. and Akman, V. (2000) 'Turing test: 50 years later', *Minds and Machines*. doi: 10.1023/A:1011288000451.

Turing, A.M. (1950) 'Computing machinery and intelligence', *Mind: A Quarterly Review of Psychology and Philosophy*, LIX(236), pp. 433–460.

Chapter 6

Semi-autonomous digital objects: between humans and machines

Simon Carter

Contents

1 Introduction

In this chapter, you will be reflecting on how digital devices can alter our idea of agency and autonomy. Agency here means that people can act freely according to their own choices, intentions and desires; and autonomy, which is related to agency, refers to a person's ability to make choices unaffected by forces external to themselves. In the first part of the chapter, you will consider how some commonplace digital objects, such as apps and devices, help people navigate in unfamiliar locations and whether these can alter our idea of autonomy and agency. You will then consider agency in more detail and look at how it is possible to consider different levels of agency when examining different digital *things* and their interactions with *people*. Finally, you will consider how agency may be distributed by looking at a fairly advanced automated system – a commercial flight to Barcelona on a modern aircraft.

1.1 Teaching aims

The aims of this chapter are for you to:

- examine the role of digital objects using the concepts of agency and autonomy

- consider the ways in which digital things and devices can give rise to the idea of distributed agency

- evaluate the sociological thread of *people and things* in the context of digital technologies.

2 Where is the action?

We usually think of 'action' as something that people do in any given situation, often when dealing with a problem or difficulty, to achieve an aim. Action is something that people deliberately do, and we are therefore expected to take responsibility for these actions. For example, when a film is described as an 'action movie' we all generally have a good idea about what is involved. Normally there will be a central character or 'hero' who takes various actions, such as running, jumping, shooting or fighting. The story will often follow a set pattern or narrative structure (Propp, 1968) – the hero will be presented with a problem to be solved and villains that need to be defeated. The hero's actions, after a few set-backs, will eventually resolve the problem and lead to a successful resolution.

While the 'hero' in such films is the centre of the action, this is not the whole story. Action, in these circumstances, includes *people* interacting with a variety of *things*. It is closely coupled with the actions of planes, automobiles, weapons, and associated gadgets. The hero of the action movie would not be able to resolve the story and produce a successful resolution without all the things that they surround themselves with. So, is the hero of such films taking 'action' by themselves or are they dependant on their interaction with the things around them? The relation between *people and things* begins to call into question the status of autonomous human action, especially when many 'smart' digital things now exhibit degrees of their own **autonomy**.

Things now surround us in our homes, workplaces and everyday life that exhibit large degrees of autonomy. For example: all new cars are fitted with automated anti-lock braking systems (ABS) that intervene, without driver involvement, to prevent skidding during sudden deceleration; many homes are fitted with smart thermostats that predict when the heating needs to be turned on depending on weather conditions and the detection of occupants in the house; hospitals often have semi-automated pharmacies to dispense drugs; it is common for many industrial processes to operate with minimal human supervision. Indeed, there are few human activities, whether in the factory, office, home or hospital, that are not now potentially aided by smart digital devices.

Most of us are quite happy to hand some of our autonomy to digital devices while doing everyday activities. Driving is a good example of this. In the past, if someone wanted to visit an unfamiliar place, they would either use a paper map or ask for directions. Now, either by the assistance of dedicated 'satnav' devices or wayfaring apps on smartphones that use the Global Positioning System (GPS) technologies, people can navigate to destinations 'aided' only by this technology when before they would have had to use paper maps. These devices give spoken, turn-by-turn instructions to drivers, who follow these 'orders', often without question. Many satnavs are linked to traffic information services to 'intelligently' plan routes around potential delays and traffic jams. Some even give weather updates and warn about speed cameras or unsafe driving conditions.

Users of these devices appear to be happy to relinquish some of their autonomy to simplify finding their way to unfamiliar places. Are there, however, any potential problems with giving over our autonomy to such gadgets? One such problem has been straightforwardly described as 'death by GPS', a phrase attributed to rangers working in Death Valley national park in California. The phrase 'death by GPS' describes what happens when a satnav device gives technically correct route instructions, in the sense that a suggested path is the most direct way to get from point A to point B, but it takes the driver down roads that are entirely unsuitable for a normal vehicle. Such was the case for Alicia Sanchez and her six-year-old son, who in 2009 were driving through Death Valley when her GPS directed her down what seemed to be a normal road. After 20 miles the road disappeared, and her Jeep became buried in sand. She was not found by a ranger until a week later, by which time, tragically, her son had died (Milner, 2016).

Another problem with ceding autonomy about driving decisions to satnav devices arises when they are re-routing cars in response to traffic problems. GPS wayfinding devices direct drivers away from congestion by monitoring traffic flows. This is done by anonymously accessing data collected from other users of satnavs and mobile phones, about geographic location and speed. This data is sent back to the satnav's control centre, where software calculates a route to avoid congestion. It assumes that roads that have little evidence of traffic are good choices to send drivers along. For most of the time, this works well, and drivers are happy to relinquish decision making about route choice if it means fewer hold-ups and traffic jams. Yet in 2017 GPS-enabled route-finding systems caused some drivers to ask, on social

Figure 6.1 Using satellite navigation in a car.

media, if their satnavs 'were trying to kill them'. This happened in Southern California, where at least five wildfires had been burning, engulfing tens of thousands of acres of land. Roads in these areas understandably had no traffic on them, but automated systems began directing traffic onto routes through wildfires. As a report in USA Today said:

> LOS ANGELES—Users of popular navigation apps like Waze are warning the services directed them to neighborhoods where wildfires forced closures and evacuations. The issue stems from the way apps like Waze help users avoid commute nightmares such as heavy traffic or construction. Largely reliant on information supplied by other drivers, when the Google-owned app notices gridlock on a user's route, it will reroute the driver to quieter streets – even if they're empty because drivers have fled smoke and the threat of flames.
>
> (Graham and Molina, 2017)

So, while these GPS devices were not intentionally trying to kill their owners, under these unusual circumstances, ceding some autonomy over driving decisions, to digital objects had unintended consequences. Cases like these raise questions about human action and autonomy. If you are driving and your GPS device tells you to take a road or turning, who is making this choice? And if something bad happens as a result of this 'choice' who is responsible? These questions will be discussed further in the next section.

3 Action and agency

The advent of digital devices, self-directing machines and artificial intelligence have problematised the idea that action and autonomy are always restricted to human actors. The issue of autonomy refers to an important debate in sociology and philosophy around the ideas of agency versus **social structures** or free-will versus determination. Within sociology, debates about agency raise questions about both *people's* place in *society* and *power and inequality.* Central to these debates are questions about whether people can use their agency, or free-will, to express their power or if they are constrained by social structures. The social structures that sociologists have in mind here are those social forces found in **social institutions** and configurations of institutionalised relationships, such as: class, family, media, law, the economy and politics. Many of these social structures are interconnected, and it is argued that they have an impact on an individual's thoughts, actions, experiences and options. Against this, it could be argued that people can individually, or collectively, use their agency to express power and shape their own life experiences.

Many sociologists avoid either the position that structure determines individual agency or that individuals alone have the agency to create social worlds. Rather they take the connection between structure and agency to be an ever-changing process of co-production – which simply means that both structure and agency influence one another. So, while individuals are affected by current social structures, they also have the 'agency' to influence how these structures evolve and change. In other words, there is a degree of interdependency between people's ability to use agency to act and take action, and the constraints that social structures place on this action.

You can see therefore that the debate about structure and agency is an important one in sociology. Sociologists have always acknowledged that people have agency but have also pointed out that people face a variety of social constraints or structures that put limits on what actions they can take. The constraints that limit people's agency and capacity for action are often invisible at an individual level and are perceived as 'private troubles' rather than 'public issues'. What is more, public debate, especially around policy issues, regularly fails to recognise the limited choices faced by individuals who are constrained by social structures over which they have little control. However, when discussing structure and agency, sociologists have also regularly restricted the notion of agency to people. The advent of digital technologies into many aspects of everyday life have made this restriction increasingly difficult to sustain – is agency something that only people have or do our devices increasingly have their own agency?

In the following reading, historian Keith Barton discusses the importance of teaching agency in schools. He explains the complex relationships between agency, action and the wider contexts over which people may have little control (he does not use the phrase 'social structure' here but instead mentions 'social factors'). In this short extract, Barton describes how even in extreme situations, people still can exert some agency, but only within the limits of powerful social forces. He also points out that social structures can be both 'constraining' or 'enabling'.

Reading 6.1

Keith Barton, 'Agency, choice and historical action: how history teaching can help students think about democratic decision making'

Who is history about? Who gets placed at the beginning of sentences, as the actors – the agents – of history, the ones who initiate action and are responsible, both implicitly and explicitly, for historical events, patterns and processes? For most of us, this is probably the most familiar question about agency, because we all recognize that written history has traditionally been about elite white men and their supporters. These were the people who appeared to deserve attention as the initiators of important historical actions – thus the common observation, 'History is written by the winners'. Yet these days, most historical accounts include a wider range of actors than those long ago. Post-World War II historians have increasingly emphasized women, minorities, immigrants, the poor and other marginalized groups – literally moving them from the margins to the centre of historical writing... History is more diverse than it used to be; or more accurately, different perspectives and experiences in the past matter more, to more people, than they used to. History is no longer written exclusively by (or about) the winners...

Simply including greater diversity, however, does not necessarily alter how we think about agency, because it is possible to include marginalized groups in history without actually making them actors. Instead, they may be portrayed as largely passive victims, the objects of actions carried out by those in power (Seixas, 1998). This is particularly tempting when considering the lives of people who suffered from brutal institutional regimes or oppressive social systems – women, the enslaved, colonized populations, religious minorities and so on. Even grammatical structures can position such groups as subordinate, as when they are characterized as having been 'enslaved', 'colonized' and so on. Our natural sympathy for the abuses people suffered, or for the constraints on their lives, can lead us to highlight what was done to them, rather than what they themselves did. Yet no matter how brutal the oppression, no matter how pervasive the constraints, people always have taken action to pursue their goals: women decided how to allocate their time and resources, slaves developed vibrant cultural traditions, indigenous populations created alliances with or against colonizers and so on. Historical scholarship increasingly recognizes what has long been obvious in traditions handed down within communities: no group has a monopoly on action…

At the same time, it is important for students not to overestimate the ability of people in the past to struggle against oppression. Students are often puzzled by why all slaves did not revolt or escape, why all Jews did not resist removal to camps or even why all blacks did not leave South Africa during apartheid. To understand how people took action, students also need a realistic understanding of the powerful societal factors that limited and channelled their agency. Economics, ideology, practicality and brute force all placed limits on the extent to which people in the past both conceptualized and acted on their goals – just as they do today. Such societal factors are not necessarily negative; think, for example, of how the US Civil Rights movement depended on the institutional structure of African American churches, or how the GI Bill in the United States enabled a wider range of socio-economic classes to go to college after World War II.

Understanding historical agency requires that we constantly keep in mind this tension between people's ability to act and the reality that they will do so within a wider context over which they may have little direct control (Barton and Levstik 2004; Damico et al. 2010).

References

Barton, K. C. and Levstik, L. S. (2004), *Teaching History for the Common Good*, New York: Routledge.

Damico, J. S., Baildon, M. and Greenstone, D. (2010), 'Examining how historical agency works in children's literature', *Social Studies Research and Practice*, 5: 1, pp. 1–12.

Seixas, P. (1993), 'Historical understanding among adolescents in a multicultural setting', *Curriculum Inquiry*, 23: 3, pp. 301–25.

(Barton, 2012, pp. 134–135)

So, humans may not be fully in control of the actions they take. Agency is a complex array of relationships among individuals, groups, institutions and ideas. These often interact in overlapping and sometimes contradictory ways. And what happens to the idea of agency when we add in the role of *things* as well? Even simple objects can restrict or alter people's agency and ability to act. Take, for example, the common use of automated mechanical door closers. This well-established technology uses simple springs or hydraulic pistons to close unattended doors gently after someone has gone through them. This helps prevent draughts and thus conserves energy, and also prevents the spread of fire and smoke in an emergency. While this may seem like a straightforward and simple solution to a common problem, these devices also restrict the agency of some. This is because these 'closers' make doors more difficult to open and thus assume a user is not living with a disability. In other words, 'these doors discriminate against very little and very old persons. Also, if there is no way to keep them open for good, they discriminate against furniture removers and in general everyone with packages, which usually means, in our late-capitalist society, working- or lower-middle-class employees' (Latour, 1992, p. 152).

4 Agency and things

You have seen how even simple, mundane objects can restrict agency, particularly for those people who may be less able-bodied. But what about the objects and things that are not simple? How have complex, digital and largely autonomous systems that increasingly control production, workplaces and our homes altered the idea of human agency? One way to begin to think about this is by seeing agency as something that is distributed across multiple actors and things. Think about how agency can be distributed among humans; for example, if you join a union, pressure group or a club, actions taken will likely be decided by some form of collective democratic decision-making process. By joining an organisation, you will have agreed to share or distribute some of your agency, but at the same time, as you give up some individual agency, you may also gain greater collective agency and power.

Similarly, we have already seen how, when travelling by car, the driver can effectively share some of their agency with a satnav device – with a *thing*. So, the extent of agency and autonomy can vary depending on the situation. Where an object resists the performance of a human, such as with the door closer, or when a thing takes decisions on behalf of a human, agency no longer resides solely with the human. In other words, a distributed view of agency would see action and autonomy as having interdependency with other beings, objects and things.

In the following reading, sociologist Werner Rammert discusses three areas of interdependency that are important to consider when thinking about human agency in the context of advanced technology. He mentions three specific areas: natural forces; other people; and artificial objects.

Reading 6.2

Werner Rammert, 'Distributed agency and advanced technology: Or: how to analyze constellations of collective inter-agency'

Three areas of interdependency seem to be of importance for the discussion of human agency: the *relations to natural forces*, the relations to other people, and the relations to artificial objects.

The fundamental concept of human agency has been challenged several times by scientific concepts that view natural forces as a source of action. They argue that natural forces restrict the space for deliberate action or even reject the idea of acts of free will; for instance, instinctive reactions undermine the idea of rational action. Unconscious drives reveal talk of deliberate decision-making as an illusion. Genetic dispositions and neuronal brain activity are said to demonstrate the illusionary nature of human agency and autonomy. Yet we must not throw out the baby with the bath water. It is the capacity – no matter how small it may be – to resist, by-pass or outwit these forces that has the far-reaching consequence of allowing for agency against the power of natural forces. Even Kant defined human autonomy as the capacity to choose between different determining forces and not in an absolute sense as the capacity to govern the self by laws of its own making – as it is often misinterpreted.

The *relations to other people* are both sources and limits of human agency and autonomy. They are sources because human agency emerges and can be observed only in the interaction between people, as in play, games, or any other site of social encounter (Mead, 1963). Such areas of interaction include the social relations between mother and child, pupil and peer group, master and slave, sovereign and subject, empire and colony. Resisting the will of another, deviating from conventional expectations, or creating new ways of doing things are all activities constituting agency. By contrast, we can hardly speak of agency or, at most, of a low grade of agency when people blindly follow a leader or the masses, when they conform to habits and values in a taken-for-granted manner, or when their behavior takes on the character of routine or rituals. Agency occurs and becomes visible mainly in situations of immediate interaction and interpersonal encounters (Goffman 1983) but also in the mediated relations of telepresence via TV, mobile phones, or Internet services (Horton and Strauss 1957; Knorr Cetina 2009).

The *relations to artificial objects* constitute another area of interdependency. Artificial objects are neither just nature nor social community but bind both together to constitute artificial worlds of their own. Technologies of medicine and drugs are developed and designed to restore or to empower human agency; at the same time, however, they improve the agential power of natural substances, microbes or other transformed entities. Tools and more complex technical systems of transformation are conceived as mere means of fulfilling human goals. Yet, sometimes they turn into "unruly technology" (Wynne 1988), showing unanticipated deviations from routine operations, which raise questions of human and machine agency.

References

Goffman, E. (1983) "Presidential Address: The Interaction Order", *American Sociological Review*, 48: 1–17.

Horton, D. and Strauss, A. (1957) "Interaction in Audience-Participation Shows", *American Journal of Sociology*, 62: 579–587.

Knorr Cetina, K. (1997) "Sociality with Objects: Social Relations in Post-Social Knowledge Societies", *Theory, Culture & Society*, 14: 1–30.

Mead, G. (1963; 1934) *Mind, Self and Society*. Chicago, IL: University of Chicago Press.

Wynne, B. (1988) "Unruly Technology: Practical Rules, Impractical Discourses and Public Understanding", *Social Studies of Science*, 18: 147–167.

(Rammert, 2012, pp. 92–93)

Rammert begins here by considering how the view that natural forces, such as instinct or genetics, may restrict or determine human action. The point is made that, even if these forces are significant, there is still the capacity in human agency to resist these forces. Rammert refers to the 18th-century German philosopher Immanuel Kant who maintained that people should not be subservient to external forces and called for people to have the resolution to use their own perception 'without direction from another' (Kant, 1997, p. 17).

After this, Rammert considers relations to other people; these relations, as you have seen above, are both sources of, and set limits on, human agency and autonomy. Finally, the point is made that artificial *things* constitute another area of interdependency with *people* and these can both enhance human capacities, while at the same time restricting autonomy. Thus, the GPS navigation devices enhance our abilities to find places, but, as you saw at the beginning of this chapter, sometimes they can become 'unruly technologies' with unanticipated deviations from expected behaviour.

The suggestion that agency can be distributed between humans is relatively uncontroversial, but the idea that agency could even partially reside in *things* is more contentious. Rammert is here suggesting that there should be recognition of distribution of agency between *things* and *people*. If devices are fabricated with the capacity to take actions and make decisions on behalf of people, such as with the GPS devices considered earlier, then we have to consider that agency in some important ways is also distributed between *people and things*.

We are used to thinking of the human actor as the unit of action and the centre of autonomy. The move from simple single-use tools, such as a hammer, to digital systems that, via feedback and sensors, can comprehend situations and adapt to changing environments represents the possibility that some things are becoming pro-active agents. Under these circumstances, it may make sense to think of agency as distributed between *people and things*. However, it is possible to distinguish different levels of agency. Rammert (2012) has identified five levels of agency depending on the technical mode of operation.

- Level 1 – refers to a *passive mode* of operation: this would include simple tools or objects, often these will have a single-use and be relatively inflexible. For example, a hammer can be used to drive nails into wood, or a fence can act as a barrier or to mark a boundary.

- Level 2 – at this level things have a *semi-active mode* of operation: here we find objects that have some limited capacity for self-operation. The door closer discussed earlier would be a good example of a semi-active mode of operation. It becomes active under a specific and limited set of circumstances (e.g. when the door is opened).

- Level 3 – relates to *re-active* modes of operation: objects that respond to their environment in more complex ways, normally by having some form of feedback loop. In other words, the device allows the outputs of the system to be routed back as inputs so that the system can adjust its performance. Common examples here would be anti-lock braking systems (ABS) fitted to cars or adaptive heating systems where a thermostat turns heating on or off at the desired temperature.

- Level 4 – indicates a *pro-active* mode of operation: these would be systems with self-activating programs that are able to monitor and examine internal and external data and then initiate action based on these inputs. An example of this would be the remote monitoring systems (RMS) increasingly used in healthcare. These systems are used to remotely check on at-risk patients by linking a variety of wired or wireless medical devices (e.g. blood pressure monitors, glucose meters, heart rhythm and/or peak flow meters) and then alerting the patient or a health professional if any action needs to be taken. Some even have the potential to call emergency services. Another example would be the self-parking feature that allows a car to manoeuvre into a tight parking place with no input from the driver.

- Level 5 – is a *cooperative mode* of operation: this would be a system involving dispersed digital systems working together with a high degree of self-coordination. Examples of such systems would be autonomous self-driving vehicles – these vehicles use a multitude of internal and external sensors and **cloud computing** to act on traffic data, weather, maps, adjacent cars, and surface conditions to allow a car to travel to a location with driver involvement restricted to simple monitoring (such as the automated delivery robots operating in some areas, Figure 6.2). Another example would be a 'smart home' where several different 'intelligent' systems (e.g. heating/cooling, security, lighting, smart domestic appliances, shopping services and entertainment systems) are all coordinated to anticipate and respond to the needs of the occupants.

These levels move from single-use simple technologies towards technological systems that are designed to interact with other systems and to react flexibly to changing environments by taking 'decisions' or modifying their own behaviour as a result of inputs. As Rammert says, 'it makes sense to use the vocabulary of agency and inter-agency in order to describe the activities that go on in this world of artificial things' (Rammert, 2012, p. 97). We now exist in a world where people's ability to use agency to act and take action is coupled to technologies that are also able to act and take action.

Figure 6.2 Starship delivery robot in Milton Keynes.

5 Distributed agency in action

You can see that as you move from level one to level five, it could be argued that the agency of things increases or at least becomes more complex. However, even at the first level, it could be claimed that agency is distributed between *people and things*. Take the example of a wooden fence. A farmer or gardener may construct a fence to protect crops from being eaten by wild animals. But in the process, are not the farmer's or gardener's competence and skills transferred in some small way to the fence (Latour, 1996)? The alternative, to making a fence would be that a person would have to constantly patrol the boundary to protect crops from the appetites of wild animals. With the building of a fence, some of the farmer's or gardener's agency is distributed, and they no longer need to protect the crops in person. Thus action and some agency can be delegated to the fence which is now provided with the competence of doing something (protecting crops) that a human would otherwise have to do. Admittedly, a fence is doing something very simple, but this simple act no longer depends on a person being present. The effect of the fence will last long after the person who built it has gone. As we move through level one towards level five, the distribution of agency becomes more complex, with more scope for the autonomy of things and more interdependency between humans and things. But the distribution of agency is present in even the simplest of objects or tools.

Consider something much more complex than a fence. Suppose you wanted to take a trip, for pleasure or work, to Barcelona. You might start your trip by purchasing a ticket, like many people do, by visiting an airline website where you will be presented with various options (place of departure, class of travel, day and time of travel, how much luggage you want to take). All these will, in turn, affect the price of the ticket you purchase. Previously, all these choices facing a traveller would have been handled by a human travel agent, but now most travellers book tickets directly using an airline's website. Behind the scenes, after a customer makes a purchase, the electronic record and details of the ticket are saved onto the airline's database. This information is then passed to global databases that both coordinate reservations among major airlines and connect airlines to airports. This allows the sharing of real-time information about passenger and aircraft movements. Also, information about passenger movements will be digitally passed to border and security services at both the departure and arrival points.

The digital transmission of all this information lets airports, airlines and state agencies plan for passenger movements. It allows planning of all the mundane activities involved in travel, such as how many bags need to be handled, how much food to load onto a plane (and whether there are dietary requirements) or how much fuel an aircraft might need. But all this automatic coordination distributes and delegates the agency of humans, who would otherwise have to do all this planning, management and organising of international travel.

Once on the aircraft, surely you would now be in the hands of a human actor exercising autonomy and agency – the pilot. And in some ways, this is correct. The pilot is mindful of the need to transport the 180 passengers on the Airbus A320 to Barcelona safely and on time. He or she is trained, certified and familiar with the aircraft, its controls, instruments and procedures. And in a legal sense, it is the pilot who has overall responsibility (or agency) for the flight and the safety of the passengers on board.

Yet here, agency is already divided between several humans. Normally, even on short flights, there are two pilots who constantly cooperate and check decisions with each other. Also, the pilots are not free to fly wherever they choose. The route the aircraft takes will have been planned by the airline and approved by air traffic control (ATC). The pilots on the plane will receive constant instruction from ATC during the flight. And when not under direct ATC control the pilots will be following a set of procedures and rules defined and regulated by local statutory authorities (the Civil Aviation Authority in the UK) and international agencies (The International Civil Aviation Organization). For example, when leaving and arriving at airports, charts define the exact route the aircraft must take, as well as stipulating its speed and height while manoeuvring around the vicinity of the airport. Thus, agency is already strictly distributed between *people*, remote systems (ATC), national and international organisations, and *things* (charts).

Once the plane is underway, the pilots tend to delegate most of the tasks of flying to fully automated systems. Since the advent, around thirty years ago, of planes with fully electronic computerised cockpits (often known as 'glass cockpits'), commercial aircraft are controlled by a collection of many different linked software programs that constantly monitor, measure and compute the progress of the flight and directly

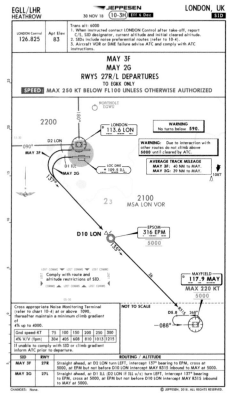

Figure 6.3 Jeppesen Chart for showing pilots how to depart from Heathrow Airport.

control the plane's speed, height and direction. The pilots will begin preparations for the flight by entering the details of the flight into a specialised computer interface (known as the Flight Management Computer or FMC (number 1 on Figure 6.4)). This sets the long-term goals of the flight (such as the destination) and is normally entered before take-off. Once underway, computerised 'autopilot' systems control most aspects of the flight, with human interaction taking place via a limited sets of dials and buttons (known as the Mode Control Panel or MCP (number 2 on Figure 6.4)). Information about the flight will be passed back to the pilots via a series of electronic displays (known as the Primary Flight Displays or PFD (number 3 on Figure 6.4)) which show the orientation of the aircraft, its speed, potential warnings of danger and the route being followed.

Figure 6.4 AirBus A320 Flight Deck.

With many commercial flights, the only time the pilots manually fly the aircraft is during take-off, with automatic systems typically engaged once the aircraft reaches around 1500 feet – the pilots may only be in direct manual control of the aircraft for a very short portion of the flight (typically the aircraft will be under fully automatic control for around 90-95% of the flight). The rest of the flight, including landing, can be carried out by either fully or semi-automated processes. This is not to say that pilots have nothing to do. Rather they now have to manage and interact with computer systems that need constant adjustments and monitoring. They also need to constantly observe their surroundings, communicate with each other and with air traffic control, who use their own digitally automated systems to manage aircraft flows. At times, managing all these systems and tasks involves intense workloads.

In the following extract, psychologist Don Harris discusses the role of automation on the flight deck, and how the increasing levels of automation over the last few decades have altered the nature and role of the commercial pilot.

Reading 6.3

Don Harris, *Human performance on the flight deck*

Automation is all pervasive on the flight deck. It isn't just about the control of the aircraft. Automation is also implicated in almost everything else, from cabin pressurisation, to engine start up, to dimming the displays at night time. Parasuraman, Sheridan and Wickens (2000) defined automation as the full or partial replacement of a function carried out by a human operator. Furthermore, the aircraft flight deck can be thought of as one huge flying computer interface. It is a relatively crude example of ubiquitous computing, where there is computer functionality everywhere but is 'hidden' behind user interfaces that look nothing like a PC. Automation falls very firmly within the realm of the *Machine* however it has profound aspects on the hu*Man* [sic] component. Not only does it change the way people do their jobs (hence the education and training requirement) it has a profound affective effect on the user....

The trend in flight deck design over the past half century has been one of progressive 'de- crewing' and increased digitisation and system integration (see Applegate and Graeber, 2001). The common flight deck complement is now that of two pilots (for operational and procedural purposes usually designated 'pilot flying' or PF and 'pilot-not-flying' or PNF), Fifty years ago, it was not uncommon for there to be five crew on the flight deck of a civil airliner (two pilots; Flight Engineer; Navigator and Radio Operator). Now just two pilots, with much increased levels of assistance from the aircraft, accomplish the same tasks once undertaken by five. There are even proposals to reduce the crew of short-range airliners to just a single pilot, with increased on-board automated assistance and surveillance from the ground (Harrris, 2007). ... The aircraft and its systems are now more usually under supervisory control, rather than manual control. The manner in which the pilots exercise control is now one of being an outer-loop controller (a setter of high-level goals) and monitor of systems, rather than that of an inner loop ('hands on', minute to minute) controller. This has changed dramatically the nature of the pilot's control task in the cockpit. Emphasis is now much more on crew and automation management rather than flight path control *per se*.

References

Applegate, J.D. and Graeber, R.C. (2001). Integrated Safety Systems Design and Human Factors Considerations for Jet Transport Aeroplanes. *Human Factors and Aerospace Safety*, 1, 201–21.

Harrris, D. (2007). A Human-Centred Design Agenda for the Development of a Single Crew Operated Commercial Aircraft. *Aircraft Engineering and Aerospace Technology*, 79, 518–26.

Parasuraman, R., Sheridan, T.B., and Wickens, C.D. (2000). A Model for Types and Levels of Human Interaction with Automation. *IEEE Transactions on Systems, Man, and Cybernetics —Part A: Systems and Humans*, 30, 286–97.

(Harris, 2011, pp. 221)

We can see that the agency of the pilot(s) flying the plane is distributed between pilot and machine, between *people and things*. But it could be argued that there is a far wider distribution on this flight to Barcelona; for example, is the agency of the many Airbus software engineers, who designed the aircraft's systems and interfaces, also present on the aircraft? Moreover, the combined agency of pilot(s) and aircraft are further nested within the complexity of the air traffic control system and international regulations governing commercial aircraft movements. And all these are also then further connected to the commercial world of the travel and tourism industries, with their complex systems of distributing agency. Rather than agency residing in a single, or even a collective, actor, this example suggests that agency is distributed over a network of interlinked organisations, actors, collective actors and things.

6 Conclusion

This chapter has examined the concepts of agency and autonomy and how these are complicated by the advent of digital objects. It argues that things can be thought of as having differing levels of agency. In particular, you were introduced to the idea that agency can be distributed between *people and things*. While this distribution of agency, between humans and objects, exists in even simple items, such as a fence, the distribution becomes more complex, with more scope for the autonomy of things as we consider more sophisticated digital devices. Thus, on the commercial flight to Barcelona agency was distributed between people, organisations and digital systems in the plane and on the ground. For many digital systems, agency is distributed over a network of interlinked organisations, actors, collective actors and things.

You will have noticed that much of this chapter concentrated on the sociological thread of *people and things*. The idea that we may be increasingly sharing agency with our devices also has implications when considering the question of how the social and the technical shape each other. Reading this chapter, it may have occurred to you that we are so closely connected to the devices that we use that it may become difficult to establish clear boundaries between people and the things that surround them. It may be quite difficult ever to find a thing or a person existing in a 'pure' state. Some have argued that the social and technical are now so entwined that it makes no sense to consider these as separate categories, but instead, we should think of hybrids (Latour, 1993) that mix elements of things, people, the natural and the social.

References

Barton, K.C. and Levstik, L.S. (2004) *Teaching history for the common good*. New York, NY: Routledge.

Barton, K.C. (2012) 'Agency, choice and historical action: how history teaching can help students think about democratic decision making', *Citizenship Teaching & Learning*, 7(2), pp. 131–142.

Graham, J. and Molina, B. (2017) 'Waze sent commuters toward California wildfires, drivers say', *USA Today*, 17 December. Available at: https://eu. usatoday.com/story/tech/news/2017/12/07/california-fires-navigation-apps-like-waze-sent-commuters-into-flames-drivers/930904001/ (Accessed: 25 February 2020).

Harris, D. (2011) *Human performance on the flight deck*. Boca Raton, FL: CRC Press.

Kant, I. (1997) *Practical philosophy*. Translated from the German and edited by M.J. Gregor. Cambridge: Cambridge University Press.

Latour, B. (1992) 'Where are the missing masses? The sociology of a few mundane artifacts', in Bijker, W.E. and Law, J. (eds) *Shaping Technology/ Building Society: Studies in Sociotechincal Change*. Cambridge, MA: MIT Press., pp. 225–258.

Latour, B. (1993) *We have never been modern*. Cambridge, MA: Harvard University Press.

Latour, B. (1996) 'On interobjectivity', *Mind, Culture, and Activity*, 3(4), pp. 228–245. doi: 10.1207/s15327884mca0304_2.

Milner, G. (2016) *Pinpoint: how GPS is changing technology, culture, and our minds*. New York, NY: W.W. Norton & Company.

Propp, V. (1968) *Morphology of the folktale*. 2nd rev. edn. Translated from the Russian by S. Pirkova-Jakobson. Austin, TX: University of Texas Press.

Rammert, W. (2012) 'Distributed agency and advanced technology. Or: how to analyze constellations of collective inter-agency', in Passoth, J.-H., Peuker, B. and Schillmeier, M. (eds) *Agency Without Actors?: New Approaches to Collective Action*. London: Routledge, pp. 100–123.

Chapter 7
Freedom, fetishes and cyborgs

Paul-François Tremlett

Contents

1 Introduction

In this chapter you will explore two of the sociological threads that form the backbone of this book: *people and things* and *power and inequality*. In previous chapters you have seen that sociology provides different frameworks through which to observe and understand different dimensions of social life.

Mead's **symbolic interactionism**, for example, focused on human beings as lively makers of meaning and culture and downplayed human interactions with things and objects in social and cultural life. For this framework, things and objects were largely inert, simply tools to be used or materials to be fashioned to carry human meaning. In this chapter, you will explore some classical and contemporary sociological theories of *people and things* and *power and inequality* that are articulated either in part or more substantially, through the idea of **fetishism**.

You will explore the writings of the 19th century sociologist Karl Marx, the film *Metropolis*, and the link they make between human relations, technological things, freedom and fetishism. You will then turn to the work of the contemporary sociologist Bruno Latour and the feminist historian of science Donna Haraway and their ideas about fetishes and **cyborgs** to explore an alternative sociological framework for understanding human relations with things. Along the way, you will consider examples of things in workplace, and educational and therapeutic contexts.

1.1 Teaching aims

This aims of this chapter are for you to:

- explore the classical and contemporary sociology of things

- introduce the concept of fetishism

- introduce the concept of the cyborg

- evaluate the extent to which power permeates human relations with things.

2 Who was Karl Marx?

Figure 7.1 Karl Marx, the
German-born socialist, philosopher,
economist and writer in *c*.1875.

Karl Marx (1818–1883) was born in Trier, in Germany. He met
Friedrich Engels in Paris in 1844, and the two struck up a life-long
friendship, famously writing *The Communist Manifesto* together in 1848.
The following year, Marx came to London as a political refugee, and
he lived there until his death in 1883. If *The Communist Manifesto* is his
most famous text, it was also a work of political propaganda. However,
Marx also composed a number of scholarly, sociological and
philosophical texts to understand the emergent, industrial society of his
day. Mid 19th century Europe was a place of considerable political,
economic and technological turmoil. He argued that history was
defined by a process of growing human freedom and, as part of that
process, industrial capitalist society would inevitably be overthrown and
replaced by a new social form he called 'communism'. Focusing in
particular on capitalism and the contradiction, as he saw it, between
the worker's demand for wages and the factory owner's demand for
profit, Marx argued that technological innovation was de-skilling
workers and transforming their labour into a series of repetitive,
mechanical movements that rendered the worker 'both intellectually

and physically to the level of a machine' (Marx, 1992, p. 285). According to Marx, capitalist society enriched the few at the expense of the mass of working men, women and children. They were simply fodder for the factories, 'dehumanized' (1992, p. 336 italics in original) and turned into machines – that is, turned into things – by labour that, under a different system, or so Marx believed, could be re-organised towards the fulfilment rather than the impoverishment of the individual human being. For Marx, then, workplace technology turned humans into machines. It deprived them of the freedom to develop themselves. Marx's solution was to try to reverse the polarity of that relationship, so that the factory machines served the interests of ordinary working people, and not the other way around.

What is fetishism?

The term 'fetishism' was coined in the late 18th century by Charles de Brosses (1709–1777) to describe the religion of West Africa. A fetish was a handmade object said to possess magical or sacred power and believed capable of enchanting the unwary or unprotected. The term subsequently became a staple of early anthropological and sociological theories of the origins of religion.

Marx was not only interested in the factory and the transformation of work by new industrial machine technologies. He was also interested in the products factories made, or what he called, 'commodities'. In particular, he was interested in a phenomenon he called the 'fetishism of commodities' (Marx, 2009, p. 39). Fetishism was a term coined by early anthropologists and sociologists as a theory for the origins of religion. It implies the worship of objects and things, with the important qualification that the objects and things in question were not seen as inert or passive, but, like living things, were understood to be manufactured, god-like and powerfully animate. Marx used the idea of fetishism to convey the notion that commodities conceal the asymmetric relationships that define labour or what he called the 'relations of production'. What did Marx mean by this complicated idea?

Fetishism and the origins of sociology

Marx was not the only sociologist interested in fetishism. Auguste Comte (1798–1857) is considered by many to be the founder of sociology (although the figure of Ibn Khaldun offers an alternative genealogy for the discipline: see Soyer and Gilbert, 2012). For Comte, writing in the aftermath of the French revolution, it seemed that a new rational, modern, industrial-scientific order was emergent. The old feudal society of aristocracy, Church and monarchy, with its arbitrary privileges, had been eclipsed in the revolution of 1789. Comte, like many of his contemporaries, saw an opportunity to bring an end to the uncertainties of the times by establishing a new industrial society on rational principles. Comte believed that, in order for this new society to be realised, a new science was needed to reorganise society by raising *politics to the rank of the sciences of observation*' (Comte, 1998, p. 81 italics in original). In his early essays Comte called this new science 'social physics' (Comte, 1998, p. 158), and did not coin the term 'sociology' until the end of the *Course in Positive Philosophy* (published 1830–1839). Comte's vision of sociology emerged not only from his analysis of the society of his day but also from his interest in the historical development of the sciences. Comte argued that the value of the sciences lay in their methods: he coined the term 'positivism' to distinguish scientific knowledge – which could be verified through the application of scientific methods such as observation and comparison – from religious knowledge, the earliest form of which, or so he believed, was fetishism. According to Comte, fetishism was the original stage of humanity, when people saw 'all the objects that attract' their 'attention as if they were living beings' (Comte, 1998, p. 147).

Next time you are shopping online, you will find yourself confronted by a world of commodities for you to choose from. Marx wants you to tear your eyes away from these commodities and the relationships that seem to exist between them, and instead focus on the unequal and exploitative human relationships that created the commodities in the first place. It is precisely the apparent ability of the commodity to conceal, mystify and obscure the real nature of capitalism that led Marx to make the link with fetishism and religion (Fraser and Wilde, 2011, p. 57). For Marx, the irrational delusions of religion – particularly the 'primitive' worship of things known to 19th-century anthropologists and sociologists as fetishism – was a metaphor for capitalist society in which things and objects were sanctified and held in a higher regard than their human makers. Now read this short extract by Marx on 'The fetishism of commodities'. Do not be deterred if you find the passage difficult; you will be able to derive its sense from the discussion above and from that which follows it.

Reading 7.1

Karl Marx, 'The Fetishism of Commodities'

A commodity appears, at first sight, a very trivial thing and easily understood. Its analysis shows that it is, in reality, a very strange thing, abounding in metaphysical subtleties and theological niceties ... It is as clear as day that man, by his industry, changes the forms of the materials furnished by nature, in such a way as to make them useful to him. The form of wood, for instance, is altered by making a table out of it. Yet, the table continues to be that common, everyday thing, wood. But, as soon as it steps forth as a commodity, it is changed into something transcendent. It not only stands with its feet on the ground, but, in relation to all other commodities, it stands on its head, and evolves out of its wooden brain grotesque ideas ... A commodity therefore is a mysterious thing, simply because in it the social character of men's labor appears to them as an objective character stamped on the product of that labor; because the relation of the producers to the sum total of their own labor is presented to them as a social relation, existing not between themselves, but between the products of their labor.... In order, therefore, to find an analogy, we must have recourse to the mist-enveloped regions of the religious world. In that world the productions of the human brain appear as independent beings endowed with life, and entering into relation both with one another and the human race. So it is in the world of commodities with the products of men's hands. This I call the fetishism which attaches itself to the products of labor as soon as they are produced as commodities, and which is therefore inseparable from the production of commodities.

(Marx, 2009, pp. 37–39)

In this short passage, Marx suggests that the commodity-fetish, even though it is nothing more than a product of human labour, does two things: first, it masks the human labour invested in its manufacture and second, it turns its creator(s) into objects. The anthropologist David Graeber neatly summarises the problem in the following terms:

> Collectively, human beings create their worlds, but owing to the extraordinary complexity of how all this creative activity is coordinated socially, no one can really keep track of the process, let alone take control of it. As a result, we are constantly confronting our own actions and creations as if they were alien powers. Fetishism is ... [when] we end up making things and then treating them like gods.
>
> (Graeber, 2007, p. 140)

Marx's approach to the commodity is supposed to unmask it for what it really is. By replacing a world of fetishes with objectively established facts about capitalism and the relations of production, Marx hoped to release us from our thraldom to commodities and things, and thereby make possible the transition to a post-capitalist society.

2.1 Metropolis

The idea that industrial society – the factory and technology of the 19th century – was turning human beings into machines, was not confined to Marx. Nor was the association between the power of machine technology and the irrational, despotic power of religion. The 1927 black and white silent film *Metropolis* – directed by Fritz Lang – depicted a dystopian future urban society, in which an elite enjoyed limitless leisure and prosperity while underground workers toiled on huge machines to power the city. At the centre of the film are the different worlds of the elite and the workers, and the problem of building a bridge of understanding between them, that might transform their relationship from one of exploitation to one of common humanity. In the first section of the film there are lengthy depictions of 'the depths', the area below the city where workers labour at the machines. They are 'mere cogs in the wheels of industry – men who have been turned into anonymous slaves whose rote actions mirror the movements of the machines' (Wosk, 2010, p. 404). The contrast drawn between the hedonism of the elite and the drab existence of the workers is dramatic. Above ground we see skyscrapers, and roads filled with cars, while aeroplanes criss-cross the sky. The city appears as the very essence of early 20th-century modernity. But while the elite pass their time in pleasure gardens or in sport, the workers are tied to their machines, their bodies compelled to endlessly repeat robotic movements. The audience witnesses this through the eyes of the film's hero Freder who, while visiting the depths, sees one of the machines explode, because the worker charged with maintaining it has collapsed from exhaustion. The explosion kills a number of workers and Freder hallucinates the machine's transformation into Moloch, a Canaanite god associated by Old Testament sources with child sacrifice. Freder watches on as workers are thrown into Moloch's gaping, hungry mouth.

Figure 7.2 'The depths' from Fritz Lang's 1927 film *Metropolis*.

Metropolis elaborates on Marx's framework according to which the factory and industrial technology threaten to transform human beings into things – that is, machines – and represents this process in part through reference to an ancient, malefic god. A world so irrational that things have power over human beings is akin to a world where

Figure 7.3 'Moloch' from Fritz Lang's 1927 film *Metropolis*.

irrational religious ideas hold sway. But *Metropolis* adds a new figure to this frightening mix: a robot that is a perfect simulacrum of a human being.

Despite the appearance of perfect order, the city is bisected by catacombs and the heroine Maria uses them to move between the depths and the city above ground, to spread the idea among the workers that someone will soon come to end their misery and unite the divided city. The catacombs form another dimension to the city that draws on medieval, Gothic and Christian religious imagery. The master of Metropolis plots to thwart Maria's message by replacing her with a demonic robot simulacrum, but his plans go awry as robot Maria spreads chaos, both in the depths among the workers who smash the machines, and above ground in the city where she drives the men of Metropolis into a frenzied state of barely restrained sexual desire (she ends up being burned at the stake). Note the double movement from technologies that transform humans into machines, to technologies that turn machines into humans, but also the gendered and religious symbolism through which technology is associated with women and with evil (and by implication, modern Metropolis is equated with men, power and control) (see Huyssen, 1982).

We will return to the question of gender, power and technology towards the end of the chapter, but for the time being let us remind ourselves of how our discussion builds on the threads of *people and things* and *power and inequality*. First, we noted a basic sociological framework (symbolic interactionism) that distinguished humans from things in the following terms:

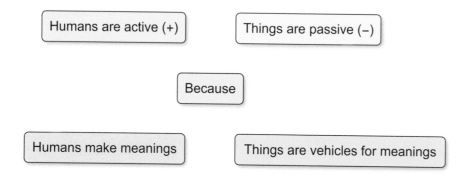

Second, following Marx, we noted the capacity of technology for domination, and the possibility that the above distinction might be reversed:

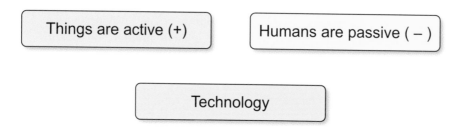

But from our everyday dealings with all kinds of technologies we know, and indeed take for granted, that technology empowers us in our learning, in our relationships and in our workplaces. At the same time, we also know that contemporary technologies are getting smarter all the time, and that these technologies are not passive in the way a hammer or a pencil is. In short, we know that things and objects can be both passive and active; so is there an alternative sociological framework we might use to help us think differently about people and things?

3 Bruno Latour

Figure 7.4 Bruno Latour, 2017.

Bruno Latour is a French sociologist who is known for his studies of scientists, science, and technology, and a key figure in the field of Science and Technology Studies (STS). His work is known for challenging taken-for-granted notions of what is involved in scientific discovery. Rather than accepting that scientific facts exist as entities waiting to be discovered by scientists, Latour argues that scientific facts are a product of inquiry. According to Latour, scientific facts and theories are the outcome of the institutions and practices that produce them and make them comprehensible. Facts are a consequence of the networks of things and people that produce them. In the 1980s and 1990s Latour wrote about laboratory culture, the impact of Louis Pasteur and an automatic personalised transport system, among other things, and more recently he has been exploring the environmental politics of nature.

For Marx, machine technology and commodities, and human relationships with things were entangled in a story about freedom, power and inequality. The idea of the fetish and a general sense of the irrational was deployed by Marx to emphasize the absurdity and upside-down nature of a world where things ruled humans. In this first of two extracts from his work, Bruno Latour shows us, in rather tongue-in-cheek fashion, how our relationships with things are implicated in our conceptions of freedom.

Reading 7.2

Bruno Latour, 'On the cult of the factish gods'

Why does Mafalda's father, in the last scene of this short comic strip … appear so terrified that he uses scissors to shred, compulsively, all the cigarettes remaining in his pack? The reason is that Mafalda, incorrigible rascal, simply used the passive form to describe the innocuous behaviour of her father.

"What are you doing?" she asks in the first scene.

"As you can see, I'm smoking," responds her father unwarily.

"Oh," Mafalda remarks in passing, "I thought the cigarette was smoking you": panic.

Whereas he thought of himself as an untroubled father, comfortably seated in his armchair after a hard day at the office, his daughter saw him as an unbearable monster: a cigarette grabbing a man to have itself smoked in a big cloud of tar and nicotine; the father as an appendage, an instrument, an extension of the cigarette, the father become cigarette to the cigarette. Nothing more is needed to unleash a crisis: I foreswear smoking forevermore. To bind me to this promise, I reduce my entire pack to unsmokable stumps; I tear apart this idol that has enslaved me, into such minute fragments that it will never again be able to take hold of me, even if the craving, as we say, seizes me again.

Mafalda's amusing story has only the appearance of profundity. Moving from the first to the last scene, we basically pass from one extreme to another: at the start, the father believes himself given to an innocent vice that he has almost completely under control; at the end, he can extricate himself from his shackles only by pulverising the cigarette, which so totally controls him that his daughter thought she had seen, in this hybrid, a cigarette smoking a man. In the two instances, both at the beginning and at the end, the reader continues to believe that we are talking about control. From the active form, "I smoke a cigarette," to the passive form, "you are smoked by a cigarette," nothing has changed other than the apportionment of master and instrument. The father alternates too drastically from one position to the other: too comfortable in the first image; too panicked in the last. … at the beginning, by thinking that he is capable of controlling his action: he acts and the cigarette does nothing: at the end—by thinking that he is completely controlled by the object—the cigarette acts and he does nothing.

(Latour, 2010, pp. 54–56)

Figure 7.5 Quino, "Le Club de Mafalda," no. 10 (Grenoble: Editions Glénat, 1986), 22.

Latour's cigarette-smoking scenario reverses the polarity of the active human versus the inert thing distinction, such that it is the object – the cigarette – that becomes all-powerful. Latour's sociology, by contrast, places humans and things on a flat or level plane, in which neither the human nor the object is dominant. Latour seeks to do away with both all-powerful humans and all-powerful things, in their stead envisioning humans and things as interacting elements or 'actants' within wider networks, assemblages and associations. Elsewhere he has described this approach as 'actor network theory' or ANT (Latour, 2005). Latour's point is that things are not passive or inert but have real effects. As such, things should be understood as co-constructors of and co-actors alongside humans, in the creation of shared social and cultural worlds. This is not the topsy-turvy world of fetishism but, according to Latour, a more faithful, empirical account of the worlds we actually live in which, he argues in the following extract, requires sociology to adapt its approach to people and things.

Reading 7.3

Bruno Latour 'On interobjectivity'

Too often sociology remains without an object. Like many human sciences, it has constructed itself so as to resist attachment to objects, which it calls fetishes. It has taken the ancient admonition of the prophets against gods, merchandise, consumer goods and objets d'art to heart: 'Idols have eyes and yet do not see, mouths and yet do not speak, ears and yet do not hear.' According to them something else animates these lifeless bodies, dead statues: our belief, the social life that we project onto them. The fetishes do not count for anything in themselves. They are merely a projection screen. However, they do indeed add something else to the society that manipulates them: objectification. Like so many overhead retroprojectors, these idols reverse the sense of action— leaving the poor humans who have given them everything they have the impression that their force comes from them alone, and that it is this force that renders humans impotent, which makes them act, which alienates them. The human sciences have for a long time been trying to reverse this reversal. Through a retroprojection symmetrical with the first, they reveal the labor of humans and their multiple animation in the lifeless body of the fetish. The deontology of sociologists demands this anti-fetishism of them. Thus it is clear why reintroducing the objects, speaking again of the weight of things, according inanimate beings real social forces is for them an error: the error of returning to objectivism, naturalism, or belief. However, we cannot make a place for objects without modifying the deontology of the social sciences, and without accepting a certain dose of fetishism. Objects do *do* something, they are not merely the screens or the retroprojectors of our social life. Their sole function is not merely to 'launder' the social origin of the forces that we project onto them.

(Latour, 1996, p. 236)

This is a challenging passage. Latour's basic point is that sociologists have assumed that the power of things rests solely in the animacy they are given by their human makers and users. According to this perspective – theology even! – to argue that things have their own agency is to invite the charge of fetishism and idolatry. Latour insists that 'objects do do something' and that they are more than just 'screens' upon which 'our social life' is projected, hence his suggestion that in order to take things seriously, sociology needs to accept 'a certain dose of fetishism'.

The sociologies of Marx and Latour offer very different accounts of human relationships with things. Marx sees those relationships as being saturated with problems of power and domination, and he uses metaphors, concepts and images drawn from early anthropological and sociological accounts of non-European religion – what was in the 19th century called fetishism – to describe an inverted, irrational world where technologies turn humans into machines. Latour sees human relationships with things and technology in very different terms, arguing that humans and things should be understood as co-producers of social and cultural worlds. Let us now examine how these different approaches to humans and things play out in accounts of contemporary workplaces and digital technologies.

4 Digital technology, robots and artificial intelligence in the Amazon warehouse

The inspiration for this chapter comes in part from the plethora of stories in newspapers and magazines about new digital technologies, and in particular robots and so-called AI or Artificial Intelligence. There seems little doubt that these new technologies are changing the nature of the workplace and work itself. Arguably, we are in the midst of a fourth industrial revolution (Schwab, 2016). A common element among contemporary reflections on new technologies is that the changes they are ushering in are on a much more fundamental scale than anything that has gone before.

> We stand on the brink of a technological revolution that will fundamentally alter the way we live, work, and relate to one another. In its scale, scope, and complexity, the transformation will be unlike anything humankind has experienced before ....
>
> The First Industrial Revolution used water and steam power to mechanize production. The Second used electric power to create mass production. The Third used electronics and information technology to automate production. Now a Fourth Industrial Revolution is building on the Third, the digital revolution that has been occurring since the middle of the last century. It is characterized by a fusion of technologies that is blurring the lines between the physical, digital, and biological spheres.
>
> (Schwab, 2016)

And:

> We now stand at a juncture where there is no pursuit that cannot in principle be undertaken by an automated system, and we need to come to terms with what that might mean for the economy, the ways in which we organise our societies, and our own psyches.
>
> (Greenfield, 2017, p. 185)

Some argue that these new technologies will usher such profound change that a new leisure society will be possible. For example, proponents of 'Fully Automated Luxury Communism' imagine a future in which work has been abolished due to the spread of automation to all sectors of the economy and society. This idea is a kind of technological utopianism that assumes new technology will bring positive outcomes to society as a whole. Others, who we might call technological pessimists, imagine a much darker future, in which a 'shrunken workforce will be asked to do more, for lower wages, at yet a higher pace' (Greenfield, 2017, p. 195). Interestingly, both groups can be described as technological determinists because both argue that technologies play such a central, determining role in shaping society and social relationships. For example, 20th-century industrial technology such as motor vehicle manufacture enabled a shared experience of labour that shaped many communities and their sense of identity and place, opportunities for social mobility and political allegiance, for decades. The steady automation of these workplaces and the ensuing disappearance of their mass human workforces, points to the emergence of a different kind of society shaped by new technological forces and experiences of identity and place.

Transnational e-commerce companies like Amazon are at the cutting edge in the development of new workplace technologies, including the use of smart wristbands to monitor employee efficiency (Solon, 2018) and the employment of robot co-workers in their warehouses and distribution centres (Harris, 2017). If the wristband conjures in our minds a dystopian workplace environment of constant surveillance and subjection to technology where human workers are transformed into robots, the robot co-workers suggest the possibility of the same process but moving in the opposite direction, where robot co-workers are transformed into persons. In an interview with the journalist John Harris in 2017, one Amazon employee at the Manchester warehouse said that robot 64117 was his 'favourite' because it had 'travelled only 164 metres the whole time it's been here. It's the laziest drive we've got. It's got the work/life balance worked out' (Harris, 2017). The attribution of a human motive to robot 64117 is telling: it is as if the robot is being socialised by its participation in the labour process. We seem to have remained firmly within the framework we encountered in Marx and *Metropolis*: new technologies threaten either to turn humans into robots or machines or, moving in the other direction, to turn machines and robots into humans.

However, robots are not just being deployed in the workplace: they can be found in a number of settings. We are now going to look at their use in educational and therapeutic contexts for working with autistic children.

4.1 Robots and autism

Autism is a complex condition and this section considers just one way of defining and treating it (the concept of 'neurodiversity' opens up a range of alternative approaches and possibilities for thinking about the condition).

Some psychologists have suggested that humans come pre-equipped with something they call 'Theory of Mind'. Theory of Mind refers to a hard-wired, shared human capacity for making predictions about the interior, intentional states of other people, based on cues such as the expressions on peoples' faces (for example, smiling, laughing, crying, grimacing, sneering, frowning, etc). Autism is regarded by some psychologists as a deficit in Theory of Mind, leading to people with autism being described as 'mindblind' and autism itself described as a 'machine state' (Richardson, 2016, p. 18). In the 2013 edition of the American Psychiatric Association's *Diagnostic and Statistical Manual of Mental Disorders*, autism is described in the following terms:

> Autism spectrum disorder is characterized by persistent deficits in social communication and social interaction across multiple contexts, including deficits in social reciprocity, nonverbal communicative behaviors used for social interaction, and skills in developing, maintaining, and understanding relationships. In addition to the social communication deficits, the diagnosis of autism spectrum disorder requires the presence of restricted, repetitive patterns of behavior, interests, or activities.
>
> (American Psychiatric Association, 2013, quoted in Richardson, 2016, p. 19)

The use of robots in educational and therapeutic contexts to treat a condition that has been described using metaphors and images of robots is one surely saturated in paradox and irony. Suffice to say, sociologists interested in autism need to be aware of the discursive production of autism as a 'machine' state, and as a topic of psychological enquiry and treatment (see Danforth and Naraian, 2007; Baker, 2010; Ochs and Solomon, 2010). The Aurora Project, begun in

1998, studies the use of robots in educational and therapeutic contexts of children with autism, framing the work in the following terms:

> Human–human interaction is multi-modal, involving not only verbal language, but a rich body language, gestures etc., many of these expressed in a subtle and unconscious manner. ... Deficits in mind-reading skills, as they have been shown in people with autism, make people's social behaviour, from the perspective of a person with autism, widely unpredictable. Different from human beings, interactions with robots can provide a simplified, safe, predictable and reliable environment where the complexity of interaction can be controlled and gradually increased. ...
>
> A core aim ... is to investigate if and how simple imitation and turn-taking games with a robot can encourage social interaction skills in children with autism. Specifically, the robot's role is considered as an object of shared attention, encouraging interaction with peers (other children with or without autism) and adults.
>
> (Robins *et al.*, 2005, p. 107)

Figure 7.6 Kaspar, the robot teaching autistic children to read faces.

Robot scientists have developed a robot called Kaspar with a limited number of facial expressions calculated to provide the opportunity for an autistic child to learn, through the robot, how to read faces and thereby recognise the inner states of others and socialise (Richardson, 2016). One question we might ask is the extent to which, in these educational and therapeutic contexts, humans and non-human things are equal co-actors in the production of social worlds. Latour might insist that we treat humans and non-humans equally, while Marx might insist that we focus on the asymmetries of power between humans and things, but which approach should we choose? It is for this reason that we turn now to the work of Donna Haraway.

5 Donna Haraway and fetishism

Figure 7.7 A still image from the film *Donna Haraway: Storytelling for Earthly Survival*, a film by Fabrizio Terranova, courtesy Icarus Films.

Donna Haraway (b. 1944) was born in Denver in the USA. She studied evolutionary philosophy and theology in Paris on a Fulbright Scholarship and completed a PhD in biology at Yale. Working at the cutting edge of feminist studies and as a historian of science, Haraway's work has continuously sought to challenge, in ways which intersect with and depart from the works of both Marx and Latour, how divisions between, on the one hand, human and animal and on the other, organism and machine, are entangled in specific political and economic configurations of power. In the essay 'Gene: maps and portraits of life itself' (2018), Haraway engages with the concept of fetishism, applying it at the level of our individual genes. According to Haraway, the genome is a battleground for the production of knowledge about the human body, and the mapping of its frailties, capabilities and possibilities. She argues that the drive to map the genome generates specific forms of power and privileges particular forms of knowledge over others (e.g. biological knowledge over social-scientific knowledge).

Haraway approaches the gene as a thing. It is an approach that is Marxist to the extent that, just as 'commodity fetishism was defined so that only humans were the real actors, whose social relationality was obscured in the reified commodity form', what she calls 'gene fetishism' requires the 'forgetting that bodies are nodes in webs of integrations' (Haraway, 2018, p. 142). However, Haraway's approach to the gene is equally Latourian to the extent that she insists we must 'remember all the nonhuman actors too' (2018, p. 143) and genes are, of course, non-human actors. In short, Haraway demands that we both understand the fetish-like animacy of things (like genes), while recognising that human relationships with things do not occur in a vacuum but are always already saturated by questions of power and inequality. By clearing a path between Marx and Latour, Haraway is able to preserve Marx's insight that human relationships with things cannot be separated from questions of power, and Latour's insight that things and objects act too.

5.1 Haraway's cyborg

Haraway's work has consistently sought to destabilise how we think of the human. In her now-famous, early essay, 'A cyborg manifesto: science, technology and socialist-feminism in the late twentieth century' (1991), Haraway celebrates the cyborg, a hybrid being for which 'the dichotomies between mind and body, animal and human, organism and machine, public and private, nature and culture, men and women, primitive and civilized are all in question' (Haraway, 1991, p. 163). Haraway provides an overview of 20th-century, women science-fiction writers who, she says, are engaged in a kind of 'cyborg writing' (1991, p. 175). She claims that cyborg writing disrupts the Western cultural imaginary, challenges patriarchy and racism, and generates new possibilities for cultural change based in the celebration of the human as an assemblage of biological and artificial elements, properties, skills and dispositions. In the challenging reading that follows, Haraway suggests that, as we welcome new technologies, we must be aware of their capacity for domination as well as their capacity to enrich and expand how we engage with one another and the non-human world around us. Understanding and enjoying Reading 7.4 is not just a matter of catching the meaning of each single word but is also about allowing yourself to be swept up in the feeling and energy of her passionate and evocative writing.

Reading 7.4

Donna Haraway, 'A cyborg manifesto: science, technology and socialist-feminism in the late twentieth century'

By the late twentieth century, our time, a mythic time, we are all chimeras, theorized and fabricated hybrids of machine and organism; in short, we are cyborgs. The cyborg is our ontology; it gives us our politics. The cyborg is a condensed image of both imagination and material reality, the two joined centres structuring any possibility of historical transformation. In the traditions of 'Western' science and politics – the tradition of racist, male-dominated capitalism; the tradition of progress; the tradition of the appropriation of nature as resource for the productions of culture; the tradition of reproduction of the self from the reflections of the other – the relation between organism and machine has been a border war. The stakes in the border war have been the territories of production, reproduction, and imagination. This chapter is an argument for pleasure in the confusion of boundaries and for responsibility in their construction. ... [most people] see deepened dualisms of mind and body, animal and machine, idealism and materialism in the social practices, symbolic formulations, and physical artefacts associated with 'high technology' and scientific culture. ... But a slightly perverse shift of perspective might better enable us to contest for meanings, as well as for other forms of power and pleasure in technologically mediated societies.

From one perspective, a cyborg world is about the final imposition of a grid of control on the planet .... From another perspective, a cyborg world might be about lived social and bodily realities in which people are not afraid of their joint kinship with animals and machines, not afraid of permanently partial identities and contradictory standpoints. The political struggle is to see from both perspectives at once because each reveals both dominations and possibilities unimaginable from the other vantage point.

(Haraway, 1991, pp. 150, 154)

Haraway's basic point is that conventional boundaries between the human and the machine and the human and the animal, are breaking down. This disintegration of once taking for granted boundaries opens up the possibility for domination – what she calls 'the final imposition of a grid of control on the planet' – but also for 'pleasure', and for a 'shift of perspective' through which to better see 'possibilities' and 'contest' power.

6 Conclusion

In this chapter you have navigated a course through the sociological threads of *people and things* and *power and inequality*, and through some classical and contemporary sociological accounts of human relationships with things and objects. You have explored two concepts: the fetish and the cyborg. The former was deployed by Marx to bring home what he thought of as the irrationality of a world where 'things are mistakenly perceived as the generators of value, while people appear as and even become un-generative things, mere appendages of machines' (Haraway, 2018, p. 135). Latour also engaged with the idea of the fetish as a means of developing an alternative framework for thinking about humans and things. Latour's insistence on conceiving of social worlds as horizontal planes of interactions involving myriad human and non-human co-actors came on the back of his provocative suggestion that 'we cannot make a place for objects without modifying … the social sciences, and without accepting a certain dose of fetishism' (Latour, 1996, p. 236) and that in order to take things and objects seriously, sociologists should treat them not merely as inert stuff but as lively matter. You then turned to the work of Donna Haraway both for her work on fetishism and for her concept of the cyborg. Haraway's work is intended to deconstruct the common-sense and taken-for-granted conceptions of nature, human and machine, and to highlight the gendered and racialised currents of power and domination that are always entangled in notions of the human and the non-human.

You also looked at the Amazon workplace where workers are increasingly subjected to surveillance technologies of different kinds, and new kinds of workplace sociality with the introduction of robot co-workers. You also considered the deployment of robots in the treatment of autistic children in specific educational and therapeutic environments. The new digital technologies and forms of AI in these different settings are simultaneously exciting and disturbing. They seem to be radically altering human relationships with things and layering those relationships with new and highly complex entanglements of power and inequality. The different engagements with the concept of fetishism by Karl Marx, Bruno Latour and Donna Haraway points to the ambiguity of things and objects and their complex political (in terms of freedom) and lively (in terms of fetishism) ramifications for how sociologists think about society, while Haraway's concept of the cyborg potentially dissolves any sense of the separability of the human and the non-human.

References

Baker, J.P. (2010) 'Autism in 1959: Joey the mechanical boy', *Pediatrics*, 125(6), pp. 1101–1103.

Comte, A. (1998) *Comte: early political writings*. Translated from the French and edited by H.S. Jones. Cambridge: Cambridge University Press.

Danforth, S. and Naraian, S. (2007) 'Use of the machine metaphor within autism research', *Journal of Developmental and Physical Disabilities*, 19(3), pp. 273–290.

Fraser, I. and Wilde, L. (2011) *The Marx Dictionary*. London: Bloomsbury.

Graeber, D. (2007) *Possibilities: essays on hierarchy, rebellion and desire*. Oakland, CA: AK Press.

Greenfield, A. (2017) *Radical technologies: the design of everyday life*. London: Verso.

Haraway, D. (1991) *Simians, cyborgs and women: the reinvention of nature*. London: Free Association Books.

Haraway, D. (2018) *Modest_Witness@Second_Millennium. FemaleMan_Meets_OncoMouse: feminism and technoscience*. 2nd edn. London: Routledge.

Harris, J. (2017) 'Meet your new cobot: is a machine coming for your job?', *The Guardian*, 25 November. Available at: https://www.theguardian.com/money/2017/nov/25/cobot-machine-coming-job-robots-amazon-ocado (Accessed: 24 April 2020).

Huyssen, A. (1982) 'The vamp and the machine: technology and sexuality in Fritz Lang's *Metropolis*', *New German Critique*, 24/25: pp. 221–237.

Latour, B. (1996) 'On interobjectivity', *Mind, Culture, and Activity*, 3(4), pp. 228–245.

Latour, B. (2005) *Reassembling the social: an introduction to actor-network-theory*. Oxford: Oxford University Press.

Latour, B. (2010) *On the modern cult of the factish gods*. Translated from the French by C. Porter and H. MacLean. Durham: Duke University Press, pp. 1–66.

Marx, K. (1992) *Early Writings*. Translated from the German by R. Livingstone and G. Benson and Introduced by L. Coletti. Harmondsworth: Penguin.

Marx, K. (2009) *Das kapital: a critique of political economy*. Washington DC: Gateway Editions.

Marx, K. and Engels, F. (1968) *The communist manifesto*. Harmondsworth: Penguin.

Ochs, E. and Solomon, O. (2010) 'Autistic sociality', *Ethos*, 38(1), pp. 69–92.

Richardson, K. (2016) 'The robot intermediary: mechanical analogies and autism', *Anthropology Today*, 32(5), pp. 18–20.

Robins, B., Dautenhahn, K., Te Boekhorst, R. and Billard, A. (2005) 'Robotic assistants in therapy and education of children with autism: can a small humanoid robot help encourage social interaction skills?', *Universal Access in the Information Society*, 4(2), pp. 105–120.

Schwab, K. (2016) *The Fourth Industrial Revolution: what it means, how to respond*. Available at: https://www.weforum.org/agenda/2016/01/the-fourth-industrial-revolution-what-it-means-and-how-to-respond/ (Accessed: 5 August 2019).

Solon, O. (2018) 'Amazon patents wristband that tracks warehouse workers' movements', *The Guardian*, 1 February. Available at: https://www.theguardian.com/technology/2018/jan/31/amazon-warehouse-wristband-tracking (Accessed 24 April 2020).

Soyer, M. and Gilbert, P. (2012) 'Debating the origins of sociology: Ibn Khaldun as a founding father of sociology', *International Journal of Sociological Research*, 5(1–2), pp. 13–30.

Wosk, J. (2010) 'Metropolis', *Technology and Culture*, 51(2) pp. 403–408.

Chapter 8

Health and digital technologies: the case of walking and cycling

Simon Carter

Contents

1 Introduction

In this chapter, you will be considering the advent of wearable digital technologies that track walking and cycling and their health implications. Initially, you will consider some of the reasons why policymakers want to increase the amount of walking and cycling in the population. You will then explore how the concepts of medicalisation ('the everyday' treated as a medical problem) and biomedicalisation (technologies that seek to enhance the biological self) are applied to the case of walking and cycling and consider how wearable digital devices have transformed these mundane activities. You will further reflect on how these processes have created new inequalities and power relations. The chapter will also be an opportunity to explore how wearables can blur the boundaries between transport, leisure, competition and work.

1.1 Teaching aims

The aims of this chapter are for you to:

- examine the role of digital wearables associated with walking and cycling

- outline the sociological concepts of medicalisation and biomedicalisation

- evaluate *power and inequality* and *individuals and society* in the context of digital technologies for recording walking and cycling.

2 Transforming everyday mobility

A few years ago, at a highway safety conference in Savannah, Ga., I drifted into a conference room where a sign told me a "Pedestrian Safety" panel was being held. The speaker was Michael Ronkin, a French-born, Swiss-raised, Oregon-based transportation planner whose firm, as his website notes, "specializes in creating walkable and bikeable streets." Ronkin began with a simple observation that has stayed with me since. Taking stock of the event—one of the few focused on walking, which gets scant attention at traffic safety conferences—he wondered about that inescapable word: *pedestrian*. If we were to find ourselves out hiking on a forest trail and spied someone approaching at a distance, he wanted to know, would we think to ourselves, "Here comes a pedestrian"?

Of course we wouldn't. That approaching figure would simply be a person.

(Vanderbilt, 2012)

Figure 8.1 Sign warning drivers about pedestrians.

The word 'pedestrian' contains a dual meaning. This duality sets up an opposition where walking is seen as being less important than other modes of travel. On the one hand, pedestrian simply refers to the act of walking, of putting one foot in front of another in order to get somewhere. However, it also portrays something slightly negative or derogatory. We would describe something, such as a speech or film, as pedestrian if it was dull, tedious and lacking creativity. Moreover, when the word pedestrian is used to describe someone who walks, it captures something of this duality. It is not a word that is commonly used in everyday speech but is normally employed to compare those people who walk to those who use motorised vehicles. Thus, the most common place that we see the word pedestrian is around road traffic. Signs warn drivers to beware of pedestrians (Figure 8.1) and people walking are directed away from traffic by signs that designate them as pedestrians rather than people. It often seems as though people walking are being subtly treated as either an urban menace to drivers or as if they may endanger themselves by sharing space with the 'favoured machines'.

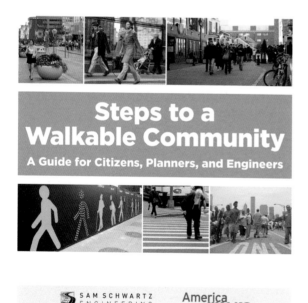

Figure 8.2 Policy document from 'America Walks' to aid citizens, planners and engineers in encouraging more walking.

The language used in warning signs about walking in urban spaces partially reflects our attitudes towards mundane methods of mobility such as walking or cycling. Walking, and to a lesser extent, cycling, have become actions inhabiting the margins in comparison to the assumed **normative** methods of transport via motor vehicles. It could be argued that in the UK and North America particularly, there is an *inequality* between these different forms of mobility with users of motorised vehicles having the *power* to define usage as normal and acceptable, while walkers and cyclists are seen as hazards.

Figure 8.3 Policy document from SWITCH, with practical advice to promote a switch from car-based travel in the European Union.

However, there have been attempts to transform the acts of walking and cycling and bring them back from the margins. These moves are often connected to concerns about people's sedentary lifestyles with evidence suggesting that significant segments of the population are taking little or no physical activity (NHS Digital, 2012). Even moderate physical activity is thought to improve health and offer physical and mental benefits, such as lowering blood pressure, reducing depression, lowering the risk of heart disease and diabetes, and lowering the risk of dementia. Hence, everyday mobility is increasingly being reframed as a public health problem, needing policy initiatives to encourage people to leave their vehicles and increase the amount of walking or cycling they do (Green, 2009; de Nazelle *et al.*, 2011; Oja *et al.*, 2011; Saunders *et al.*, 2013). This has led to national and local campaigns in many countries to encourage what has become known as 'active travel' or mobility that relies on getting from point A to point B using only the power of the human body by either walking or cycling (Figures 8.2 and 8.3). As well as health benefits, active travel has significant environmental benefits. Private car use is a grossly inefficient way to travel around urban spaces; walking and cycling are both highly efficient means of transport. Given that transport is a major contributor to greenhouse emissions, encouraging active travel could dramatically reduce carbon emissions.

Figure 8.4 Digital devices for monitoring mobility.

At the same time as a lack of walking and cycling has been **framed** as a public health problem, there has been a simultaneous proliferation of digital technologies and things which also attempt to transform the walking and cycling that *people* do. These include applications (apps) that can be downloaded to smartphones or tablets, and even smartwatches that aid wayfinding by providing constantly updated route maps designed specifically for walkers or cyclists (Figure 8.4).

Also, of increasing popularity are dedicated digital wearables that record activity such as steps (e.g. devices like the Fitbit) and there are even more sophisticated multifunction wearables that additionally record multiple data streams, including biomarkers (such as heart rate) and use GPS to record distance and speed travelled. Many of these apps and devices allow users to keep an online record of their activities and share their achievements with other users. In addition, many of these online services allow users to analyse their efforts and provide symbolic awards, badges or medals for achievements.

3 From medicalisation of the social to biomedicalisation of the individual

Both the campaigns to encourage more active travel and the digital technologies associated with walking and cycling could be seen as contributing to the idea that physical activity is a social good in its own right. Physical activity is being framed as desirable both for the individual and, collectively, for society. So, as well as extolling the benefits of increased physical activity for *individual* users, campaigns to encourage walking and cycling often refer to *societal* benefits. Thus active travel, as well as improving population health, is seen as having the benefit of reducing traffic pollution and greenhouse gases. Furthermore, having more people walking or cycling on the streets is thought to reduce crime (Gilderbloom, Riggs and Meares, 2015) and has the economic benefit of encouraging the use of local retail outlets.

While not denying the obvious benefits of increasing active travel, a sociological understanding of the phenomenon would also wish to examine how the promotion of physical activity is socially framed and the social processes that lead to people wanting to quantify and record their everyday physical activities. Two concepts from the **sociology of health and illness** are relevant here: medicalisation and biomedicalisation.

Medicalisation describes social processes by which activities in everyday life, and social problems, are increasingly viewed as 'medical' or 'public health' problems. As sociologist Irving Zola said, medicalisation is a 'process whereby more and more of everyday life has come under medical dominion, influence and supervision' (Zola, 1983, p. 295). Sometimes this entails the direct involvement of the medical profession. For example, menopause could be thought of as a part of natural ageing, yet over the last century it has become increasingly medicalised with middle-aged and older women often being encouraged to view menopause as a deficiency condition requiring 'treatment' with replacement hormones under medical supervision (Bell, 1987; Meyer, 2001). In other cases, the medical profession may only be marginally involved, or uninvolved, but a social problem becomes defined using 'medical terms, using medical language to describe a problem, adopting a medical framework to understand a problem, or using a medical intervention to 'treat' it (Conrad, 1992). For example, alcoholism is often treated as a private problem of *individuals* living with a disease or illness rather than a *societal* problem of a legal drug, with minimal controls, being promoted by powerful commercial interests. So medicalisation, via health promotion and public health initiatives, may lead to people believing that certain ways of thinking about social problems are appropriate, with people carrying out 'self-surveillance' of their behaviours (Foucault, 1980). For example, the desire of individuals to maintain a 'healthy lifestyle', may lead people to engage in behaviours such as monitoring the number of units of alcohol they consume or limiting their dietary intake of fats.

Campaigns to promote active travel certainly seem to couch the issue in medicalised terms. For example, the American Public Health Association produced a policy document in 2012 to promote active transportation, and the preface begins by saying:

> The connection between transportation and health is indisputable — as a science, discipline and matter of policy. Transportation systems impact health for better or worse. ... There are limited opportunities to get out of the car to walk or bicycle. Unnecessary congestion and air pollution have become customary and our waistlines are growing. Obesity could edge out tobacco as public enemy No. 1 in our lifetime.
>
> (American Public Health Association, 2012, p. 2)

So here, the lack of active travel is defined as a public health problem leading to air pollution and obesity. Indeed, the final implication in this statement seems to equate a lack of active travel as a similar public health problem to tobacco use. Similarly, a 'Let's get Scotland Walking' campaign was launched in Scotland in 2014. The introduction uses dramatic language to link inactivity to health problems, specifically the connection of inactivity, as a social problem, to smoking and also high blood pressure:

> Physical inactivity contributes to over 2,500 premature deaths in Scotland each year (that is around 7 a day) and costs the NHS in Scotland around £94.1 million annually.... Research illustrates that physical inactivity is the second biggest cause of global mortality (joint with smoking, after high blood pressure [Blair (2009) and Khan and Tunaiji (2011) cited in the original]). Furthermore, it is estimated that getting Scotland active would increase life

expectancy by more than a year given our current inactivity levels. Walking, given its accessibility, has been highlighted as the most likely way all adults can achieve the recommended levels of physical activity [National Institute for Health & Care Excellence (2012, 2013) cited in the original].

(Scottish Government, 2014)

While policy initiatives to encourage people to participate in active travel in their daily lives often use the language of medicalisation, there seems to be something slightly different going on with the framing of digital *things* and devices to monitor *people's* walking and cycling. Here, it is more useful to consider the concept of biomedicalisation. The idea of biomedicalisation extends some of the concepts found in medicalisation to take account of the dynamic relationship between new technologies and society. In particular, it looks at how increasing reliance on developments in the biological sciences and digital technologies extends and reconstitutes many medicalisation processes. Adele Clarke and colleagues (Clarke *et al.*, 2010) suggest five closely connected social processes which characterise biomedicalisation:

1   novel forms of economic organisation based on biomedical knowledge, technologies, and services

2   a new emphasis on health that focuses on optimisation, enhancement, risk and surveillance (including self-surveillance)

3   increasing reliance on science and new technologies (referred to as the technoscientisation of medicine)

4   transformation of knowledge production, distribution and consumption within the biological science and medicine

5   the possibilities that new technologies (including digital technologies) have for transforming bodies and identities.

Here the preface 'bio' is of importance because it signifies new social processes that in turn imply new forms of (bio)power, **(bio)politics** and (bio)economics that increasingly impinge on human activities and human bodies. This, as explained in the following extract by Clarke and colleagues, is the significant point about biomedicalisation. Rather than a social problem being defined, described and 'treated' using a medical framing, as with medicalisation, biomedicalisation is concerned with those **technoscientific** ventures that seek to enhance the biological self:

> The shifts from medicalization to biomedicalization [are] cobbled and webbed together through the increasing application of technoscientific innovations. One overarching analytic shift is from medicine exerting clinical and social *control over* particular conditions to an increasingly technoscientifically constituted biomedicine also capable of effecting the *transformation of* bodies and lives [Clarke (1995) cited in the original]. Such transformations range from life after complete heart failure to walking in the absence of leg bones, to giving birth a decade or more after menopause, to the capacity to genetically design life itself—vegetable, animal and human. Of course, many biomedically induced bodily transformations are much less dramatic, such as Botox and laser eye surgery, but these are no less technoscientifically engineered.

> (Clarke *et al.*, 2003, p. 165)

So here, Clarke and colleagues are emphasising that the shift from medicalisation to biomedicalisation involves various transformations and enhancements of bodies. If we look at some of the digital technologies associated with walking and cycling, we can discern that the theme of enhancing the biological self is common. At the time of writing, two of the most well-known technologies connected with walking and cycling are Fitbit and Strava. Fitbit manufactures a range of wearable devices that primarily record the number of steps a user has taken, with some of the latest models recording GPS as well as biomarkers such as heart rates. This data can then be uploaded and stored on an online website where users are urged to link with friends ('Fitbit is more fun with friends') so that achievements can be shared and users can 'encourage each other to stay fit and active!'. On their website, the following is given as an answer to the question 'why Fitbit?'

> On the walk to work, at the weight room or in the last mile. Somewhere between first tries and finish lines. Pillow fights and pushing limits. That's where you find fitness. Every moment matters and every bit makes a big impact. Because fitness is the sum of your life. That's the idea Fitbit was built on – that fitness is not just about gym time. It's all the time. How you spend your

day determines when you reach your goals. And seeing your progress helps you see what's possible. Seek it, crave it, live it.

(Fitbit, 2019)

Strava, on the other hand, does not manufacture material devices but instead produces apps for smartphones, that can record activities directly, such as running or cycling. In addition, the online site can link with a variety of cycling computers and digital devices to allow recorded information to also be collated on the site. The online site then allows users (referred to as 'athletes') to analyse their recorded data and produce charts and graphs to display how they are progressing (see Figure 8.5). However, Strava is perhaps most well known for enabling cyclists to track and share their times for specific segments of a route they have ridden and awards a 'Queen/King of the Mountain' badge/medal to those who ride the fastest over these segments. In a press release from Strava, to mark Stephanie Hannon taking over as Chief Product Officer, she describes the site as follows:

> Sport can be an empowering and unifying force in the world at a challenging moment in history …. Becoming active and fit transformed my life–it made me a happier, healthier, more resilient person both physically and emotionally. Being part of a company that brings useful analytics, community and inspiration to tens of millions of athletes is easy to get excited about.

(Strava, 2018)

Both these quotes use the idea of fitness to suggest a transformation of users as they attempt to reach their fitness goals. The transformation here is firmly linked to *people's* use of digital *things*. Both also hint that 'fitness' is not a separate endeavour from other everyday activities, rather 'it's all the time' and may even be a 'unifying force' in challenging times. These digital technologies, apps and devices link to online sites that monitor the body in motion reflect a move beyond the 'medicalised' sphere of mobility. These digital technologies are not couched in the language of public health as the active travel campaigns were, and health is rarely mentioned. Instead, we can see that the idea of biomedicalisation comes into play as they address a body project with the prospect of perfectibility and biological enhancement.

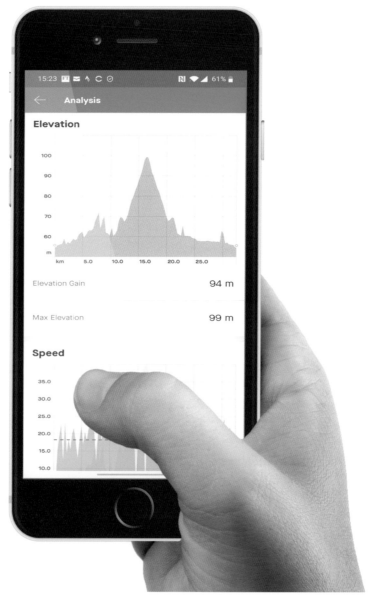

Figure 8.5 Typical data presented back to users.

These technologies both assume and encourage citizens to be orientated to self-surveillance and the encouragement to share endeavours also hints at competitiveness between individual users (Carter *et al.*, 2018). This is another difference with the campaigns for active travel where the emphasis was on the health benefits that active travel will bring to *society* as a whole. Digital technologies associated with walking and cycling on the other hand, often stress the benefits that their use will bring to the *individual* – about how the individual can enhance and transform themselves by the use of these technologies. Digital technologies, in other words, can transform the mundane activities of walking and cycling into behaviours that seek to enhance the biological self, rather than just being about travelling between places. To do this, many of the apps or online services are specifically designed to be 'persuasive technologies' or '**nudge** technologies': that is, they are explicitly intended to change the user's behaviour, utilising one or more techniques such as goal setting, providing feedback on performance, or self-monitoring. These include representations of activity such as visualisations and motivational messages, which act as conditional rewards for goals achieved (Fritz *et al.*, 2014).

4 Quantification: counting steps and tracking cycling

Many of the digital technologies that intersect with walking and cycling share one characteristic – they take the physical activity associated with walking or cycling and reduce the experience to a number: the number of steps taken; the distance travelled; the calories expended, or the fastest speed or time achieved. We could ask what the appeal of physical activities being reduced to a single numerical value is? This could be seen as a move from the 'haptic' (e.g. based on physical sensations) to the 'optic' as numbers and visualisation become more meaningful than bodily sensations (Carter *et al.*, 2018).

The 'counting of steps' in many of the wearable devices that monitor walking is one of the ways that digital technologies have foregrounded the 'optic,' and enabled the quantification of everyday mobility. At the time of writing, many of the devices to monitor walking currently set a default target of 10,000 steps. This figure is seen as a reasonable goal to ensure that a person receives the benefits of leading an active life. However, the origin of this value derives from older mechanical pedometers and lies in 'the popularity of Japanese walking clubs and a pedometer manufacturer (Yamasa Corporation, Tokyo, Japan) slogan from the 1960s… a pedometer came onto the Japanese commercial market in 1965 under the name of manpo-kei (literally translated, 'ten thousand steps meter')' (Tudor-Locke and Bassett Jr, 2004). The persistence of the 10,000-step figure is probably due as much to the ease of the number to remember as any evidence-based link with health outcomes (Tudor-Locke and Bassett Jr, 2004); also, perhaps, the gratifyingly 'collectable' virtue of steps that can be amassed.

For cyclists, there were pre-digital cycling meters and paper charts for recording distance, but these required much greater effort to set up and to maintain – only the most serious athletes bothered. Now digital cycling devices are widely available, relatively cheap and easy to set up, and record a greater variety of metrics: some external to the rider (speed, distance and height gained); others relating to biomedical aspects of the body (heart rate, cadence and power). These metrics are often combined to allow users to calculate an overall numeric 'fitness value'. Thus, the quantification of recorded steps or 'fitness values' allow users access to a simple numerical value with which to measure potential enhancements to the biological self.

What are the effects of these quantifications of everyday mobility? Considering walking first: it is possible to think of travel on foot in two ways. First would be those 'integrative walking practices' that are focused on walking itself – as an activity which is noteworthy in its own right. For example, hiking, rambling, hillwalking, or going for a walk in the country would be activities that are noteworthy in a sense that you may comment on having done one of them to friends or family. Second, there are 'dispersed walking practices' where walking is part of other activities, such as shopping or moving about an office while working. Dispersed walking practices are not normally distinguished as remarkable in themselves. Yet one effect of quantification is that it renders these dispersed practices as social entities in themselves, meaning that they become remarkable: participants become aware of their incidental walking (the steps they take while walking around the office literally 'counted'). However, these digital *things* or devices to count steps allow *people* to engender new desires as users became orientated towards 'taking a walk' to increase their step count as a practice in itself (Carter *et al.*, 2018).

Figure 8.6 Cycling has recognisable health benefits.

In contrast to walking, the role of digital technologies in the biomedicalisation of cycling has been less positioned as transforming an everyday transport activity into 'exercise'. Many people who cycle daily already understand this activity as beneficial to health. Rather, the move to recording and quantifying this activity has reframed recreational cycling and everyday commuting by bike as a competitive endeavour. In doing so, the quantification of cycling has foregrounded some ideas of health and potential users, while marginalising others. The reconfiguration of recreational cycling as a competitive activity compounds existing perceptions that see cycling as disproportionately an activity of affluent, white men (Figure 8.6). Also, the competition feeds into a certain 'assertive' style of riding that helps protect against the risks of sharing space with other road users in urban settings. Such ways of riding a bike may be less attractive to those who are not affluent, white or male (Steinbach *et al.*, 2011). It may be that digital devices, by encouraging a more competitive form of cycling, are introducing new *inequalities* and *power* dynamics into everyday mobilities.

5 Gamification and resistance

That digital technologies have made recreational cycling more competitive relies on a particular aspect of the quantification of the self – gamification. This refers to the idea that elements of game-design and principles are used in non-game contexts. Thus, the use of rewards, badges or medals, commonly found in the digital technologies that monitor walking and cycling introduce a competitive game-like element into these activities. Such gamification can operate for the lone user who may compete with the self, to improve upon their own performance, but it also has important communicative aspects with others. This has led Lomborg and Frandsen (2016) to argue that digital self-tracking is primarily a communicative activity. It allows users to share their achievements with an audience of other users. Thus, a lone cyclist or walker can be part of a wider community of walkers or cyclists.

As a communicative activity, Lomborg and Frandsen (2016, p. 9) see self-tracking as a 'lived informatics', with three dimensions:

- First is 'communicating with the digital system'. *People* must communicate with *things*. Users must often learn how to integrate several technologies that 'speak to one another'. Thus, to take full benefit of a service that provides feedback to the user, several different technologies such as mobile phones, apps, wearable devices and online sites must be made to communicate with each other and the user.

- Second is 'communicating with and acting on the self'. Here, data about the *individual* and their activities are stored on online sites, enabling analysed data to be presented back to the walker or cyclist reflexively. Some of the data presented back to users allows detailed analysis of their performance – this allows users to reflect on their biological enhancement (biomedicalisation) and record their individual progress as athletes.

- Third is 'communicating with peers' or a wider *society* of cyclists or walkers. Most of the self-tracking sites allow the user to establish contacts and communicate with other users. 'In that sense, self-tracking embeds key functionalities from social media, for networking, sharing, liking and commenting that are further shaped by the users' communicative practices onsite (Lomborg and Frandsen, 2016, p. 9).

The communicative aspects of digital technologies, therefore, enable new communities, of both known and unknown followers, to coalesce around cycling and walking practices. Users can employ competition to take 'responsibility' and self-reflect on their biological performativity. However, the competitive gamifications associated with these technologies also perform exclusions as well as inclusions. The competitive gamification may be making some user less likely to use the technology or to abandon its use. A question here is whether technologies get 'domesticated' into everyday use or how they may become abandoned or discarded (Carter, Green and Thorogood, 2013). The questions are whether these digital objects are routinely incorporated into life as stabilised *things* that *people* use or are they deserted for a variety of reasons, including being uncomfortable about the competitive aspects of gamification. Hence, some digital devices fail to stabilise into regular use by people and never become fully domesticated.

A good example comes from Copelton's (2010) study of a hospital-sponsored walking group for older women, the 'Walkie Talkies'. This group is perhaps a characteristic case of the medicalisation of walking (digital devices suggested for health and organised by the hospital), with the women encouraged to use a pedometer, which was supplied by the hospital, to track their activity and to promote more walking. However, for the women in Copelton's study, although health was typically the motivation for joining the group, what kept them returning was the friendship and companionship. This companionship was helped by engaging in joking chat that focused on community and acceptance. These friendship bonds were thought to be weakened by the use of devices that counted steps. This is because monitoring individual achievements, and giving a numerical value to these achievements, was thought to set up competition and hierarchy within the group of women.

Reading 8.1

Denise Copelton, 'Output that counts: pedometers, sociability and the contested terrain of older adult fitness walking'

Most contemporary walking programmes quantify walking with pedometers, set target step counts, and monitor progress towards that target. However, Walkie Talkies members expressed little interest in pedometers, step counts, and fitness targets. This case study reveals the central function of the club for most walkers was less about health promotion and more about building and maintaining social capital. For group leaders and fitness promoters, walking and steps are what count, but for walkers, talking and sociability count more. These differing priorities highlight the contested terrain of older adult fitness walking.

Organised walking was meaningful to participants because it facilitated pleasurable interactions that most referred to as camaraderie. Though walkers were motivated to join the club by health concerns, it was the sociability of the group that mattered for continued participation. The non-competitive nature of the club precluded the formation of hierarchies based on speed or step counts, and the 'come as you are' ethos reassured women walkers, in particular, that status distinctions common in other fitness activities would not arise in the Walkie Talkies. Time and again, walkers disparaged the perceived competitiveness of health clubs, aerobics classes, and gyms. Within this moral economy, pedometers, which quantify walking, permit hierarchies based on step counts and symbolise competition, appeared antithetical to group norms.

Although based on a small qualitative study, these findings suggest that health campaigns that structure walking as a *social* activity may find a more receptive audience among older adults, especially older women. While medical sociologists have documented that social connections contribute to health maintenance (House *et al.* 1988, Klinenberg 2001, 2002), my research goes one step further by demonstrating the importance of *sociability* in leisure pursuits for exercise adherence and health maintenance. Similar to casino gambling, Red Hat Society membership, and frequenting fast-food restaurants, exercise, for the older adult participants in this study, was really about having fun in an environment free of ageism, hierarchy and competition. If the non-competitive nature of walking is what attracts older adults to it, especially older women, then 10,000 steps programmes, with their exclusive focus on step counts, may be counterproductive. Instead of focusing on quantifiable exercise outputs, health and fitness researchers should pay greater attention to the social process of exercise. Outreach efforts that highlight the positive opportunities for sociability found through organised fitness activities such as group walking, may be more effective for recruiting older adults to these and similar programmes.

References

House, J., Landis, K. and Umberson, D. (1988) Social relationships and health, *Science*, 241, 540–5.

Klinenberg, E. (2001) Dying alone: the social production of urban isolation, *Ethnography*, 2, 499–529.

Klinenberg, E. (2002) *Heat Wave: a Social Autopsy of Disaster in Chicago*. Chicago: University of Chicago Press.

(Copelton, 2010, pp. 314–315)

Thus, few adopted or continued to use the pedometer supplied by the hospital. These were not, as Copelton notes, women who were necessarily averse to technology as they utilised technologies freely in other areas of their lives. However, wearing a pedometer 'is simultaneously a very intimate and social act that contributes to one's symbolic presentation of self' (Copelton, 2010, p. 313). The presentation of self, associated with the use of pedometers, was not resonant with the collective identity of the group. Thus, digital devices that highlight facets of identity (in this case, competitiveness) not corresponding to a group or self-identity may get abandoned or never get adopted in the first place. Another way of looking at these women's non-use of digital devices to record walking is to note that the women feared that recording of steps would introduce competition and hierarchy into the group. In other words, it would have led to *inequalities* and *power* dynamics in the group, and the women were afraid that this would threaten the cohesiveness of their social world.

6 Turning leisure into work

One further consequence of turning the mundane aspects of mobility practices into something noteworthy and recordable through self-tracking is that the boundaries between transport, leisure, competition, and work become blurred. This is the insight provided by sociologist Christopher Till, who argues that digital self-tracking has started the social process where the recording of exercise activity is being reconfigured as work (Till, 2014). This, he argues, is because while users can collate and share information about their mobilities online, the corporations that own and control these online sites 'can aggregate data or share with others within their "corporate umbrella"' (Till, 2014, p. 449) and disseminate aggregated data with third parties, with obvious appeal to many commercial organisations. This may be particularly significant for many mobility self-tracking sites where users can enter significant information about themselves, their locations, and the equipment they have purchased.

Reading 8.2

Chris Till, 'Exercise as labour: quantified self and the transformation of exercise into labour'

The few sociological approaches to digital self-tracking have tended to focus on surveillance or the micro-level impact on individuals and their relationship to the self. These have been valuable and look likely to inspire useful empirical work; however, a focus on the macro level tactics of the corporations who are largely in control of the data provides different insights. By considering self-tracked exercise activity in terms of its corporate value, we can see how it is digitized, quantified, accumulated and analysed in order to generate commercially valuable data on the population. These data are particularly valuable to the corporations who are collecting it, because it has been ideologically constituted as 'not work' and, therefore, not being worthy of payment. It has been suggested above that there are 'structural similarities' between the 'digital labour' or 'free labour' that is conducted online and the digitally-tracked exercise activities of users of self-tracking devices. When approached through a Marxist frame of analysis, it is possible to see the digital tracking of exercise activities as a form of the accumulation of labour, which enables the extraction of surplus value. The transformation of exercise activities into digital data enables individual users to see their activities as a particular kind of 'formative activity' through the representation of their achievements as digital data in the form of statistics or 'medals', which constitute a kind of objectification of the labour of the exerciser, which is relatively new to the amateur athlete. For corporations who are compiling these data, however, by transforming heterogeneous exercise activities into a standardized, quantified form, they are able to be made into a valuable resource; data that can be sold to advertisers. The exercise activities in which people engage are therefore seen as productive potential energy by corporations, who are likely to be using the design of hardware and software to subtly structure the behaviour of users to produce the kinds of data that will be of commercial value. Prior to the existence of easily available digital tracking technologies, there were few ways in which every day exercise activities could be quantified and standardized in such a form that they are amenable to the accumulation and comparison of the data of large amounts of people. These developments are currently in their early stages but may be indicative of not only a new form of surveillance, but an epistemological change in how exercise is understood, as well as signalling the potential commercialization of the exercising bodies of the population.

(Till, 2014, p. 458)

In this reading Till is using a Marxist frame of analysis, and he speaks of digital tracking as being able to extract 'surplus value'. For Marxists, one of the characteristics of capitalism is its 'Mode of Production' which is riven with *inequalities* of *power*. Within this view, capitalist commercial organisations, such as factories and companies, are privately owned, and the possession of these organisations generates profits for the owners. Private money is used by the owners (or 'capitalists') of factories and companies to buy labour and other inputs, such as raw materials, and these are combined to produce new goods and services. These new goods and services are then sold at an economic value that is greater than the inputs used to produce them. It is this that produces the profit for the owners. For Marxists, one of the most important inputs is the labour of workers. The key issue here is that the labour of workers produces a surplus-value because when the commodities or services are sold, they generate greater economic value than the wages paid to the workers. The capitalists have thus extracted surplus value from the labour of the workers by paying them less than the value of the work they have finished. Capitalists can extract this surplus value from workers because they own the means of production.

People using digital devices to record their walking and cycling are not workers in any conventional sense, as most are not being formally paid for their walking and cycling. However, they are often being symbolically rewarded by the use of 'medals' or 'badges'. Even the presentation of statistical data about themselves could be seen as a benefit in kind for their willingness to allow their data to be used. People who use digital devices to record their activities are mostly doing so for reasons we have explored above, such as wishing to improve their fitness and enhance the biological self. However, the companies that market devices for recording walking and cycling also collect the data generated by these objects. On an individual level, this is presented back to users so that they can monitor their progress but, at the same time, companies can aggregate large quantities of data that is of considerable commercial value, for example in advertising and marketing. This, according to Till, allows companies to extract surplus value from the users' walking and cycling activities. They, according to this view, are doing labour from which it is possible to extract a surplus value for profit.

7 Conclusion

This chapter has outlined the concepts of medicalisation and biomedicalisation as they have been used by sociologists in the analysis of health and technology. You saw how the concept of medicalisation was drawn on to explain the promotion of active travel as a policy initiative that attempts to improve the health of the population. When we turned to assess the use of digital devices to monitor, record and quantify walking and cycling you will have seen how the notion of biomedicalisation was in play as these devices appear to offer users the prospect of biological enhancement and 'perfectibility'.

You will also have seen how the sociological thread of *power and inequality* can be used in the analysis of walking and cycling: how there is an inequality in attitudes to walking as opposed to motorised forms of transport; and how the competitive gamification of walking and cycling may be introducing new *inequalities* and *power* dynamics into everyday mobilities, for example with the 'Walkie Talkies'. The sociological thread of *individuals and society* was also drawn on during the chapter: campaigns to increase active travel were framed as desirable both for the individual and collectively for society; the contrast was highlighted between policy initiatives to increase active travel as a benefit to society, and digital technologies associated with walking and cycling, which often stress the benefits that their use will bring to the individual; and when considering the communicative aspects of digital technologies you saw how these both act on the individual as they record their progress as athletes and as a way to establish contact with a wider society of walkers or cyclists. Finally, as the chapter focused on digital devices to record walking and cycling, there were many references to *people and things*.

References

American Public Health Association (2012) *Promoting active transportation: an opportunity for public health.* Available at: https://www.saferoutespartnership. org/sites/default/files/pdf/The_Final_Active_Primer.pdf (Accessed 22: April 2019).

Bell, S.E. (1987) 'Changing ideas: The medicalization of menopause', *Social Science & Medicine*, 24(6), pp. 535–542. doi: 10.1016/0277-9536(87)90343-1.

Carter, S., Green, J. and Speed, E. (2018) 'Digital technologies and the biomedicalisation of everyday activities: the case of walking and cycling', *Sociology Compass*, 12(4), pp. 1–12. doi: 10.1111/soc4.12572.

Carter, S., Green, J. and Thorogood, N. (2013) 'The domestication of an everyday health technology: a case study of electric toothbrushes', *Social Theory & Health : STH*, 11(4), pp. 344–367. doi: 10.1057/sth.2013.15.

Clarke, A.E., Shim, J.K., Mamo, L., Fosket, J.R. and Fishman, J.R. (2003) 'Biomedicalization: technoscientific transformations of health, illness and U.S. biomedicine', *American Sociological Review*, 68(2), pp. 161–194.

Conrad, P. (1992) 'Medicalization and Social Control', *Annual Review of Sociology*, 18(1), pp. 209–232.

Copelton, D.A. (2010) 'Output that counts: pedometers, sociability and the contested terrain of older adult fitness walking', *Sociology of Health & Illness*, 32(2), pp. 304–318.

Fitbit (2019) *Why Fitbit.* Available at: https://www.fitbit.com/uk/whyfitbit (Accessed: 23 April 2019).

Foucault, M. (1980) *Power/knowledge: selected interviews and other writings 1972–77.* Reprint. Translated from the French by C. Gordon. Harlow: Harvester Press. 1980.

Fritz, T., Huang, E.M., Murphy, G.C. and Zimmermann, T. (2014) 'Persuasive technology in the real world: a study of long-term use of activity sensing devices for fitness', *Proceedings of the SIGCHI Conference on Human Factors in Computing Systems*, April. pp. 487–496.

Gilderbloom, J.I., Riggs, W.W. and Meares, W.L. (2015) 'Does walkability matter? An examination of walkability's impact on housing values, foreclosures and crime', *Cities*, 42(PA), pp. 13–24. doi: 10.1016/j. cities.2014.08.001.

Green, J. (2009) '"Walk this way": Public health and the social organization of walking', *Social Theory & Health*, 7(1), pp. 20–38.

Lomborg, S. and Frandsen, K. (2016) 'Self-tracking as communication', *Information, Communication & Society*, 19(7), pp. 1015–1027. doi: 10.1080/ 1369118X.2015.1067710.

Meyer, V.F. (2001) 'The medicalization of menopause: critique and consequences', *International Journal of Health Services*, 31(4), pp. 769–792. doi: 10.2190/M77D-YV2Y-D5NU-FXNW.

de Nazelle, A., Nieuwenhuijsen, M.J., Antó, J.M., Brauer, M., Briggs, D., Braun-Fahrlander, C., Cavill, N., Cooper, A.R., Desqueyroux, H., Fruin, S. and Hoek, G. (2011) 'Improving health through policies that promote active travel: a review of evidence to support integrated health impact assessment', *Environment International*, 37(4), pp. 766–777. doi: http://dx.doi.org/10.1016/j.envint.2011.02.003.

NHS Digital (2012) *Health Survey for England - 2012*. Available at: https://digital.nhs.uk/data-and-information/publications/statistical/health-survey-for-england/health-survey-for-england-2012 (Accessed: 20 April 2019).

Oja, P., Titze, S., Bauman, A., De Geus, B., Krenn, P., Reger-Nash, B. and Kohlberger, T. (2011) 'Health benefits of cycling: a systematic review', *Scandinavian Journal of Medicine and Science in Sports*, 21(4), pp. 496–509. doi: 10.1111/j.1600-0838.2011.01299.x.

Saunders, L. E., Green, J.M., Petticrew, M.P., Steinbach, R. and Roberts, H. (2013) 'What are the health benefits of active travel? A systematic review of trials and cohort studies', *PLoS One*, 8(8), p. e69912.

Scottish Government (2014) *Let's get Scotland walking - the National Walking Strategy*. Available at: https://www.gov.scot/publications/lets-scotland-walking-national-walking-strategy/pages/3/ (Accessed: 21 April 2019).

Steinbach, R., Green, J., Datta, J. and Edwards, P. (2011) 'Cycling and the city: a case study of how gendered, ethnic and class identities can shape healthy transport choices', *Social Science and Medicine*, 72(7), pp. 1123–1130. doi: 10.1016/j.socscimed.2011.01.033.

Strava (2018) *Strava names Stephanie Hannon as Chief Product Officer | Business Wire*. Available at: https://www.businesswire.com/news/home/20180104006194/en/Strava-Names-Stephanie-Hannon-Chief-Product-Officer (Accessed: 23 April 2019).

Till, C. (2014) 'Exercise as labour: quantified self and the transformation of exercise into labour', *Societies*, 4(3), pp. 446–462.

Tudor-Locke, C. and Bassett Jr, D.R. (2004) 'How many steps/day are enough?', *Sports Medicine*, 34(1), pp. 1–8.

Vanderbilt, T. (2012) 'Why don't Americans walk more? The crisis of pedestrianism', *Slate*. Available at: http://www.slate.com/articles/life/walking/2012/04/why_don_t_americans_walk_more_the_crisis_of_pedestrianism_.html?via=gdpr-consent (Accessed: 17 April 2019).

Zola, I.K. (1983) *Socio-medical inquiries: recollections, reflections, and reconsiderations*. Philadelphia, PA: Temple University Press.

Section 4

Uses and abuses of the digital

Introduction to Section 4

Simon Carter and Jessamy Perriam

Welcome to Section 4. In this section, you will be examining some of the uses and abuses of the digital. Earlier sections of the book have tended to focus on one thread in particular: Section 1 emphasised *individuals and society*; Section 2 *power and inequality*; and Section 3 *people and things*. In contrast, this section will address all of the threads more or less equally.

In previous sections, you will have already come across examples of how digital devices have empowered people in various ways. For example, most people would acknowledge that it is good that digital devices allow people to stay in contact, even when they are dispersed globally. Similarly, connected digital devices make life easier by automating mundane tasks. Yet almost as soon as the internet became more widely available via mobile and domestic connections, stories began to emerge about how this connectivity may have harms as well as benefits. While urban dwellers enjoyed the advantages and convenience of easy access to the internet, many living in more remote areas struggled to get online, raising a new form of inequality. The internet allows people access to an enormous knowledge base, but it has also been accused of allowing the spread of misinformation and **disinformation**. People have the convenience of shopping, banking and making travel arrangements from their mobile devices, but now also have to face new forms of cybercrime and new threats to their privacy. Social media has given people who were previously ignored a voice, but it has also been accused of contributing to bad mental health among young people.

Societal acceptance of new technologies

Anyone who has spent time online has probably come across things that they find troubling or distasteful and even innocent searches can sometimes bring up unexpected or disturbing results. Also, online digital games are often blamed for inciting violence or even mass shootings, with the then President of the United States saying 'We must stop the glorification of violence in our society, this includes the gruesome and grisly video games that are now commonplace' (Draper, 2019). But is this any different to what happened before the internet or video games existed? People have often been upset by novel forms of communication. For instance, in the 1890s in Victorian Britain, there was one of the first examples of mass-produced popular fiction known as the 'penny dreadfuls' or 'penny bloods'. These were stories, typically published in weekly instalments, costing one penny. The subject matter was often shocking, featuring violent crimes, supernatural entities or sometimes both (Figure 1). Their target audience was working-class boys who had been taught to read in the newly set-up state schools. The penny dreadfuls were blamed for everything from youth violence and suicide, even social unrest, in much the same way as video games and social media are blamed for these things today. As the Motherwell Times said in 1895, 'Tons of this trash is vomited forth from Fleet Street every day, and inwardly digested by those whose mental pabulum is on a level with the stuff for which it craves.' (quoted in Summerscale, 2016).

Social harm and the digital

One of the central concepts that we will be referring to in this section, as we examine different aspects of digital societies, is social harm. The idea of social harm emerged from the discipline of criminology, and, in particular, from critical sociological understandings of crime. Explanations of criminal activity often narrowly focus on the individual as either the perpetrator or victim of harms, such as interpersonal violence or theft. In contrast, sociological approaches accept that crime is not just about who breaks the law but also about how society frames crime in terms of who makes the law and how it is enforced. Thus issues of *power and inequality* can be seen as having a bearing on not only what actions are seen as illegal, but also which people are more likely to be seen as offenders. Power can be used to influence The State about what is to be legally defined as harmful and what counts as a crime. This reminds us that crime and criminal law have no independent existence outside of the social processes that produce and construct them. 'It is in fact difficult if not impossible to conceive of any act that in all circumstances, in all places, at all times, appears as a crime' (Hillyard and Tombs, 2017). Even extreme events, such as the taking of life or property, can take legal forms. Also, the activities that are undertaken by powerful groups or organisations are far less likely to be defined as crimes than those actions carried out by the less powerful.

Figure 1 Varney the Vampire, a typical penny dreadful.

A good example of this can be seen by looking at different causes of death. There were around 700 deaths from murder in the UK in the year ending 2018 (Office for National Statistics, 2019), and these could all be defined as crimes. This is an example of physical harm that leads to loss of life and devastation for those connected to the victims. But consider other forms of physical harm. In the UK it is estimated that between 28,000 to 36,000 people die every year from human-made air pollution (Public Health England, 2019). Many of these deaths would be preventable if powerful organisations, such as vehicle manufacturers or industry, took different decisions about their products or activities. Or to take another example, it is estimated that roughly 8000 people die of cancer every year from past occupational contact with known carcinogens, with the leading exposure being to asbestos. These deaths would also be preventable if the management of industries in which these people worked had taken different decisions. Death from exposure to air pollution is not treated as a crime, and while allowing someone to be exposed to occupational carcinogens would count as a crime under health and safety legislation, prosecutions are rare and often result in fines rather than custodial sentences. This also raises issues of *power and inequality*, as Jen Remnant has said about asbestos:

> Permitting the use of asbestos corresponds with wider occupational health inequalities. The policy makers that allow the use of asbestos, and those individuals who buy it cheaply for construction, despite the dangers it represents, are not those expected to handle it. They are not the people heading home with the fibres in their lungs or on their clothing. They are not the people hoping to enjoy retirement when they notice a persistent cough, pain or breathlessness. Diseases caused by asbestos will be experienced by workers at the bottom of the labour chain; in the US, likely to be immigrant construction workers.
>
> (Remnant, 2018)

The social harm approach, instead of concentrating on crime, rather focuses on the harm that activities may do to society or the environment. Advocates of social harm analysis argue that illegal or criminal acts can be harmful, but sometimes are not, and on the contrary, many legal activities present great harm to societies or the environment. The approach asks that we take a step back from looking at activities in terms of their legal status and instead concentrate on processes that are harmful or damaging, but that also have the potential to be prevented. As Hillyard and colleagues argue:

> for the person who dies, whether it is from a deliberate act, 'accident' or indifference they are still dead with all the social and economic consequences for their family and friends. ... Thus, it is a central premise ... that it makes no sense to separate out harms, which can be defined as criminal, from all other types of harm. All forms of harm we argue must be considered and analysed

together. Otherwise a very distorted view of the world will be produced.

(Hillyard *et al.*, 2004, pp. 1–2)

The social harm approach allows analysis to move between the local and global to look at harmful activities that are not limited to individual countries. Thus it lends itself to the study of environmental damages that cross national boundaries or those that are produced by transnational corporations. For example, as we write this book in 2020, there is widespread concern that we are facing a climate emergency due to human activities that release the gases responsible for global warming, such as carbon dioxide. Left unchecked, climate change will lead to a variety of serious social harms, such as significantly increased health risks (Watts *et al.*, 2019), or sea-level rises that will threaten low-lying communities where over one billion people now live (Kulp and Strauss, 2019). Some of the major contributors to climate-change gases are well known, such as the petrochemical industry, the automotive industry or the aviation industry.

Other contributing activities are not so obvious. A lot of work and leisure activities that we do are now delivered via digital technologies. The documents, data, images and videos that we use are often stored outside of our own phones or laptops, in the cloud (Figure 2, overleaf). We also no longer watch videos via physical media such as tapes or DVDs, as films and television series are now commonly 'streamed' directly to televisions or mobile devices. The original media is also located in the cloud. When we use words such as 'the cloud' to describe data storage, we tend to create an abstraction of the physical locations where this data is stored. But the films we watch on streaming services, the documents we store and the photographs we have taken on our smartphones reside in data centres scattered all over the world. These data centres use large amounts of energy to power the servers that run the cloud, as well as cooling systems to keep the technology at an optimum temperature. The ways we use, create and enjoy data can have serious repercussions for the environment which in turn will cause significant social harm. The French environmental think-tank 'The Shift Project' argue that online video viewing is no longer sustainable because it 'represents 60% of the world's data traffic, generated more than 300 $MtCO_2e$ during 2018, i.e. a carbon footprint comparable to the annual emissions of Spain' (The Shift Project, 2019). While some have disputed the figures used by the Shift Project

(Le Page, 2020), it is likely that some social harm results from enjoying something as simple as watching an online film or television programme.

Figure 2 A server room in a data centre delivering streaming services.

Reading the section

To address what some of the possible harms of the digital are, we will be looking at some specific examples in the coming section. In Chapter 9, you will have a chance to examine the material infrastructure that makes digital connections feasible. You will also see where some of the things needed for the manufacture of digital devices come from and how their extraction might harm people. In Chapter 10, we will examine some of the disinformation, and so-called 'fake news' circulated via digital means and how this differs from a pre-internet era. In Chapter 11, we will look at digital failures, data accidents and cybersecurity. In Chapter 12, you will also have a chance to access the claims that social media can cause mental health problems for young people. Finally, in Chapter 13, we will look at the ubiquity of digital algorithms and the potential biases that can reinforce existing inequalities.

References

Draper, K. (2019) 'Video games aren't why shootings happen. Politicians still blame them', *The New York Times*, 5 August. Available at: https://www.nytimes.com/2019/08/05/sports/trump-violent-video-games-studies.html (Accessed: 6 February 2020).

Hillyard, P., Pantazis, C., Tombs, S. and Gordon, D. (2004) 'Introduction', in Hillyard, P., Pantazis, C., Tombs, S. and Gordon, D. (eds) *Beyond criminology: taking harm seriously*. London: Pluto Press, pp. 1–9.

Hillyard, P. and Tombs, S. (2017) 'Social harm and zemiology', in Liebling, A., Maruna, S. and McAra, L. (eds) *The Oxford Handbook of Criminology*. 6th edn. Oxford: Oxford University Press, pp. 284–305.

Kulp, S.A. and Strauss, B.H. (2019) 'New elevation data triple estimates of global vulnerability to sea-level rise and coastal flooding', *Nature Communications*, 10(1), pp. 1–12.

Le Page, M. (2020) 'Binge watching TV isn't as bad for the climate as some reports suggest', *New Scientist*. Available at: https://www.newscientist.com/article/2235713-binge-watching-tv-isnt-as-bad-for-the-climate-as-some-reports-suggest/ (Accessed: 14 January 2021).

Office for National Statistics (2019) *Homicide in England and Wales: year ending March 2018*. Available at: https://www.ons.gov.uk/peoplepopulationandcommunity/crimeandjustice/articles/homicideinenglandandwales/yearendingmarch2018 (Accessed: 7 February 2020).

Public Health England (2019) *Review of interventions to improve outdoor air quality and public health*. Available at: https://assets.publishing.service.gov.uk/government/uploads/system/uploads/attachment_data/file/795185/Review_of_interventions_to_improve_air_quality.pdf (Accessed: 16 November 2020).

Remnant, J. (2018) 'White fluff', *Cost of living*, 5 December. Available at: https://www.cost-ofliving.net/white-fluff/ (Accessed: 7 February 2020).

Summerscale, K. (2016) *The wicked boy: the mystery of a Victorian child murderer*. London: Bloomsbury.

The Shift Project (2019) *Climate crisis: the unsustainable use of online video*. Available at: https://theshiftproject.org/wp-content/uploads/2019/07/2019-02.pdf (Accessed: 16 October 2019).

Watts, N. *et al.* (2019) 'The 2019 report of The Lancet Countdown on health and climate change: ensuring that the health of a child born today is not defined by a changing climate', *The Lancet*, 394(10211), pp. 1836–1878.

Chapter 9
Material digital technologies

Jessamy Perriam and Simon Carter

Contents

1 Introduction

In the previous chapters, we have been looking at various aspects of digital societies and how the digital has touched individuals, communities and everyday life. In this chapter, we will study the material elements that make up digital societies – the physical things that allow us to use digital devices and connect to the internet. In the first part of the chapter, we will look at the infrastructures that make digital connections viable. Then you will have a chance to explore the materials that make digital objects, such as smartphones, possible. We want you to examine the things that allow people to connect digitally and some of the possible **social harms** that can result from this. Also, we will examine the different ways in which power and inequality can play out as a result of the development, manufacture and distribution of these physical objects that make up digital societies.

1.1 Teaching aims

The aims of this chapter are for you to:

- examine the networks of infrastructure that make up the internet to determine why some places have better internet access than others

- consider the inequalities resulting from the way that digital connections are socially and politically organised

- explore the environmental and human impacts of mineral extraction associated with digital devices.

2   Digital squirrels

When we use the word 'infrastructure', what comes to mind? Perhaps you think of roads, bridges, pipes and electrical cables. Infrastructure forms part of our day-to-day lived experience. In a typical day, you are likely to use many different kinds of infrastructure. When you turned the light on or when your alarm went off this morning, you were making use of electricity-generating systems that may make use of the sun, the wind, water, nuclear energy or fossil fuels. When you took a shower, flushed the toilet or filled the kettle, you were interacting with a network of pipes, taps and sewerage systems. All of this happens without much thought on your part. Far from only being an individual, the practice of going about your daily routine connects you to a network of *people and things*. This is no different when we consider our use of digital technologies. The following extract from Andrew Blum's book *Tubes* illustrates this point. A few years ago, Blum's internet service in his Brooklyn home was patchy. As he describes it:

> The repairman arrived the next morning, full of assurances. He attached an electronic whistle—it looked like a penlight—to the living room end of the cable, and then began to trace its path, searching for clues. I followed him, first outside to the street, then down into the basement and through a hatch to the backyard. A rusty switch box was caught in a web of black cables and bolted to a brick wall. Disconnecting them one at a time, he screwed a tiny speaker into each one until he found the one that whistled: audible proof of a continuous path between here and there.
>
> Then his eyes lifted ominously to the sky. A squirrel scampered along a wire toward a battleship gray enclosure affixed like a birdhouse to a pole. Anemic urban vines wrapped around it. Animals chew on the rubber coating, the repairman explained. Short of rewiring the whole backyard, there was nothing he could do. "But it might get better on its own," he said, and it did. But the crude physicality of the situation astonished me. Here was the Internet, the most powerful information network ever conceived! Capable of instantaneous communication with anyplace on earth! Instigator of revolutions! Constant companion, messenger of love,

fountain of riches and beloved distraction. Stymied by the buckteeth of a Brooklyn squirrel.

(Blum, 2013, pp. 1–2)

In *Tubes*, Blum recounts his journey to try to find out what caused this disconnection, and he uncovers all of the physical objects that make our daily life online work seamlessly. While we find out that a squirrel in Blum's garden was responsible for damaging the cable, we also realise that we cannot take internet infrastructure for granted. Blum takes the reader on a journey to try to locate the internet. This journey incorporates visits to disparate sites, such as a data centre in rural America and a cable on the Atlantic coast. The point of Blum's book is to highlight how the internet is a physical thing, located at many points across the world.

3   Internet infrastructure

To show how the internet is a physical thing, located in many points and places, we will now consider the infrastructures that allow digital connections. In the following section, you will be reading how two writers, Susan Leigh Star and Nicole Starosielski talk about infrastructure. When considering infrastructure from a social sciences perspective, we need to think about the attributes it might have and how people interact with the things that make up the infrastructure.

Figure 9.1 Fibre-optic cables.

In the second part of this section, you will see how Starosielski talks about common misconceptions of the distributed and egalitarian nature of internet infrastructure. First, you will be reading an extract from Susan Leigh Star, who has spent a lot of time thinking about infrastructure. In the following reading, she describes fieldwork with biologists, who were building an electronic shared laboratory, and attempts to define key attributes of infrastructure. Like many of the readings in *Understanding Digital Societies* it is not necessary to understand all of the terms used in the extract. Rather, we would like you to consider the main points about infrastructure that Star raises. When reading this, it may also be helpful for you to consider some of the ways you have observed infrastructure yourself.

Reading 9.1

Susan Leigh Star, 'The ethnography of infrastructure'

People commonly envision infrastructure as a system of substrates —railroad lines, pipes and plumbing, electrical power plants, and wires. It is by definition invisible, part of the background for other kinds of work. It is ready-to-hand. This image holds up well enough for many purposes—turn on the faucet for a drink of water and you use a vast infrastructure of plumbing and water regulation without usually thinking much about it.

The image becomes more complicated when one begins to investigate large-scale technical systems in the making, or to examine the situations of those who are *not* served by a particular infrastructure. For a railroad engineer, the rails are not infrastructure but topic. For the person in a wheelchair, the stairs and doorjamb in front of a building are not seamless sub tenders of use, but barriers (Star, 1991). One person's infrastructure is another's topic, or difficulty. As Star and Ruhleder (1996) put it, infrastructure is a fundamentally relational concept, becoming real infrastructure in relation to organized practices (see also Jewett & Kling, 1991). So, within a given cultural context, the cook considers the water system as working infrastructure integral to making dinner. For the city planner or the plumber, it is a variable in a complex planning process or a target for repair: "Analytically, infrastructure appears only as a relational property, not as a thing stripped of use" (Star & Ruhleder, 1996, p. 113).

In my own research, this became clear when I did fieldwork over 3 years with a community of biologists, in partnership with a computer scientist who was building an electronic shared laboratory and publishing space for them (Schatz, 1991). I was studying their work practices and travelling to many laboratories to observe computer use and communication patterns. ... It seemed the difficulty was not in the interface or the representation of the work processes embedded in the system, but rather in infrastructure—incompatible platforms, recalcitrant local computing centres, and bottlenecked resources. We were forced to develop a more relational definition of infrastructure, and at the same time, challenge received views of good use of ethnography in systems development.

We began to see infrastructure as part of human organization, and as problematic as any other. ... Ruhleder and I came to define *infrastructure* as having the following properties ....

Embeddedness. Infrastructure is sunk into and inside of other structures, social arrangements, and technologies. People do not necessarily distinguish the several coordinated aspects of infrastructure. ...

Transparency. Infrastructure is transparent to use, in the sense that it does not have to be reinvented each time or assembled for each task, but invisibly supports those tasks. ...

Reach or scope. This may be either spatial or temporal—infrastructure has reach beyond a single event or one-site practice. ...

Learned as part of membership. The taken-for-grantedness of artefacts and organizational arrangements is a *sine qua non* of membership in a community of practice (Bowker & Star, in press; Lave & Wenger, 1991). Strangers and outsiders encounter infrastructure as a target object to be learned about. New participants acquire a naturalized familiarity with its objects, as they become members. ...

Links with conventions of practice. Infrastructure both shapes and is shaped by the conventions of a community of practice (e.g., the ways that cycles of day-night work are affected by and affect electrical power rates and needs). Generations of typists have learned the QWERTY keyboard; its limitations are inherited by the computer keyboard and thence by the design of today's computer furniture (Becker, 1982). ...

Embodiment of standards. Modified by scope and often by conflicting conventions, infrastructure takes on transparency by plugging into other infrastructures and tools in a standardized fashion. ...

Built on an installed base. Infrastructure does not grow *de novo*; it wrestles with the inertia of the installed base and inherits strengths and limitations from that base. Optical fibres run along old railroad lines; new systems are designed for backward compatibility, and failing to account for these constraints may be fatal or distorting to new development processes (Hanseth & Monteiro, 1996). ...

Becomes visible upon breakdown. The normally invisible quality of working infrastructure becomes visible when it breaks: the server is down, the bridge washes out, there is a power blackout. Even when there are back-up mechanisms or procedures, their existence further highlights the now-visible infrastructure. ...

Is fixed in modular increments, not all at once or globally. Because infrastructure is big, layered, and complex, and because it means different things locally, it is never changed from above. Changes take time and negotiation, and adjustment with other aspects of the systems are involved. Nobody is really in charge of infrastructure. ...

References

Becker, H. S. (1982). *Art Worlds*. Berkeley: University of California Press.

Bowker, G., & Star, S. L. (in press). *Sorting things out: Classification and its consequences*. Cambridge, MA: MIT Press.

Hanseth, O., & Monteiro, E. (1996). Inscribing behavior in information infrastructure standards. *Accounting, Management & Information Technology*, 7, 183-211.

Jewett, T., & Kling, R. (1991). The dynamics of computerization in a social science research team: A case study of infrastructure, strategies, and skills. *Social Science Computer Review*, 9, 246-275.

Lave, J., & Wenger, E. (1991). *Situated learning: Legitimate peripheral participation*. Cambridge, UK: Cambridge University Press.

Schatz, B. (1991). Building an electronic community system. *Journal of Management Information Systems*, 8, 87-107.

Star, S. L. (1991). Power, technologies and the phenomenology of conventions: On being allergic to onions. In J. Law (Ed.), *A sociology of monsters: Essays on power, technology and domination* (pp. 25-56). London: Routledge.

Star, S. L., & Ruhleder, K. (1996). Steps toward an ecology of infrastructure: Design and access for large information spaces. *Information Systems Research*, 7(1), 111-134.

(Star, 1999, pp. 380–382)

From the reading above, you can see that Star describes some key aspects of infrastructure. For example, we often take infrastructure for granted, and it is invisible until it breaks down. We also do not need to rebuild any given infrastructure, such as water supply, from scratch each time we want to use it. Today, you may take it for granted that Wi-Fi and mobile data services will mean that you are always connected to the internet, almost to the point of feeling bereft if there is a short outage in service. For those of you who used the internet in the 1990s, you will remember the sounds of the internet infrastructure as noisy modems tried to connect to the internet. In those days, we also had to accept the fact that using the internet often meant that you could not make or receive calls at the same time. If you wanted to use the internet away from your home, you would have had to find an internet café, or similar specific dedicated venue, because phones with mobile data were not widely available until later in the 2000s.

When we think of the internet, it is often difficult to picture the infrastructure that makes it possible to send emails, browse websites or make video calls. We often think of internet infrastructure being egalitarian and connecting everyone equally. But the reality of this is quite different. As Nicole Starosielski describes in her book *The Undersea Network*, the infrastructure that makes up the internet is highly political, built on historical telegraph networks, determined by geography and dependent on millions in financial investment. 'It is wired rather than wireless; semi-centralized rather and distributed; territorially entrenched rather than deterritorialized; precarious rather than resilient; and rural and aquatic rather than urban' (Starosielski, 2015, p. 10).

To illustrate this point, Starosielski describes the history and challenges presented by the geography of the internet:

> Early telegraph networks were mapped over colonial geographies, and the majority of companies that laid telephone cables through the 1980s were government-owned or -affiliated monopolies. These extensive investments shaped the contours of cabled environments and provided traction for Internet infrastructure. The two fiber-optic cables connecting New Zealand to the outside world, for example, are located in the same zones as telegraph cables from the early twentieth century.... Major transpacific cable

hubs in the United States are located at sites established during the Cold War.

Although our digital environment appears to be a space of mobility, radically changing every few years, the backbone for the global Internet continues to be sunk along historical and political lines, tending to reinforce global inequalities.

(Starosielski, 2015, p. 12)

When we think about digital infrastructure, we end up at an intersection where *power and inequality* and *people and things* collide. We need the infrastructure to carry out many transactions and activities that are increasingly only available online. But inequality begins to occur when we are unable to access that infrastructure. Some of the reasons why people may not have access are due to geography. This may not be so obvious if you live in large urban hubs such as London or New York City where there are significant data exchanges. However, if you live in remote areas in countries such as Canada, Australia or even the Highlands of Scotland (BBC, 2019), it can become difficult to connect reliably to the internet, and therefore the wider world.

Figure 9.2 Underground pipes and cables.

In Canada, remote **First Nations** groups have experienced difficulty in getting connected to the internet because of what is called the problem of the 'last mile' of infrastructure required to get online (McMahon, 2014). Many corporate telecommunications providers find it geographically difficult or unprofitable to connect the last mile – the portion of the telecommunications network that reaches the end-users' properties. The last mile (which may be a lot shorter than a mile) is the most expensive because this is where connections are most numerous as well as having to co-exist with many other infrastructure connections. Similarly, if any repairs are required to the infrastructure, this can be difficult to arrange in remote areas if, for example, weather conditions are often poor or extreme. This lack of access to digital infrastructure has ongoing impacts for communities as they have trouble keeping up with digital literacy in comparison to their urban, **settler** counterparts.

Additionally, when digital literacy is mentioned, it does not solely refer to simply knowing how to operate a computer, smartphone or another piece of technology effectively. It is also about having experience of how to integrate technology use into everyday tasks and being able to identify when that use starts to become problematic, for example in situations like trolling, misinformation or identity theft. Even searching the internet takes some practice and skill to do efficiently. If you have not been able to easily access the internet due to the tyranny of distance or affordability, you will likely not have had the opportunity to gain good levels of digital literacy.

In discussing the 'last mile' problem with digital infrastructure, Rob McMahon raises two interesting points. Firstly, he asks how First Nations communities might be self-determining in installing, governing and maintaining their internet infrastructure. And secondly, he raises a key point: how might First Nations communities understand digital infrastructure within their broader socio-technical arrangement? This second point is important when considering digital literacy because it confronts the trap that there is only one way of being digitally literate. McMahon argues that each community needs to determine for themselves what it means to be digitally literate along with the risks and opportunities that present themselves when introducing internet infrastructure to a community.

Meanwhile, in Australia, the National Broadband Network – an internet infrastructure project that promised to deliver fast broadband to the majority of the Australian population faced delays because of the costs of rolling out the cables across an entire continent. Australian residents face a 'postcode lottery' when accessing broadband infrastructure, so much so that real estate advertisements actually highlight access to broadband internet as a selling point – location matters when it comes to getting online.

In the following reading, Nicole Starosielski discusses some of the issues of providing internet infrastructure in remote regions. Here, Starosielski examines how cities and urban dwellers have exerted influence over the way digital infrastructure has developed. Yet, connecting regions that are geographically distant has implications both for other users of the spaces that the infrastructure passes through and the uncabled peoples who may want to access the benefits of digital connections.

Reading 9.2

Nicole Starosielski, *The Undersea Network*

Geographies of digital media tend to focus on the city as it has been intertwined with the development of information flows. Indeed, the destination of signal traffic is often the urban user, and the city has exerted a gravitational effect on infrastructural development. Most of the undersea cable network's routes and pressure points, however, are nestled in natural environments, and the system has been profoundly shaped by the politics of rural, remote, and island locations. Much of Australia and New Zealand's cable infrastructure is routed through and shaped by the histories of Hawai'i and Fiji. A significant amount of U.S.-Asia traffic moves through Guam. On California's west coast, traffic often exits the country via remotely located hubs in San Luis Obispo and Manchester rather than Los Angeles or San Francisco. As a result, the local investments of environmentalists in California, fishermen in Southeast Asia, and deep-sea marine biologists in Canada have come to inflect cable networks in unexpected ways. Although cable traffic is often destined for larger urban areas (very little material drops off in these remote locales), the channels through which it flows nonetheless depend on investments in and reorganizations of aquatic and coastal environments—sites that have rarely been studied in relation to media distribution. As the ocean becomes subject to increasing spatial pressures, with the acceleration of shipping, underwater mining, and alternative energy projects, such environmental negotiations will continue to be integral to network development.

...

Over the past decade, as the Arctic ice has retreated with global warming, the Northwest Passage has opened up new pathways, not only for shipping and for oil extraction, but also for cables carrying digital communications signals. The proposed Arctic Fibre cable would link London and Tokyo via the Arctic Ocean, a shorter path than the Atlantic and Pacific routes, and provide a new source of Internet connectivity for northern communities.[41] There had been a number of attempts to lay a transarctic cable prior to this, including a telegraph stretching between Alaska and Russia (before the transatlantic telegraph was laid in the 1860s) and Project Snowboard, initiated by British Telecom in the 1980s. In the 1990s the Russian Ministry of Posts and Telecommunications even devised a plan to use a nuclear submarine to lay a fiber-optic cable under the Arctic. It was not until the large-scale environmental transformation of climate change, however, that a trans-arctic cable route became feasible.

Between the route's endpoints in London and Tokyo lie a disparate set of environments—frigid Arctic waters in which deep oil reserves are nested, Canadian and Alaskan communities, and locations where scientific research on global warming is being conducted. Through these predominantly rural environments extend a range of human and nonhuman circulations, from atmospheric currents to the movements of container ships. Such circulations could generate friction for Arctic Fibre, a form of resistance that Anna Tsing describes as simultaneously productive and enabling.[43] The reactions of previously uncabled populations, from the indigenous people of the Canadian north to the oil companies that seek to drill off the coast, are still unknown. Icebergs scouring the coastal seafloor might disrupt shallow cables. Fisherman's nets threaten to hook and sever them. Even along well-traveled routes, environments have always generated friction for undersea networks. Throughout the telegraph era, fishermen regularly dragged their nets along the densely cabled transatlantic route, disconnecting links and scattering signal traffic.

Notes

41. Cunningham, "Can the Arctic Provide an Alternative Route?"

43. Tsing, *Friction*.

(Starosielski, 2015, pp. 14–16; some notes omitted)

The reading illustrates how digitally connecting remote regions also entails links between disparate human and non-human entities. These include not only the remote communities through which infrastructure passes, but also atmospheric and oceanic circulations, oil companies, icebergs, fishing nets and other natural environments. It is also clear that while new digital infrastructures may offer the opportunity for remote communities to become connected, the social impacts of such connections are often quite difficult to predict.

4 Raw mineral shortages and digital technologies

So far in this chapter, we have been considering infrastructures and how they impact on *power and inequality* in access to digital services. Most of what you have read so far in this chapter relates to how global connections affect local communities and environments. However, it is also important to consider the materials that make up the digital objects we use. For example, the components of a typical smartphone will include a screen, battery, a central processor or 'system on a chip', digital system storage, camera and a variety of sensors. These will be fabricated in different places, and all will require specific raw materials in their manufacture.

In a while, you will see where some of these raw materials originate. But first, let us consider what these raw materials are. Everything around us is made up of around 90 naturally occurring building blocks, known as chemical elements. These chemical elements are substances that cannot be broken down into any other substance and chemists have organised these elements into a periodic table that groups elements together with similar properties (Figure 9.3).

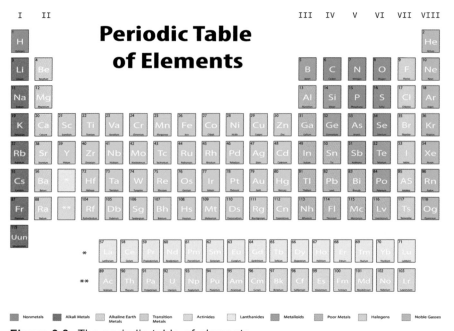

Figure 9.3 The periodic table of elements.

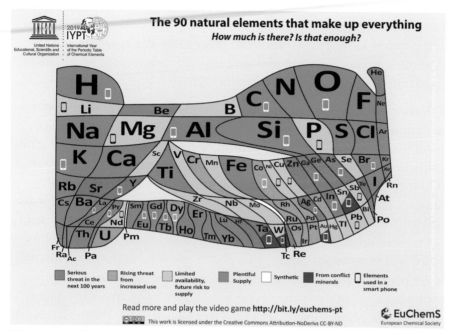

Figure 9.4 The elements that make everything, how much there is, and how fast we are using them.

In 2019 the European Chemical Society produced a completely new version of the periodic table (Figure 9.4). Rather than each element in the table occupying the same space, the table is redrawn so that the area of each element indicates the amount of that element available on the planet, with a colour code to indicate how fast we are using these elements. Also indicated on the table (with a small phone symbol) are the 31 elements needed to make a smartphone. As you can see from the table, many of the elements needed to make digital devices are not plentiful, and many will be under a serious threat of shortages in the coming years.

Efforts can be made to preserve existing stocks of these elements and fall into three broad options: replace, recycle or reduce. While efforts are being made to find alternatives to replace some of these elements, many will have unique properties that make finding alternatives difficult. Recycling and recovery of elements from mobile phones could help alleviate potential shortages of raw materials. Yet this process is not without significant problems. The attempt to recover materials from recycled phones often occurs in low to middle-income countries and these activities can take place under appalling conditions. Phones are typically broken up and then dissolved in acid, with the most valuable elements being recovered. The remainder of the acidic

313

brew is then discarded. These recovery efforts are fraught with social and physical harms: they expose workers to toxic chemicals; and discarding excess toxic effluent exposes the environment and humans to harmful waste (Lim and Schoenung, 2010).

Efforts to reduce the use of these materials would mean lowering the number of smartphones that people buy. This goal presents considerable challenges. At present, it is estimated that around 1.5 billion mobile phones are purchased worldwide every year (Gartner Inc, 2019). To maintain and satisfy this level of demand requires immense quantities of raw materials, many of which are also needed for other uses. Mobile phones are sometimes referred to as 'up-to-date products' because they are typically replaced while still functional (Cox *et al.*, 2013). This is due partly to users' desire for the latest products but also to service contracts that allow users to replace their phones constantly. Surveys estimate that users typically replace their mobile phones every 1.5 to 3 years (Wieser and Tröger, 2018). At the time of writing, the rate of growth in smartphone purchases appears to be slowing very slightly (Gartner Inc, 2019) but to diminish the harmful environmental and human impact of phone use will require a far greater reduction in demand than that currently seen.

5 Conflict minerals and digital technologies

High worldwide demand for mobile phones, combined with restricted supplies, has tended to increase demand for these limited resources with a corresponding increase in price. The rising value of certain raw materials needed in digital devices means that mining of these minerals has become increasingly lucrative. What effect has this had on the regions where these minerals are extracted? It may seem like rising prices would be a good thing for these regions, but there is evidence that mining of these minerals can lead to social harm by exacerbating existing conflicts in some regions where rebel groups, warlords and outside actors can profit from mining. Thus the extraction of raw materials can contribute to violence and exploitation during conflicts. This has led to these raw materials becoming known as 'conflict minerals'. Examples include the so-called 'blood diamonds' mined in the war zones of Sierra Leone and Angola and used to finance an insurgency, or a warlord's activity.

Key chemical elements, such as tungsten and tantalum, needed for the manufacture of smartphones and other digital devices are found in conflict-prone areas in several African countries, such as the Democratic Republic of Congo (DRC). Growing concerns over how the rising demand for key raw materials may be fuelling conflicts persuaded policymakers of the need to devise interventions to cut the links between conflict and resources. Further pressure was brought to bear by campaign groups like the 'Enough Project' and 'Stand with Congo', who worked with celebrities and sports stars to encourage the introduction of policies to limit the funding of conflict. The Enough Project's provocative campaign directly connected the DRC's mineral economy, western consumers and the use of rape and sexual violence by rebel groups.

Many of the growing concerns expressed by policymakers and campaign groups can be traced back to a United Nations report by a panel of experts on the 'Illegal exploitation of natural resources and other forms of wealth of the DRC' (United Nations Security Council, 2001). This report urged an immediate ban on the trade in raw materials from the DRC due to their use in financing armed groups. The combination of this report, and the campaigning activities, led to policy interventions by both the European Union and in the

United States. The US policy was incorporated into Section 1502 of the Dodd–Frank Act (2010) that obliges companies to divulge the sources of raw minerals, from the eastern DRC or neighbouring countries, used in the manufacture of goods.

These campaigns and policy interventions were certainly based on good intentions and could be seen as an attempt by Western governments and campaign groups to address issues of global *power and inequality*. Yet there has also been some criticism of these interventions for the seemingly negative impact and unintended consequences that they have had. As you will see, policy initiatives to reduce social harm can have unintended consequences. For example, some have pointed out that such approaches make no distinction between different types of mineral extraction (Radley and Vogel, 2015). In the DRC there are two main types of mineral extraction – artisanal and industrial mining. Artisanal mining is locally based and largely uses manual extraction techniques and employs large numbers of local workers (around 20 million people in Africa are employed this way). In contrast, industrial mining is largely automated, organised by large international companies, has close associations with national elites and employs few local people.

Figure 9.5 Artisanal miners work at a cobalt mine pit in the Congo.

Artisanal and industrial mining are associated with different forms of violence and conflict. With artisanal mining, it was found that when mineral prices rose that there was a corresponding increase in violent conflicts between groups over resources. On the other hand, when industrial mining was instituted there were fewer conflicts between groups but an increase in civil disturbances and violence against civilians (Radley and Vogel, 2015). This is almost certainly due to the way that these two methods of extraction are socially organised; industrial mining organisations can protect themselves with private security forces and their close association with local elites allows for the involvement of the state police and army – this level of protection is not available to artisanal miners. Also, policy interventions tend to favour industrial mining activities because of their higher revenue-generating potential and their apparent lower levels of conflict. Yet the lower levels of conflict are due to political choices to protect industrial mining concessions – there is no reason why artisanal mining could not be given enhanced security from state actors if the state decided to do so. If artisanal extraction enjoyed higher levels of security, it would also have the added advantage of greater employment prospects for local people. As Radley and Vogel conclude:

> If a more nuanced analysis can contribute to reshaping currently existing rules and policies within broader processes of state and governance reform … a reliable and viable system ensuring more ethical products are produced and consumed and leading to improvements in the daily lives of the Congolese is possible.
>
> (Radley and Vogel, 2015, p. 409)

In the following reading, Ben Radley discusses further some of the unintended consequences of Western campaigns to address the social harms associated with conflict minerals. In the reading, he lays out some of the shortcomings of DRC-focused advocacy organisations. In the reading excerpt he refers to a film, 'We Will Win Peace' (2015), that he helped produce. As you read the piece, as well as looking at how he identifies shortcomings, also see how he critiques the relationship between advocacy organisations (activist groups that attempt to influence public opinion and policy) in the West and those they claim to represent and the solutions he proposes to resolve the tension.

Reading 9.3

Ben Radley, 'The problem with Western activists trying to do good in Africa'

It is important not to conflate the work of all DRC-focused advocacy organisations under the same umbrella. But central to the success of the "conflict minerals" campaign was the emergence of a dominant narrative that placed Western consumers at the heart of the solution.

A key element of the storyline is that armed groups in the eastern DRC are raping women to access and control mineral resources. If Western consumers exerted pressure on electronic giants like Apple and Samsung to stop buying these minerals, they could prevent rape and help end the conflict.

In the US, celebrities and sports stars are engaged by organisations such as the Enough Project and Stand With Congo to help promote the campaign. The message appeals particularly strongly to student groups and middle- and upper-class liberals.

The campaign has led to policy successes in both Washington and Brussels. The US policy – Section 1502 of the Dodd-Frank Act – requires companies to reveal their supply chains when sourcing minerals from the eastern DRC or neighbouring countries.

The foundations of the "conflict minerals" campaign can be traced back to 2001. It was then that a United Nations panel of experts recommended an immediate embargo on the trade in minerals from the eastern DRC due to their systematic exploitation by armed groups as a means to finance their activities. This was followed by numerous NGO reports pursuing a similar line of argument.

Shortcomings

But there are three shortcomings to the "conflict minerals" campaign that came out of this work.

- It misrepresents the causal drivers of rape and conflict in the eastern DRC;

- It assumes the dependence of armed groups on mineral revenue for their survival; and

- It underestimates the importance of artisanal mining to employment, local economies and therefore – ironically – security.

Compounding these shortcomings was a fatal flaw in the US legislation enacted in 2010. When Section 1502 of the Dodd-Frank Act was passed it was not possible for companies sourcing minerals from the eastern DRC to determine whether those minerals were or weren't contributing to conflict.

As a result and due to confusion over the implications of the legislation, international buyers withdrew, and an effective mineral boycott enveloped the region. The socioeconomic impact on Congolese living in this mineral-dependent region was severe.

Today the policy solution pursued in the DRC by a range of foreign companies, NGOs and donors revolves around an expansion of the Congolese state into areas formerly beyond its control. The aim is to establish and oversee mineral certification, traceability and validation systems that can attest to their "conflict-free" status.

Early evidence suggests this process is catalysing the previously lethargic formalisation of artisanal mining and, with it, the establishment of formal land tenure agreements. In doing so, it provides conditions that might be amenable to forms of state-led development that have eluded the region for so long.

But the establishment of property rights and formal titling unleashes new processes of dispossession, economic exclusion and social differentiation built on pre-existing inequalities. Thus, such changes often benefit wealthy and powerful elites, and negatively affect the lowest classes of labour and already marginalised social groups.

Dissonance

Herein lies the main tension in the work of Western advocacy organisations, and the reason they invite critique: there is a heavy dissonance between their stated constituency and their actual constituency, or who they work for and who they work with.

...

Yet the relationship between advocacy organisations headquartered in Western cities and their marketed constituency of marginalised and disadvantaged African groups is far more tenuous.

One of the most striking elements during the making of the film was the difficulty of finding Congolese groups in rural and peri-urban areas who knew about and supported the "conflict minerals" campaign. This suggests a lack of engagement with the people who stand to be most directly affected by campaign outcomes.

Instead, many Western advocacy organisations use short visits to the DRC to work predominantly with government, business and other elites in national and provincial capital cities. The result is that the disruptive and contingent process of state-building and formalisation they engage in and promote often works against the very people they claim to represent.

And so organisations such as the Enough Project claim that progress is being made, and critics counter that harm is being done. There is truth to both perspectives, but they are focused on different aspects of the same process.

How to resolve the tension

Western advocacy organisations could change how they market their interventions and talk about their work. Helping bring the state back into local development processes in peripheral countries such as the DRC is an entirely legitimate and valuable pursuit. Yet they may not want to do this because it will likely be difficult to mobilise people and funding around long-term and socially disruptive goals.

Alternatively, they could reorient their efforts to working with, not just for, the non-elites they use to promote their public image and in whose name they justify their external interventions. What their work would lose in structural impact, it would gain in honesty, legitimacy and local impact. The groups and classes of artisanal miners, peasants and other workers we spoke with would come to know more concretely who the organisations are. They would also provide more appropriate solutions to their own problems and struggles than the pursuit of overseas policy change, which fails to respond to their immediate needs.

(Radley, 2016)

Radley, in this reading, makes the point that well-intentioned attempts by advocacy groups to reduce social harm can have unintended consequences. For example, the activist campaigns and policies used by Western governments had the effect of introducing a mineral boycott of the region with a resulting severe impact on the socio-economic conditions of the Congolese living there. Also, the establishment of mineral certification and traceability encouraged the instituting of formal land-tenure agreements and state-led development in artisanal mining areas. Yet this also tended to favour the wealthy and powerful elites and reinforce pre-existing inequalities.

The relationship between campaigning organisations and those they claim to represent was also seen as problematic, with local people having no involvement, or even knowing about, the campaigns that were supposed to represent them. Instead, advocacy organisations made brief visits, where they worked with business and other elites in urban centres. Their interventions, Radley argues, resulted in policies that often worked against 'the very people they claim to represent'. Radley ends by suggesting that advocacy organisations should work more closely with the non-elites such as artisanal miners, peasants and other workers. This would result in more appropriate solutions that would have greater legitimacy and local impact.

This reading also identifies that one of the key shortcomings of the activist campaigns was the narrative that saw a direct causal relationship between armed rebel groups, sexual violence and access to mineral resources. Radley claims that this misrepresents the causal nature of the relationship, without going further to explain the reasoning behind his claim of misrepresentation.

As the alleged link between sexual violence and mineral extraction was a key and emotive argument made by activist campaigns, it is worth examining this in more detail. Examination of this reveals a nuanced interplay of *power and inequality*. The links between armed conflict and sexual violence are well established (Brownmiller, 1975), and this was certainly the case in the DRC (The *PLoS Medicine* Editors, 2009). Yet the narrative that sees a simple causal link focuses attention on a narrow set of actors (rebel groups) while obscuring the role of others. The geographers Charlotte Mertens and Ann Laudati (2018) argue that the connection between resource extraction and sexual violence is complicated for three reasons. First, artisanal mining represents a space of opportunity as well as a risk for both men and women. The focus on rebel groups fails to consider the (sexual) violence enacted by others, including corporate, state agents, and foreign NGOs, as well as the miners themselves. Second, it obscures other gender vulnerabilities (women's access to employment and women's working conditions) in mining sites and positions women as victims rather than recognizing the active role they play in extractive communities. Third, the focus on sexual violence in mining sites masks other forms of violence such as murder, forced labour, and looting, while at the same time suggesting that mining sites are a major place of sexual violence. This overlooks and obscures the documented and widespread rapes associated with conflict away from mining areas. As Mertens and Laudati conclude:

> The narrative of rape as a weapon of war to access minerals, resonates with western audiences because it establishes a clear victim-perpetrator setup: racialized and gendered rebels and soldiers against a terrorized population. In this sense it gives clarity and simplicity to an otherwise very complex, multi-actored and multi-layered conflict. While rape has indeed been used as part of a military or political strategy and 'conflict minerals' do play a role in the continuation of the armed conflict or at least partially fund some armed groups and state forces … it remains crucial to understand the construction of this narrative, its political work and what it hides.
>
> (Mertens and Laudati, 2018)

6 Conclusion

In this chapter, you have considered the intersection of where *power and inequality* and *people and things* collide. You started by thinking about the material infrastructure that digitally connects people to the internet and how this involves a lot of physical things at many points across the world. You saw how the material construction of the internet infrastructure could augment existing inequalities, especially for those indigenous peoples living in remote regions. You also explored differing notions of what infrastructure is; about how infrastructures are taken for granted until they fail; and how connecting remote regions also entail links between disparate human and non-human entities. You then went on to look at where the raw materials (things) in digital devices come from and how their extraction raises complex issues of *power and inequality*. It was shown here that sometimes attempts to reduce social harm can have unintended consequences.

References

BBC News (2019) 'Scottish areas with "best and worst" broadband', 22 January. Available at: https://www.bbc.co.uk/news/uk-scotland-highlands-islands-46945879 (Accessed: 23 January 2020).

Blum, A. (2013) *Tubes: behind the scenes at the internet*. London: Penguin Group.

Brownmiller, S. (1975) *Against our will: men, women and rape*. New York: Simon and Schuster.

Cox, J., Griffith, S., Giorgi, S. and King, G. (2013) 'Consumer understanding of product lifetimes', *Resources, Conservation and Recycling*, 79, pp. 21–29. doi: 10.1016/j.resconrec.2013.05.003.

Gartner Inc (2019) *Gartner says global smartphone sales stalled in the fourth quarter of 2018* [Press Release]. 21 February. Available at: https://www.gartner.com/en/newsroom/press-releases/2019-02-21-gartner-says-global-smartphone-sales-stalled-in-the-fourth-quart (Accessed: 27 January 2020).

Lim, S.R. and Schoenung, J.M. (2010) 'Toxicity potentials from waste cellular phones, and a waste management policy integrating consumer, corporate, and government responsibilities', *Waste Management*, 30(8–9), pp. 1653–1660. doi: 10.1016/j.wasman.2010.04.005.

McMahon, R. (2014) 'From digital divides to the first mile: indigenous peoples and the network society in Canada', *International Journal of Communication*, 8, pp. 2002–2026.

Mertens, C. and Laudati, A. (2018) *Resources and rape: the DRC's (toxic) discursive complex*. Available at: https://africasacountry.com/2018/11/resources-and-rape-the-drcs-toxic-discursive-complex (Accessed: 1 February 2020).

Radley, B. (2016) 'The problem with Western activists trying to do good in Africa' *The Conversation*, Available at: https://theconversation.com/the-problem-with-western-activists-trying-to-do-good-in-africa-57917 (Accessed: 30 January 2020).

Radley, B. and Vogel, C. (2015) 'Fighting windmills in Eastern Congo? The ambiguous impact of the "conflict minerals" movement', *The Extractive Industries and Society*, 2(3), pp. 406–410. doi: 10.1016/j.exis.2015.05.005.

Star, S.L. (1999) 'The ethnography of infrastructure', *The American Behavioral Scientist*, 43(3), pp. 380–391. doi: 10.1177/00027649921955326.

Starosielski, N. (2015) *The undersea network*. Durham: Duke University Press.

The *PLoS Medicine* Editors (2009) 'Rape in war is common, devastating, and too often ignored', *PLoS Medicine*, 6(1) pp. 0001–0003. doi: 10.1371/journal.pmed.1000021.

United Nations Security Council (2001) *Report of the panel of experts on the illegal exploitation of natural resources and other forms of wealth in the Democratic Republic of Congo*, S/2001/357 (12 April). English. doi: S/2001/357.

Wieser, H. and Tröger, N. (2018) 'Exploring the inner loops of the circular economy: replacement, repair, and reuse of mobile phones in Austria', *Journal of Cleaner Production*, 172, pp. 3042–3055. doi: 10.1016/j.jclepro.2017.11.106.

Chapter 10

Disinformation, 'fake news' and conspiracies

David G. Robertson

Contents

1 Introduction

This chapter explores the relationship between the internet and 'truth'. In an age of 'fake news', who should we trust? Conspiracy theories and **disinformation** existed long before the internet, but to many it seems like they have become more prevalent, and possibly more extreme, in the 21st century. The internet has become a major site – perhaps THE major site – for contemporary contestations over matters of truth. This issue introduces the central questions of the section: has the internet been the cause of a change in the way we view 'truth', or merely made disinformation more visible? What is the connection between the internet, conspiracy theories and disinformation? What larger social processes underlie these changes to our relationship with 'truth'? Such questions are more than academic, as we have seen how they have real-world ramifications, from personal harassment, to affecting elections, and in extreme cases, to violent outcomes.

We start the chapter by thinking about what terms like 'conspiracy theory', 'disinformation' and 'fake news' mean. As you will see, this is not as simple a question as it might at first seem! We will look at several different academic approaches to conspiracy theories, beginning with early political science approaches which pathologise them as evidence of paranoia, something which underpins much popular and academic work even today. We will then look at some more contemporary sociological approaches, which see conspiracy theories as a cultural phenomenon with much to potentially tell us about the modern sociological imagination. Underlying these sociological understandings is the intersection of knowledge and power – who do we trust, and how do they know?

Then we will look at the relationship between conspiracy theories and the internet. We will look briefly at the assassination of John F. Kennedy – a foundational event in the development of modern conspiracy culture – as an example of how these ideas developed and spread pre-internet. We then turn to a more contemporary example, Pizzagate, a web-based conspiracy theory in which pro-Trump activism merged with anti-elitism and paedophilia panic. Pizzagate demonstrates how such ideas can lead to extremism, but it also shows the importance of internet groups in spreading these narratives. It also reflects how popular conspiracy theories are ultimately about power, and typically reflect widespread but disenfranchised political views.

Next, we will consider research that challenges some of the common-sense ideas about conspiracy theories and the internet – as well as underlining their links to broader social concerns and power. Our final case study, the Cambridge Analytica scandal, is not on the fringes but right at the centre of politics and shows that these issues of trust and power are not entirely unfounded. Technology provides the powerful with new, clandestine ways to control the flow of information which reaches us, and potentially to influence our political decisions. The chapter concludes that there is a relationship between the internet, the flow of information and power, but that focusing on conspiracy theories may be missing the greater threat to democracy.

1.1 Teaching aims

The aims of this chapter are for you to:

- explore sociological understandings of conspiracy theories

- consider the relationship between conspiracy theories, disinformation and the internet

- understand how conspiracy theories represent concerns over *power and inequality* in society.

2 Thinking about conspiracy theories and disinformation

Figure 10.1 Social media is often considered a major driver of disinformation and conspiracy theories.

2.1 What are conspiracy theories?

Conspiracy theories are everywhere today it seems; yet conspiracy theories are one of those issues that the closer you look, the less clear they become. We will begin to unpack the concept in this section.

Most approaches to conspiracy theories start with their content, presenting it as irrational or paranoid, and attempt to extrapolate the mental processes that lead to such conclusions. Such portrayals in the media and popular culture derive, in part, from one of the foundational scholarly texts on conspiracy theories, Richard Hofstadter's *The Paranoid Style in American Politics* (1964). Hofstadter thought that the centrist political consensus of the day was threatened by the conspiracy theories that were being promoted by small but organised right-wing groups like the John Birch Society and so portrayed them as unscientific, undemocratic and pathologically paranoid (1964, pp. 36–39). Hofstadter's work set much of the agenda for the research that followed, which has tended to see conspiracy theories in pathological terms – that is, as evidence of irrationality, ignorance or mental illness. The philosopher Fredric Jameson famously described conspiracy theories as 'the poor person's cognitive mapping … a degraded figure of the total logic of late capital' (Jameson, 1988, p. 356), and the historian Daniel Pipes writes that we are dealing 'not with the cultural elite but its rear guard, not with the finest mental creations but its dregs' (Pipes, 1997, p. 49).

The problem is, however, that defining a conspiracy theory by its content is not so simple as it might at first seem. For one, there cannot simply be a theory which posits a conspiracy – conspiracies certainly happen, all the time. Nor is it the case that conspiracy theories are demonstrably groundless, unscientific or bizarre. For one thing, it is not unusual for ideas labelled 'conspiracy theories' to turn out to have been correct: that the US and UK intelligence services are monitoring all telecommunications; that the CIA was funnelling money from the sale of arms to Iran to Nicaraguan Contras; that the CIA dosed unsuspecting people with LSD in the 1960s; that the dossier on 'weapons of mass destruction' was 'sexed up' to justify the invasion of Iraq after 9/11; that world leaders meet in secret Bilderberg meetings every year – to take just a few, clear examples. Moreover, governments will themselves support untrue conspiracies when those conspiracies help their agendas, or powerful groups within them. Neither Joseph McCarthy's crusade against communist 'sleepers' in the US in the 1950s and '60s, or satanic ritual abuse in the 1980s and '90s, were referred to as conspiracy theories at the time, though with hindsight it is clear that they were ungrounded theories about a group working to a secret plan to change society.

Social scientific approaches, on the other hand, focus on the function of conspiracy theories, instead of the content; what is the appeal of conspiracy theories for particular individuals, and what do they get out of it socially? Rather than identify cognitive mechanisms, sociologists are more interested in identifying the social processes conspiracy theories are linked to, and this points to the issues of power which most sociological approaches see as being at the root of the idea of conspiracy theories. For example, Mark Fenster's *Conspiracy Theories: Secrecy and Power in American Culture* (1999) sees conspiracy theories as driven by utopian political aims. The desire to bring to light the hidden hand behind corrupt governments, Fenster argues, is no more than an unusually determined desire to speak truth unto power, and a commitment to democracy and openness. Catherine Olmsted takes this further, arguing that the reason that conspiracy theories became so popular in the US in the late 20th century was that the government had long been accusing Germans, communists and Muslims of conspiring against the US (2009, p. 9).

As Joseph Uscinski puts it, 'Conspiracy theories are for losers' – not in the sense that 'people who believe conspiracy ideas are losers, i.e. lacking power', but rather in the sense of 'only ideas not held by those with power are described as conspiracy theories' (Uscinski, 2017). We should therefore think very carefully when we choose to describe certain ideas as 'conspiracy theories', as this is not a neutral or objective act.

So, there is nothing unusually paranoid or irrational about conspiracy theorising. Rather, this chapter takes the position of the sociologist Stef Aupers – that conspiracy theories are not the symptom of irrational or anti-modern currents in society, but rather 'a radical and generalised manifestation of distrust that is deeply embedded in the cultural logic of modernity' (Aupers, 2012, p. 24).

In this extract, sociologist Stef Aupers argues that the defining feature of contemporary conspiracy theories is a particular response to a **secularised**, disenchanted world in which radical scepticism is combined with the desire to find some ultimate cause or structure underlying world events.

Reading 10.1

Stef Aupers, '"Trust no one": modernization, paranoia and conspiracy culture'

In the *X-Files* agents Mulder and Scully develop theories about possible relations between phenomena, test hypotheses and try to rationally explain seemingly inexplicable and mysterious events. While encountering various supernatural and mysterious agents in a network of conspiracies, they remain true to the scientific method of enquiry. And yet, Mulder's motto 'I want to believe' expressed in the *X-Files* movie 2008 exemplifies a modern tension between belief and non-belief; the secular and the religious; rationality and enchantment, that is at the heart of contemporary conspiracy culture.

It is a truism that belief has become utterly problematic in modern societies (Bruce, 2002; Wilson, 1976). Max Weber famously wrote about a 'disenchantment of the world' – a long-standing process in the West that eroded mysterious accounts of nature, magic and, ultimately, the belief in every metaphysical '*Hinterwelt*' that once provided the western world with solid meaning. This is the tragic dimension of modernity: science describes the world 'as it is' but can, by its very nature, say nothing about what the world's processes really mean and what the meaning of life actually is. The intellectual imperative to pursue the truth contributes to a world devoid of existential meaning – a world in which 'processes ... simply "are" and "happen" but no longer signify anything', as Weber (1978 [1921]: 506) writes. Peter Berger et al. (1973: 82) commented on the existential implications of this development: 'Modern man has suffered from a deepening condition of "homelessness" – a metaphysical loss of "home".' Weber and contemporary advocates of secularization, however, prove to have a serious blind spot for the fact that exactly these problems of meaning invoke the rise of new forms of religion, spirituality and re-enchantment (Aupers and Houtman, 2010). Already in Weber's time, many of his fellow intellectuals took refuge in alternative religions – like Steiner's anthroposophy, Blavatsky's new theosophy or spiritism – and this trend only increased over the last century: in most countries in Western Europe the Christian churches are in decline, but affinity with esotericism, occultism, paganism and New Age spirituality is rapidly growing (e.g. Aupers and Houtman, 2006; Campbell, 2007; Heelas et al., 2005; Houtman and Aupers, 2007).

Notwithstanding its scientific ambitions and (often) atheist pretentions, conspiracy culture, too, is a response to existential insecurity in a disenchanted world. Those engaged in it 'want to believe' and, just like contemporary spiritual seekers, their 'grand narratives' about the nature of reality serve to construct ultimate meaning. But there is a crucial difference: premodern people and contemporary New Age participants locate mysterious forces in the natural world – in human bodies, the earth and the universe as a whole. Nature is considered sacred: it is an overpowering force that invokes religious feelings of 'awe' – a typical combination of fear and fascination (Marett, 1914 [1909]). Conspiracy theorists relocate such mysterious forces from nature to modern society: invisible, yet immensely powerful forces are operative *behind* the cultural screens, *underneath* and *beyond* the empirical surface of modern life. Such a worldview generates meaning: it reverses the Weberian 'disenchantment of the world' since the (cultural) world is *not* 'as it is' – 'processes' do *not* 'simply happen' but *do* 'signify' *something*. The conspiracy theorist suspects there is intention where others find coincidence and contingency; they detect structure where others see chaos; they find meaning where others do not. Conspiracy theories 'require a form of quasi-religious conviction, a sense that the conspiracy in question is an entity with almost supernatural powers' (Melley, 2000: 8). It is considered a calling to unravel such mysteries through rational enquiry, by critically looking into every detail that may lead one to the ultimate truth 'out there' where 'everything is connected'. Based on these considerations we can understand conspiracy theorizing as a hybrid of scepticism and belief – as a 'religion for atheists' or a form of 'rational enchantment'. The scientific discourse in conspiracy culture may even function as an indispensable alibi for atheists who 'want to believe' to immerse themselves freely in mysterious matters without retreating into 'irrational' belief. Like spiritual seekers – often anchoring their esoteric claims in natural sciences to support the authority of their arguments – conspiracy theorists use 'scientism as a language of faith' (Hammer, 2001: 201–321).

References

Aupers S and Houtman D (2006) Beyond the spiritual supermarket: The social and public significance of New Age spirituality. *Journal of Contemporary Religion* 21(2): 201–222.

Aupers S and Houtman D (eds) (2010) *Religions of Modernity: Relocating the Sacred to the Self and the Digital*. Leiden: Brill Publishers.

Berger PL, Berger B and Kellner H (1973) *The Homeless Mind: Modernization and Consciousness*. New York: Random House

Bruce S (2002) *God is Dead: Secularisation in the West*. Oxford: Blackwell

Campbell C (2007) *The Easternization of the West: A Thematic Account of Cultural Change in the Modern Era*. Boulder, CO: Paradigm Publishers.

Hammer O (2001) *Claiming Knowledge: Strategies of Epistemology from Theosophy to the New Age*. Leiden: Brill

Heelas P, Woodhead L, Seel B et al. (2005) *The Spiritual Revolution: Why Religion is Giving Way to Spirituality*. Oxford: Blackwell

Houtman D and Aupers S (2007) The spiritual turn and the decline of tradition: The spread of post-Christian spirituality in fourteen western countries (1981–2000) *Journal for the Scientific Study of Religion* 46(3): 305–320.

Marett R (1914 [1909]) *The Threshold of Religion*, London: Methuen and Co. Ltd.

Melley T (2000) *Empire of Conspiracy: The Culture of Paranoia in Postwar America*. Ithaca, NY and London: Cornell University Press.

Weber M (1978 [1921]) *Economy and Society*, 2 vols. Berkeley: University of California Press

Wilson B (1976) *Contemporary Transformations of Religion*. Oxford: Oxford University Press

(Aupers, 2012, pp. 29–31)

As Aupers notes, scepticism is a key component of the **'disenchantment'** of the modern world; the rise of scientific rationalism has meant that absolute 'grand narratives' and metaphysical 'ultimate truths' are no longer universally accepted. At the same time, however, this has not lessened the human need to find meaning in our lives, and Aupers suggests that conspiracy theories function as a way of constructing meaning in a disenchanted world, as a sort of 'rational enchantment'.

This underlines the point that there are social factors in conspiracy theories, and that they reflect widespread concerns about how we understand the societies we live in. In fact, we can gain a better understanding of conspiracy theories if we understand them as part of the sociological imagination, in which 'neither the life of the individual nor the history of a society can be understood without understanding both' (Mills, 2000, p. 1).

2.2 Fake news and disinformation

All organisations wish to be seen in the best possible light, and in the present media-saturated world, that means controlling the information available about them. This is not new; Edward Bernays, 'the Father of Public Relations', codified these principles in the 1920s; Margaret Thatcher worked with advertising agency Saatchi and Saatchi to improve her presentation; and Tony Blair employed Peter Mandelson as New Labour's 'spin doctor' in the 1990s. Presenting information and events in such a way as to support a particular party's ideological position is one thing; however, when a group is knowingly presenting as truth something they know to be incorrect, we can consider it to be disinformation.

There is nothing new about disinformation and false reporting, of course – groups have always sought to discredit their opponents. In the run up to the 2016 US Presidential election, this issue – under the newly-minted term 'fake news' – became a central talking point. Groups across the political spectrum accused each other of peddling fake news. It was even added to the dictionary in 2017: 'false news stories, often of a sensational nature, created to be widely shared or distributed for the purpose of generating revenue, or promoting or discrediting a public figure, political movement, company, etc ...' ('Fake news', no date). In some contexts, the accusation of fake news

Figure 10.2 Many see President Trump as evidence that we are living in an age of conspiracy theories.

operates a lot like 'conspiracy theory' as a tool to discredit one's opponents, and indeed, we often find them used together.

Concerns about the potential for disinformation to damage society have risen sharply in recent years, as social media has come to dominate how we interact with the news. You can see these concerns in Data & Society's 'Media Manipulation and Disinformation Online' report, published in 2017, which identifies six key issues in 'why the media was vulnerable to manipulation from radicalized groups that emerged from a variety of internet subcultures in 2016':

1   Internet subcultures take advantage of the current media ecosystem to manipulate news frames, set agendas, and propagate ideas.

2   Far-right groups develop techniques of "attention hacking" to increase the visibility of their ideas through the strategic use of social media, memes, and bots—as well as by targeting journalists, bloggers, and influencers to help spread content.

3   The media's dependence on social media, analytics and metrics, sensationalism, novelty over newsworthiness, and clickbait makes them vulnerable to such media manipulation.

4 While trolls, white nationalists, men's rights activists, gamergaters, the "alt-right," and conspiracy theorists may diverge deeply in their beliefs, they share tactics and converge on common issues.

5 The far-right exploits young men's rebellion and dislike of "political correctness" to spread white supremacist thought, Islamophobia, and misogyny through irony and knowledge of internet culture.

6 Media manipulation may contribute to decreased trust of mainstream media, increased misinformation, and further radicalization.

(Marwick and Lewis, 2017, p. 1)

All of these points are certainly true, but do they only apply to these 'internet subcultures'? Using techniques to win the attention of the audience is not exclusive to the **alt-right**, nor something that only developed with the internet, as we have already discussed. Should we similarly challenge charity campaigns, online petitions, church websites, environmentalists and any group that makes use of modern technology for creating community, consciousness raising and activism?

Often, the difference is that these groups cannot draw on scientific consensus to support their claims. Yet most do claim scientific support, as Aupers discussed above, sometimes claiming that this science is silenced for not agreeing with the New World Order agenda. While it is relatively easy for those with some scientific training to debunk these claims, many of us lack the skills to do so. Furthermore, it can sometimes be difficult to untangle actual facts from things accepted as true in particular groups – so while we can say that climate change is a fact, it is difficult to find scientific proof for some ideas which are considered central to liberal democratic thinking, such as Human Rights. Moreover, this also assumes that science is the primary source of 'truth' – but much as we may prefer it to be otherwise, not everyone agrees with this. Religious beliefs are similarly unable to muster scientific support, but religious groups have a significant influence on public policy – and Christian beliefs in particular are seldom described using terms like **'radicalisation'** or irrationality. In fact, most Western states consider the freedom to hold religious beliefs to be central to modern secular democracy, regardless of their lack of scientific support. Which is to say, when thinking sociologically about conspiracy theories, we need to remain aware of how the term can reflect our own **unconscious biases**, and not only the biases of others.

The report states that the media is vulnerable to reporting fake news and suggests this is a problem because it leads to 'decreased trust of mainstream media' (Marwick and Lewis, 2017, p. 1). However, could we not also see that vulnerability as evidence that such mistrust is entirely warranted? If 'trolls, white nationalists [and] men's rights activists' can manipulate the media so easily, then perhaps we might legitimately ask about what other groups and interests are manipulating what they report.

3 Conspiracy theories and the internet

Conspiracy theories and disinformation existed long before the internet, but as we saw in the preceding section, many believe that the internet has made them more prevalent and perhaps more extreme. Has the faster dissemination and development facilitated by the internet affected their potential for challenging the status quo, or is it more likely to lead to extremism and violence? Or are they simply more visible than they were before the internet?

3.1 Conspiracy theories, pre-internet

To answer this, we need to look at how conspiracy theories emerged and spread in the days before the internet, in particular the 1963 assassination of President John F. Kennedy in Dallas, Texas (Figure 10.3). This is the paradigmatic example of conspiracy theories pre-internet, and indeed many writers identify it as the starting point for contemporary conspiracy culture.

Figure 10.3 The 1963 assassination of JFK remains the prototype for modern conspiracy theories.

One such scholar is Peter Knight, who describes it as 'synonymous with conspiracy theory' in his book *Conspiracy Culture: From Kennedy to The X-Files* (Knight, 2000, p. 77). In the chapter 'Plotting the Kennedy assassination', he charts the development of conspiracy theories around the assassination (Knight, 2000, pp. 76–116). Polls showed that belief in a conspiracy was widespread immediately, even before the much-criticised Warren Commission report was published in 1964 and remained consistently high. Yet the theories were never static, but developed over time, with an ever-branching constellation of different theories proliferating. Rather than in internet chatrooms and blogs, early JFK conspiracy theories were published in independent magazines, typically with a left-liberal leaning. Conspiracy narratives often become established when they can be linked to broader concerns about corruption, inequality or uncertainty, and in this case, these were concerns about the threat of communism and war in East Asia and the size and power of the security services. The latter became particularly important after the Watergate scandal in 1972–74 and the Church Committee investigation in 1976. By the time of Oliver Stone's 1991 movie *JFK*, around three-quarters of Americans believed in a conspiracy or cover-up of some kind. The 1990s were, coincidentally or not, also the period in which both conspiracy theories and the internet began to become highly visible parts of our society.

3.2 Pizzagate

Let's turn to a more recent, internet-based conspiracy theory, Pizzagate, in which pro-Trump activism merged with fear of paedophilia among Washington's elites. Though not a typical series of events, it nevertheless demonstrates how such conspiracy theories can gain traction by combining with already existing conspiracies, and how such ideas can lead to extremism and even violence.

In November and December 2016, online accusations of a paedophile ring operating out of a Washington pizza restaurant, Comet Ping Pong, spread rapidly after leaked emails from Hillary Clinton's campaign manager, John Podesta, were suggested to contain coded language by a number of users on web forums. Theories began to develop that this was evidence of a nationwide satanic paedophile ring involving numerous politicians and other power brokers – even the Serbian performance artist Marina Abramović. This conspiracy narrative, known as Pizzagate, was centred on the discussion boards on the website 4chan, which has also been connected to the gamergate controversy (a harassment campaign targeting women in the video game industry in 2014), the Incel community (short for involuntary celibate, an online community of male supremacists connected to several mass shootings), and the election of Donald Trump in 2016 (Nagle, 2017, pp. 11–16). Pizzagate was then picked up by the larger conspiracist outlets including Alex Jones' Infowars and made it to the mainstream media by late November 2016. The peak was 4 December, 2016, when Edgar Welch arrived at Comet Ping Pong armed with an assault rifle. He was arrested after threatening staff and firing several shots in an apparent attempt to find underground holding cells and liberate 'child sex slaves'.

We can easily identify Pizzagate as a critique of political elites, given that it centred on Democratic politicians and was spread predominantly on right-wing media at a time when the Republican Party was out of office. Nevertheless, it is rare for an online conspiracy theory such as this to escalate into violence, especially so quickly. How did Pizzagate catch fire so quickly?

One reason was because it was able to tie the contemporary political critique to existing conspiracy narratives about Satanic paedophiles, so people who already subscribed to those ideas would be quick to pick up on this new development. Principally, Pizzagate was a revival of the 'satanic panic', which was widespread in the US, UK and elsewhere in the 1980s and 1990s, and was intimately tied to a millenarian evangelical Christian worldview. It initially took the form of a generalised concern about the influence of horror movies and heavy metal music, and their links to Satanism. The fact that the Satanism of these accounts was largely imaginary didn't stop this narrative from spreading through police departments, psychologists and policy makers however. Like the promoters of Pizzagate theories, they saw secret codes, symbols and connections between popular culture, Satanism, and social problems, becoming increasingly preoccupied with reading clues into the problems of the world. By the late 1980s, this had enveloped and framed fears over child sexual abuse and developed into the Satanic Ritual Abuse (SRA) scare, in which (secret) groups of Satanists were claimed to be running organised paedophile rings, often on a huge scale and involving powerful individuals. Court cases including the McMartin preschool trial (then the largest in US history), the Franklin Scandal and, in the UK, the Orkney child abuse case all centred on organised abuse (La Fontaine, 1998). None of these cases produced convictions. While the panic produced real victims when justice failed, official support for this narrative had collapsed by the mid-1990s as it became clear that the accusations were groundless. But for some conspiracy theorists and fundamentalist Christians of the cultic milieu, it never went away (Robertson, 2016, pp. 86–88).

Pizzagate was certainly also part of the wave of right-wing populism that swept the US in the run-up to the 2016 presidential election, but whether it was cause or symptom is a harder question to answer. Certainly, once Trump took office in 2017, the fact that Podesta and Hillary Clinton were not arrested or even questioned ensured that Pizzagate fizzled out. Yet despite the novelty of the medium, the message of Pizzagate, like the Satanic Panic that it recapitulated, saw those who make up the institutions of power personified as evil in a language familiar to us for hundreds if not thousands of years, in witch trials and pogroms and crusades (Frankfurter, 2006).

4 Rethinking conspiracy theories and the internet

How then has the internet changed conspiracy theories, and they ways in which they spread? Many people – such as the authors of the Data & Society report cited previously – think that it has made people more vulnerable to disinformation, less likely to trust the media and more susceptible to 'radicalisation'. Many good reasons can be given for this belief. For one, the internet allows for faster and wider dissemination and development of conspiracy theories and fake news, meaning more people come into contact with them. It therefore follows that these ideas would spread more quickly and widely than before. Further, the internet allows formerly isolated individuals to form ideological communities, in ways that could never happen previously. This can help to give extremely unusual views and behaviours a much greater profile and influence than ever before, and as a result even increase their attractiveness to potential new recruits. You can't join a group you've never heard of, after all. Finally, social media creates information bubbles in which our existing ideologies are reinforced, no matter how marginal or mainstream, and dissenting information is filtered out. This has the effect of entrenching people ever deeper into their existing ideologies, because they never have to interact with people with dissenting views. Furthermore, they are likely to only come into contact with material that actively demonises the other, leading to the kind of angry polarisation we see in politics in the Trump era.

But are these assumptions true?

In the following article, social psychologist Joseph Uscinski looks at the evidence for three ideas about the relationship between conspiracy theories and the internet which are generally taken as fact: that conspiracy theories have increased since the birth of the internet, that the internet is dominated by unreliable information, and that the internet brings people into contact with unexpected ideological material. What are the implications of Uscinski's findings for the way we usually think about conspiracy theories online?

Reading 10.2

Joe Uscinski, 'Is the internet driving a new age of conspiracy theory?'

We're often told we're living in a post-truth world where conspiracy theories have replaced facts, expertise, and rationality. This may or may not be true, but there is no strong evidence showing that people today reject facts in favour of conspiracy theories more than they have in past historical eras.

The assertion that we are living in the age of conspiracy theory is often taken as an article of faith. To support the idea that conspiracy theories have hit an apex, the ability of the internet to effortlessly spread misinformation far and wide is often trotted out as exhibit A.

Since the unlikely election of Donald Trump to the presidency, many blamed the spread of online conspiracy theories and 'fake news' for Hillary Clinton's unexpected loss. Their basic argument is that because voters were exposed to incorrect information, they made choices they otherwise would not have made in the voting booth. If those voters had the right information, they would have made better choices (and presumably not for Trump).

Some evidence suggests voters were exposed to a great deal of conspiracy theories and fake news in 2016, but it is not clear what effect – if any – exposure to these falsehoods had on their political decision making. Nonetheless, social media companies have been pressured by Congress to police the information on their sites, often in ways that severely limit the free transference of ideas. The public has been all too willing to cede this power to legislators. As could have been predicted whenever government threatens information purveyors, much of the speech that has been banned is critical of government. But if the internet has not had the negative effects on people that its critics claim, then government intervention is unwarranted (I would say that it probably wouldn't be warranted anyway, but that is another matter).

It is unquestionably true that the internet has given us the ability to communicate unfiltered ideas instantaneously to the far reaches of the planet. But what do we really know about the role of the internet in changing people's beliefs? Is the internet making conspiracy theories more popular than before? Has the internet turned people into conspiracy-mongers? The simple answer to these questions is *probably not*, and here are three reasons why.

1) There is no evidence that beliefs of a conspiratorial kind —i.e., conspiracy beliefs—have increased since the dawn of the internet age.

As I argue in my book *American Conspiracy Theories*—co-written with Joseph M. Parent—it is not clear that beliefs in conspiracy theories are increasing. While one conspiracy theory is not representative of the whole, consider for example belief in Kennedy assassination theories. Immediately following the assassination of President Kennedy, polls showed that belief in a conspiracy to kill the president was a majority belief; in the decades that followed as many as 80 percent of Americans believed there was a conspiracy rather than a lone gunman. None of this required the internet.

If the internet increases conspiratorial thinking, we would have expected the internet age to bring with it an uptick in people believing JFK assassination conspiracy theories or at least to have maintained belief around 80 percent. But since the roll-out of the internet in the 1990s, belief in JFK assassination conspiracy theories has declined about 20 points. Yes, the assassination has become more distant in our collective past, but there continues to be no shortage of talk about Kennedy conspiracy theories on the internet or in more traditional media to keep it alive. Belief is down regardless.

Kennedy assassination theories are just one small slice of the conspiracy theory pie, but conspiracy beliefs writ large don't show much evidence of having gone up as the internet made its way into everyone's home. The level of belief in conspiracy theories is an empirical issue, and such levels could conceivably rise and fall over time. Perhaps in a few years their levels will markedly rise or precipitously fall, but until we have evidence of such dynamics we should not assume conspiracy beliefs are higher or lower now than at any other time.

2) The internet has authoritative information too.

One might get the impression from much journalism that the internet is populated exclusively by conspiracy theories, 'fake news', and dubious information. It isn't. The internet allows for unprecedented access to the best and most authoritative information humans have from doctors, lawyers, governments, and scientists. Prior to the advent of the internet, it was much more tempting to rely on village wisdom because experts were hard to come by. That's just not the case anymore, and we need to thank the internet for that.

However, it's true that the internet comes with a lot of content dedicated to conspiracy theories and other forms of dubious information. Dubious information is always a problem and we should not gloss over its impact. But just because a conspiracy theory is available on the internet does mean anyone is looking at it. For example, the *New York Times* website is currently ranked about 33rd in the U.S. and 118th globally for web traffic; Alex Jones' *InfoWars* site, perhaps the most popular conspiracy theory dedicated website is ranked a distant 942 in the U.S. and 3,454th worldwide.

Social media allows people to develop and share their own conspiracy theories too, but the effect of this should not be overrated either. One can go onto social media any time of day and find new conspiracy theories brewing, but most of those theories will fail to make it to dawn of the next day. As much as Twitter and Facebook allow new conspiracy theories to be openly shared; they are great at squashing conspiracy theories as well. Consider for example the theory that Barack Obama killed Justice Antonin Scalia in 2016. That theory attracted attention for a short while, but quickly became sterile. Part of the issue is that sharing conspiracy theories on social media can generate new believers, but it can also lead to immediate ridicule and rebuttal. Some scholars suspect that the internet may be better at killing conspiracy theories than it is at propagating them.

3) Ideologies still matter.

The internet allows people to invent their own information environments; they pick their friends, who they follow, what websites they access. People's ideologies tend to drive these choices so that people immerse themselves into online environments that favor what they already believe. Even when they do come into contact with unwanted conspiracy theories, it is not clear that these theories have the sweeping effects that critics claim because people's ideologies are good at rejecting discordant ideas anyway.

This is not to say that dubious ideas are harmless or have no effects. People who absorb inaccurate information will sometimes believe it, and worse, act on it. Once dubious ideas are lodged in a person's head, they can be difficult to dislodge. But these effects are much more nuanced than they are often made out to be.

The internet has been widely used in the U.S. for more than 20 years. If the impact was what some accounts say it is, we would have fallen off of the conspiracy theory cliff years ago (we haven't). No doubt the internet has changed society in many ways, but it is unwarranted to blame the internet for every perceived social ill. To put this in perspective, the invention of paper, the printing press, telephone, radio, and television all led contemporary critics to claim that each of these was to blame for a breakdown of public opinion and/or morals. The truth is that more and better communication has been accompanied by social improvements along numerous dimensions. We should all fight dubious ideas when we see them, but at the same time we should not blame old problems on new technologies.

(Uscinski, 2019)

It seems that much of our thinking about conspiracy theories and the internet is wrong, or at least, over-simplified. Given our discussion of the JFK assassination as the archetypal conspiracy theory, it is particularly interesting to note that belief in an assassination conspiracy actually dropped following the ascendency of the internet. The internet makes access to authoritative information easier too, and while it might make it easier to share conspiracy theories, it also makes it easier to challenge them.

5 The Cambridge Analytica scandal

Yet there may be other ways in which the internet threatens democracy other than the promulgation of conspiracy theories. At the same time as Pizzagate was emerging from 4chan, investigative reporters were uncovering details of a real conspiracy involving one of the biggest tech companies in the world, with ramifications cutting to the heart of contemporary political debates. The Cambridge Analytica scandal combines several issues of trust in relation to the internet, including public trust in social media platforms, the relationship between government and the internet, and the general public's understanding of the sources of disinformation. Less obviously, it shows why some of the larger issues underlying the social imagination around issues of trust and transparency may not, in fact, be misguided.

Figure 10.4 Facebook were at the centre of initial reports of the Cambridge Analytica scandal.

In December 2015, *The Guardian* published a report by Harry Davies which said that the British political consultants, Cambridge Analytica, who were working for the Republican presidential candidate Ted Cruz, had gained access to personal data on millions of people's Facebook profiles without their consent (Davies, 2015). Investigative journalist Carole Cadwalladr began publishing on Cambridge Analytica's role in the Brexit campaign in February 2017, but these initial reports were received with scepticism. A little over a year later, however, Cadwalladr managed to persuade a former employee, Christopher Wylie, to come forward as a whistle-blower. On 17 March 2018, *The Guardian*, The New York Times and Channel 4 News published the story simultaneously, to mitigate the threat of legal action from Cambridge Analytica and Facebook.

Cambridge Analytica distributed a Facebook app called This is Your Digital Life, which included a survey presented as being for academic use. The user's consent, however, allowed the app to harvest not only the user's data, but that of all of those in their network of friends. In this way, Cambridge Analytica was able to profile at least 50 million Facebook users (Graham-Harrison and Cadwalladr, 2018). The data included the user's age and location and allowed a political campaign to target their advertisements with unprecedented specificity (Rosenberg, Confessore and Cadwalladr, 2018). As well as Ted Cruz and the Brexit campaign, Cambridge Analytica also worked for Donald Trump's presidential campaign, which at its peak was spending a million dollars a day on Facebook ads (Rosenberg, Confessore and Cadwalladr, 2018). The 2019 Netflix documentary *The Great Hack* revealed that Cambridge Analytica had been co-founded by Steve Bannon, former executive chairman of the far-right outlet Breitbart News, and White House Chief Strategist for the first seven months of Donald Trump's presidency. The implication of this is that Cambridge Analytica was not merely a neutral 'hired gun', but part of a strategy aimed specifically at supporting the political right. Congress launched an investigation into the scandal, during which Facebook CEO Mark Zuckerberg was called to testify; he took personal responsibility and apologised for the breaches of personal data (Figure 10.5). Facebook was eventually fined approximately $5 billion dollars by the Federal Trade Commission (Wong, 2019).

We have a responsibility to protect your information. If we can't, we don't deserve it.

You may have heard about a quiz app built by a university researcher that leaked Facebook data of millions of people in 2014. This was a breach of trust, and I'm sorry we didn't do more at the time. We're now taking steps to make sure this doesn't happen again.

We've already stopped apps like this from getting so much information. Now we're limiting the data apps get when you sign in using Facebook.

We're also investigating every single app that had access to large amounts of data before we fixed this. We expect there are others. And when we find them, we will ban them and tell everyone affected.

Finally, we'll remind you which apps you've given access to your information – so you can shut off the ones you don't want anymore.

Thank you for believing in this community. I promise to do better for you.

Mark Zuckerberg

Figure 10.5 Facebook CEO Mark Zuckerberg's apology to the public over the data breaches.

The degree to which the techniques spearheaded by Cambridge Analytica affected the outcomes of these elections is not yet clear; in closely fought elections, such as the Trump–Clinton race or the Brexit referendum, even a relatively small swing can have larger knock-on effects if it affects marginal seats. What it has shown beyond a doubt, however, is that the internet is central to how politicians run campaigns today. Privately owned platforms like Facebook provide new techniques of surreptitious data-gathering and information targeting which are revolutionising how the public can be understood – and manipulated. At the same time, it shows that both these companies and our governments are failing to develop adequate policies and moderation techniques to deal with disinformation.

6 Conclusion

Many commentators continue to argue that the popularity of conspiracy theories means that democracy itself may be at stake (Castellano, 2019; Ebner, 2019). Sunstein and Vermule's influential 2008 report argued that conspiracy theories created such 'serious risks, including risks of violence' that they proposed a government program of 'cognitive infiltration' of groups involved with conspiracy theorizing (2008, p. 1). After writing that the government should covertly infiltrate and discredit groups it deemed as peddling conspiracy theories, Sunstein became head of the White House Office of Information and Regulatory Affairs under Barack Obama.

This chapter has shown that the idea that dangerous conspiracy theories spread as a result of the unregulated internet is an over-simplification. Rather, the larger threat to democracy comes from powerful and wealthy individuals and organisations, those with the wealth and power to control what we read, whether through controlling media outlets, hijacking our Facebook feeds, or marginalising opinions we disagree with as conspiracy theories or fake news. While silencing dissenters may seem attractive when we agree with these ideas, we should remember what can happen when the state uses those mechanisms to enforce hatred. We need to carefully consider if our society remains a democracy if we deny people the right to oppose democracy.

Either way, conspiracy theories need not be true for us to see them as a significant part of the sociological imagination, a manifestation of the distrust embedded in 'the cultural logic of modernity' (Aupers, 2012, p. 24). While politicians and media outlets decry conspiracy theories and disinformation, these are a symptom, rather than a cause, of the underlying distrust in institutions and authorities. The Cambridge Analytica scandal is just one example of how these institutions and authorities have been instrumental in creating this distrust, through a lack of transparency and evasion of accountability. Technology certainly has influenced society and the integrity of democracy, but if we focus our attention on marginal conspiracy theories, rather than speaking truth unto power, we may miss the greater threat.

References

Aupers, S. (2012) '"Trust no one": modernization, paranoia and conspiracy culture', *European Journal of Communication*, 27(1), pp. 22–34. doi.org/10.1177/0267323111433566 .

Castellano, O. (2019) *Conspiracy theories and algorithms are hurting democracy*. Available at: https://medium.com/@orge/conspiracy-theories-and-algorithms-are-hurting-democracy-c15ef6d52f71 (Accessed: 25 November 2020).

Davies, Harry (2015) 'Ted Cruz campaign using firm that harvested data on millions of unwitting Facebook users', *The Guardian*, 16 February. Available at: https://www.theguardian.com/us-news/2015/dec/11/senator-ted-cruz-president-campaign-facebook-user-data (Accessed: 25 November 2020).

Ebner, J. (2019) 'Stop the online conspiracy theorists before they break democracy', *The Guardian*, 18 February. Available at: https://www.theguardian.com/commentisfree/2019/feb/18/online-conspiracy-theorists-democracy (Accessed: 25 November 2020).

'Fake news' (no date) Available at: https://www.dictionary.com/browse/fake-news (Accessed: 10 October 2019).

Fenster, M. (1999) *Conspiracy theories: secrecy and power in American culture*. Minneapolis, MN: University of Minnesota Press.

Frankfurter, D. (2006) *Evil incarnate: rumors of demonic conspiracy and ritual abuse in history*. Princeton, NJ: Princeton University Press.

Graham-Harrison, E. and Cadwalladr, C. (2018) 'Revealed: 50 million Facebook profiles harvested for Cambridge Analytica in major data breach', *The Guardian*, 18 March. Available at: https://www.theguardian.com/news/2018/mar/17/cambridge-analytica-facebook-influence-us-election (Accessed: 25 November 2020).

Hofstadter, R. (1964) 'The paranoid style in American politics', *Harper's Magazine*, November, pp. 77–86.

Jameson, F. (1988) 'Cognitive Mapping', in Nelson, C. and Grossberg, L. (eds) *Marxism and the Interpretation of Culture*. Urbana, IL: University of Illinois Press, pp. 347–360.

Knight, P. (2000) *Conspiracy culture: from Kennedy to the X-Files*. London: Routledge.

La Fontaine, J.S. (1998) *Speak of the devil: tales of Satanic abuse in contemporary England*. Cambridge: Cambridge University Press.

Marwick, A. and Lewis, R. (2017) *Media manipulation and disinformation online*. Data & Society. Available at: https://datasociety.net/pubs/oh/DataAndSociety_ExecSummary-MediaManipulationAndDisinformationOnline.pdf (Accessed: 25 November 2020).

Mills, C.W. (2000) *The sociological imagination.* New York, NY: Oxford University Press.

Nagle, A. (2017) *Kill all normies: the online culture wars from Tumblr and 4chan to the alt-right and Trump.* Lanham: John Hunt Publishing.

Olmsted, K.S. (2009) *Real enemies: conspiracy theories and American democracy, World War I to 9/11.* New York: Oxford University Press.

Pipes, D. (1997) *Conspiracy: How the Paranoid Style Flourishes and Where it Comes From.* New York, NY: Free Press.

Robertson, D.G. (2016) *UFOs, conspiracy theories and the New Age: millennial conspiracism.* London: Bloomsbury.

Rosenberg, M., Confessore, N. and Cadwalladr, C. (2018) 'How Trump consultants exploited the Facebook data of millions', *The New York Times,* March 17. Available at: https://www.nytimes.com/2018/03/17/us/politics/cambridge-analytica-trump-campaign.html (Accessed: 25 November 2020).

Sunstein, C.R. and Vermeule, A. (2008) *Conspiracy theories. Harvard public law working paper no. 08–03; U of Chicago, Public Law Working Paper No. 199; U of Chicago Law & Economics, Olin Working Paper No. 387.* Available at: SSRN: http://ssrn.com/abstract=1084585 (Accessed: 25 November 2020).

Uscinski, J. (2017) *Conspiracy theories are for losers.* Available at: https://www.pitzer.edu/mcsi/2017/11/14/joseph-uscinksi-conspiracy-theories-losers/ (Accessed: 25 November 2020).

Uscinski, J. (2019) *Is the internet driving a new age of conspiracy theory?.* Available at: https://arcdigital.media/is-the-internet-driving-a-new-age-of-conspiracy-theory-5c956ddc16cd (Accessed: 25 November 2020).

Wong, J.C. (2019) 'Facebook to be fined $5bn for Cambridge Analytica privacy violations', *The Guardian,* 12 July. Available at: https://www.theguardian.com/technology/2019/jul/12/facebook-fine-ftc-privacy-violations (Accessed: 25 November 2020).

Chapter 11

Cybersecurity, digital failure and social harm

Simon Carter and Jessamy Perriam

Contents

1 Introduction

Cybersecurity is an increasing concern as more of our everyday life is conducted in digital settings and more of our household objects become connected to the internet. However, the narratives around cybersecurity still feature clichéd images of a hacker sitting in a dark room trying to break into secure systems. But most people's everyday experience of cybersecurity is more likely to resemble the last time they were on the phone to their bank because a credit card they tried to use had been locked following 'unusual activity'. Or perhaps you can think of one of the many incidents when people could not access their online accounts, sometimes for days on end, because a bank was experiencing 'technical difficulties'. Or maybe you can even recall news stories about data breaches from a secure system leaking the addresses and personal details of users.

It is likely that your definition of cybersecurity is both simpler and more complex than the reality. This chapter starts by providing some basic definitions of cybersecurity and then describing the *people and things* involved in cybersecurity, both from the perspective of preventing incidents and those taking part in cybercrime. You will probably notice that the network of *people and things* is incredibly complex. As the chapter progresses, you will begin to see that *individuals and society* also have a role to play in ensuring cybersecurity.

1.1 Teaching aims

The aims of this chapter are for you to:

- identify the basic terms around cybersecurity and cyber incidents

- describe why terms such as 'cyberwar', and 'cyberterrorism' are problematic

- understand and apply normal accident theory (NAT) to digital societies

- consider social harm in relation to cybersecurity incidents.

2 What is cybersecurity?

As cybersecurity expert Harry Metcalfe explains:

> If you define cyber as the security of things that are connected to the Internet then actually the underlying concepts there have been around for a very long time and before they were called cyber they were just called Internet security and in fact there are quite a lot of people who think they should still be called that because it brings a kind of clarity that sometimes cyber as a term loses. But cyber is quite important as an idea … because it's been a piece of terminology that people have really rallied around and that has allowed people who think that this is important and have been making a case for it over the years to get more traction than they have had in the past when it's been called things like information assurance which are a bit kind of obscure …
>
> Some of those things are very technical and are about the protocols and the way that things are implemented. Others are more process orientated and they're about how organisations behave and what policies they have. Some of it is about capability and the skills that organisations have in their teams and the way that they think about what they do and what supplies to use and how to govern and assure what they do.
>
> So really it's a very broad term when you're thinking about the things that you need to do in order to make things secure as part of a cybersecurity approach. But at a top-level I think it's about the security of things that are connected to the Internet which I think we could sort of take one step further and we could say that that is about making sure that the behaviour of things that are connected to the Internet is effectively governed by people who own those things and not by other people.
>
> (Metcalfe, 2018)

Here, Metcalfe is making the point that cybersecurity can be rather technical as it involves protocols and specialised procedures. Yet it is also something far simpler than this; it is about how to make sure that things connected to the internet remain safe and carry on functioning the way they were intended to. However, cybersecurity does not just refer to preventing the intentional activities of people who wish to harm or interfere with things that are connected to the internet. It can also refer to problems (also known as vulnerabilities) that may arise from unintended interactions and failures.

Failures of this type may still involve people, but their intentions may not have been to harm. For instance, on Christmas Eve 2012, the Netflix services to Canada, the United States and Latin America were severely disrupted for several hours. The disruption began because Netflix relies on Amazon Web Services (AWS), which is a subsidiary of Amazon that provides cloud computing facilities to individuals, companies and governments. Even though Netflix and Amazon are competitors, AWS provides storage capacity for Netflix's streaming services. The disruption to service began when a software engineer inadvertently deleted a small piece of code from an Elastic Load Balancing service (ELB). ELBs are purpose-built services for allocating workloads across multiple computing resources: they distribute and match demand between users – in this case, people wanting to watch streaming videos and providers of online services, such as Netflix. After this accidental deletion, the disruption began to spread with an impact on people watching on a variety of devices. Initially, the operators were unable to determine the cause of the problem, and the interruption in service continued for several hours.

The Christmas Eve Netflix disruption caused a minor inconvenience to people living in a few locations. Yet the example shows how there are multiple dependencies with things connected to the internet. Accidental deletion of a piece of computer code by one person, in one commercial organisation, then affected another commercial organisation, which in turn had a negative impact on many customers who wanted to spend their holiday watching movies. However, with the current multiple dependencies on the internet, such failures have the potential to be catastrophic in both the short and long term. For example, suppose a failure caused widespread disruption to banking or health services rather than affecting those just wanting to be entertained. You will read more about the societal impacts of failure on complex digital systems later in this chapter.

3 'Normal accidents' and technological failure

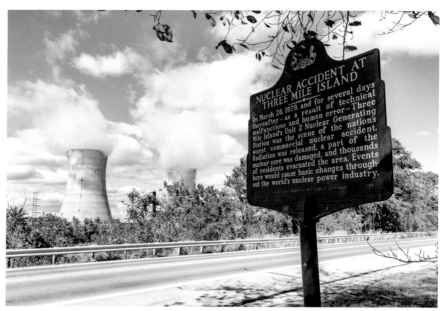

Figure 11.1 Three Mile Island.

One sociologist who has examined technological failures as a consequence of complex interacting systems is the sociologist of organisation, Charles Perrow, who in 1984 first published the influential book *Normal Accidents* (Perrow, 1999). Perrow developed his theories on technological accidents after being asked to provide a background paper for the President's commission on the accident at Three Mile Island. In 1979, the nuclear power station at the Three Mile Island facility near Harrisburg, Pennsylvania underwent a catastrophic accident that resulted in a partial meltdown of the reactor core. The accident started with the failure of a seal that allowed a cup-full of water to enter an instrumentation system. This very small leak of water triggered an escalating series of coupled events that led to a major loss of coolant to the reactor.

The important point is that there was no single cause of this accident, rather numerous trivial events combined to confound the plant's safety systems. The plant designers did not predict these events, and for most of the incident, the operators were baffled by what was happening. Perrow concluded that the failure was not due to the abnormal effects of poorly designed or ill-managed technologies but rather the system's interactive complexity. Complex technological systems, such as Three Mile Island, were disposed to catastrophic failure or what he termed 'normal accidents'.

Perrow's theory was that catastrophic failures are unavoidable in those systems that are 'tightly coupled' and 'interactively complex'. These two concepts were novel and are important in understanding normal accident theory (NAT). Tight coupling means that a system can respond quickly to external inputs; what happens in one part of the system directly and rapidly affects what happens in another part of the system. For example, in most homes, the central heating thermostat is tightly coupled to the boiler. If you turn the thermostat up, the boiler responds immediately and soon after the radiators heat up. Yet, tight coupling is itself not a cause of accidents. Many industrial processes are tightly coupled, such as assembly or productions lines. Here, tight coupling leads to a more efficient system that is cost-effective, responsive and fast. Loosely coupled systems, in contrast, tend to react slowly to inputs. What happens in one part of the system will still affect other parts of the system, but at a much slower rate. For example, universities are loosely coupled systems, where inputs from one part of the system tend to spread very slowly through the rest of the system. If something goes wrong in a loosely coupled system, as there is a slow reaction to inputs, there is time to correct things before problems spread to the rest of the system.

The potential for a 'normal accident' arises when tight coupling is combined with interactive complexity. This means that a technological system is both complex and has many subsystems that interact with each other. Thus interactive complexity refers to those systems where the components of a subsystem perform multiple functions or have 'common modes', where there is a dependence between subsystems. For example, suppose a building had all the pumps for its fire sprinklers in a single room that also contained the fire alarm control box. This room is a 'common mode' for the sprinkler pumps and the fire alarm, and if the room becomes too hot for the equipment to operate (e.g. due to a fire), then this one event could cause multiple failures with dire consequences. Interactively complex systems may have many such common modes, and the components of such a system may interact with one another in unpredictable ways when a failure occurs.

In contrast to the interactively complex are linear systems. These are systems where a series of defined operations follow each other in sequence. For example, the production or assembly line, mentioned previously, needs to be tightly coupled to be efficient. But the manufacturing process on an assembly line has a sequence of events laid out in a linear sequence, one after the other. If something goes wrong (e.g. a component falls into the production process) then the line is stopped, the fault is fixed, and the line restarted.

Figure 11.2 An automobile production line, tightly coupled but linear.

So for Perrow, there are two dimensions to normal accidents – loose versus tight coupling and linear versus complex interactions. Accidents become all but inevitable, or normal, in systems that are 'tightly coupled' and 'interactively complex'. In these systems, small faults can propagate quickly through the system and, due to the interactive complexity, unexpected interactions can occur, which often leads to a significant degree of incomprehensibility for the operators.

If you look at Figure 11.3, there is a graphical representation of the relationship between tight coupling and complex interactions. This image shows various industries and activities. On the vertical scale is the degree of coupling, going from loose at the bottom towards tight at the top. On the horizontal scale is the nature of interactions going from linear, on the left, to complex on the right. So, for example, in cell 4 are universities which are complex but loosely coupled, whereas nuclear plants, in cell 2, are both complex and tightly coupled. Those industries and activities in cell 2 are, according to Perrow, prone to 'normal accidents'.

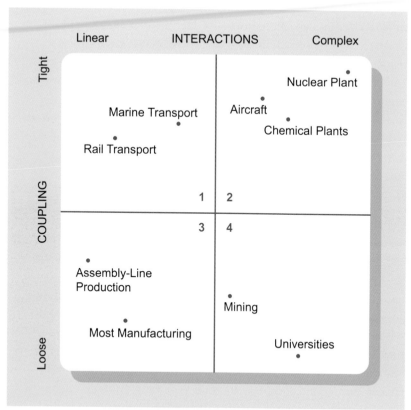

Figure 11.3 Chart showing Tight coupling/Interactive complexity (Adapted from Perrow, 1999, p. 98).

In the following reading, Perrow gives an example of the difference between a linear, tightly coupled system experiencing failure and one where an interactively complex system experiences a common-mode failure.

Reading 11.1

Charles Perrow, *Normal Accidents: Living with High-Risk Technologies*

Almost any organization of any size, whether public or private, will have many parts that interact once we look closely at them. The existence of many parts is no great trouble for either system designers or system operators if their interactions are expected and obvious. If a part or a unit fails in an assembly line, it is quite clear what will happen to the parts and units "downstream" of the failure, and we know that the products "upstream" will start piling up fast. We can shut down the line and fix it, or bypass that work station and assemble the missing parts later on, or temporarily shunt the product into a storage bin. These are "linear" interactions: production is carried out through a series or sequence of steps laid out in a line. It doesn't matter much whether there are 1,000 or 1,000,000 parts in the line. It is easy to spot the failure and we know what its effect will be on the adjacent stations. There will be product accumulating upstream and incomplete product going out downstream of the failure point. Most of our planned life is organized that way.

But what if parts, or units, or subsystems (that is, components) serve multiple functions? For example, a heater might both heat the gas in tank A and also be used as a heat exchanger to absorb excess heat from a chemical reactor. If the heater fails, tank A will be too cool for the recombination of gas molecules expected, and at the same time, the chemical reactor will overheat as the excess heat fails to be absorbed. This is a good design for a heater, because it saves energy. But the interactions are no longer linear. The heater has what engineers call a "common-mode" function—it services two other components, and if it fails, both of those "modes" (heating the tank, cooling the reactor) fail. This begins to get more complex.

...

Common-mode failures are just one indication of interactiveness in systems. Proximity and indirect information sources are two others. For a graphic illustration of complexity in the form of unanticipated interactions from these sources, let us go to a different system, marine transport. A tanker, the *Dauntless Colocotronis*, traveling up the Mississippi River near New Orleans, grazed the top of a submerged wreck. The wreck had been improperly located on some of the charts. Furthermore, it was closer to the surface than the charts indicated because its depth had been determined when the channel was deep, and the listing for mariners had not been corrected for those seasons when the river would be lower. The wreck, only a foot or so too high for the tanker, sliced a wound in the bottom of the tanker, and the oil began to seep out. Unfortunately, the gash occurred just at the point where the tank adjoined the pump room. Some of the oil seeped into the pump room. At first it was probably slow-moving, but the heat in the room made it less viscous, allowing it to flow more rapidly, drawing more oil into the pump room. When enough accumulated it reached a packing "gland" around a shaft near the floor that penetrated into the engine room next to it. The oil now leaked into the engine room. In the hot engine room, evaporation was rapid, creating an explosive gas. There is always a spark in an engine room, from motors and even engine parts striking one another. (In fact, nylon rope can create sparks sufficient to cause explosions in tanker holds.) When enough gas was produced through evaporation, it ignited, causing an explosion and fire.

In this example, an unanticipated connection between two independent, unrelated subsystems that happened to be in close proximity caused an interaction that was certainly not a planned, expected, linear one. The operators of the system had no way of knowing that the very slight jar to the ship made a gash that would supply flammable or explosive substances to the pump and engine rooms; nor of knowing, until several minutes had passed, that there was a fire in the engine room; or of the extensive amount of oil involved. They tried to put it out with water hoses, perhaps not realizing it was an oil fire, but the water merely spread the oil and broke it up into finer, more flammable particles.

(Perrow, 1999, pp. 72–74)

Here Perrow explains the different problems that may occur after a failure in a linear as opposed to a complex system. A failure in a linear system is immediately obvious and understandable. The operators of such a system will be immediately able to see where the problem is and take action to correct it. Alternatively, a single failure in the more interactively complex system can cause multiple failures, and because components or subsystems often perform multiple functions, it will not always be immediately obvious where the failure originated. The operators of such a system may initially be baffled as the failure worsens, and because of tight coupling, the spread of the failure may be very rapid.

4 Normal accidents, cybersecurity and data accidents

Accidents and disasters have always occurred in societies. However, the linked and complex nature of many modern technologies have created the need for awareness and vigilance of where, and how, things may go wrong. While Perrow's normal accident theory (NAT) explains the potential for catastrophic failures in modern technologies, it was largely formulated before the internet age. Now others have begun to analyse how NAT may be applied in the context of the increasing and widespread use of the internet to connect *people and things*. In the following reading, Daniel Nunan and Marialaura Di Domenico apply NAT to the growth of **big data**, and they define this as a term 'to encapsulate both the technical and commercial aspects of this growing data collection activity' (Nunan and Di Domenico, 2017, p. 481). In this reading, the authors discuss the example of the Christmas Eve Netflix outage in 2012, previously mentioned, and draw attention to three aspects of this event that are illuminated by NAT.

Reading 11.2

Daniel Nunan and Marialaura Di Domenico, 'Big Data: a normal accident waiting to happen?'

The first of these components is that big data has the characteristics of a tightly coupled system. This may appear to be a counterintuitive argument considering that the internet itself is an archetype of a loosely coupled system, designed in a cold war era to survive the destruction of any one of its parts. However, behind big data lies tightly connected infrastructure and firms that bind together the organisations reliant on this technology. This is characterised by a shift away from organisations exerting full control over their technology 'stack' and towards cloud computing, where storage and processing power is treated as a utility. Although organisations may develop the software that runs, and collects data, to maximise efficiency, they are increasingly reliant on the use of large data centres run by firms such as Amazon, Microsoft or Google. For all but the very largest firms, the efficiency and perceived resilience offered by these multi-billion dollar data centres make it a necessity to use third party storage for technology. Yet, when there is a failure in data centres, the consequences are far more widespread, unexpected and unpredictable than when firms had more control over their own infrastructures. For example, an accidental deletion of a small amount of data by a developer in the software that balances traffic between different servers using Amazon Web Services on Christmas Eve 2012 resulted in a chain of events that rendered online services, including Netflix, unavailable on Christmas morning (Cockcroft 2012). In their apology for the incident (Amazon 2012), Amazon highlighted that only a very small number of developers had access to this data, the developer did not initially realise the mistake and, for the first few hours, the technical teams were puzzled by the error messages being generated by their system. This issue was fixed not through technical means, but by implementing a process to ensure changes to systems were double-checked to avoid accidental deletion in the future.

Secondly, related to this loose coupling, the distributed nature of the way in which big data is collected and stored creates inherent complexity with multiple organisations and multiple technologies. Going back to the example given previously of the Netflix failure, what is even more significant is that Netflix was reliant on another organisation's infrastructure to deliver much of its content. In this case, an organisation with which it competes directly, Amazon's Instant Video service. Whilst a few firms can achieve a degree of vertical integration, most are reliant on an increasing web of third parties. Taking a theoretical example of a mid-size online retailer in addition to hosting the website, reliance upon other websites might include payment services (such as credit cards Paypal, Apple Pay), integration with social media, content delivery networks for video content, integration with a third party CRM, courier and delivery services, web analytics tools and advertising servers, to name but a few. This is on top of the complexity inherent in the data itself, a complexity reflected in the increasing concern over the ability to find suitably skilled employees with the ability to effectively analyse such data (Brown *et al.* 2014).

Thirdly, a distinguishing characteristic of normal accidents and big data is the lack of a shared understanding over risk. Organisations that have previously been used as cases of normal accidents can be characterised by a clear understanding of what constitutes an accident, even if they may disagree with the extent to which such accidents can be considered as 'normal'. Furthermore, previous organisations that collected very large amounts of data were often governments who had clear incentives to maintain privacy because, in the absence of a commercial incentives, ensuring limited access to the data also meant increasing levels of control. By contrast, the commercial demands of many of the firms that enable big data are built around both the indiscriminate collection of data and encouraging sharing of data. When Facebook CEO Mark Zuckerberg says, 'privacy is dead', even looking beyond the rhetoric, they are signalling that the underlying culture relating to data risk and privacy is different. This creates a tension in the types of activity that generate commercial value that can also be responsible for the forms of normal accidents we describe in this paper.

References

Amazon (2012). Summary of the December 24, 2012 Amazon ELB service event in the US-East Region. Retrieved April 2, 2015 from http://aws.amazon.com/message/680587/.

Brown, B., Court, D. & McGuire, T. (2014). *Views from the front lines of the data-analytics revolution*. Mckinsey.com. Retrieved June 10, 2014 from http://www.mckinsey.com/insights/business_technology/views_from_the_front_lines_of_the_data_analytics_revolution.

Cockcroft, A. (2012). *The Netflix tech blog: A closer look at the Christmas Eve outage*. Retrieved June 10, 2014 from http://techblog.netflix.com/2012/12/a-closer-look-at-christmas-eve-outage.html.

(Nunan and Di Domenico, 2017, pp. 485–486)

Nunan and Di Domenico start by observing that the internet could be thought of as a loosely coupled system, in that it is designed to function even when individual parts are failing. Yet the need to manage ever greater amounts of data means that organisations increasingly rely upon data centres and third-party storage centres. This creates hidden 'common modes' and dependencies in systems that appear to be independent but are closely connected or tightly coupled. If, on top of this, are added the various other components that organisations are increasingly dependent on (e.g. payment services, social media, content delivery networks, web analytic tools, etc.) then we have a highly complex and tightly coupled system. The authors finally allude to a new type of accident, specifically related to big data: many of the commercial organisations that 'enable big data are built around both the indiscriminate collection of data and encouraging sharing of data' to the extent that the Facebook CEO suggested that 'privacy is dead'.

The authors, later in the paper, suggest that normal accidents involving big data could be thought of as 'data accidents', where multiple unrelated datasets are released into the public domain in such a way that reidentification of data is possible. The example of Edward Snowden is given as an example of a data accident. Snowden was a Central Intelligence Agency (CIA) employee and subcontractor, and in 2013 he leaked highly classified information from the US National Security Agency. These leaks exposed various worldwide surveillance systems conducted by the US government. Many regard Snowden as a hero and his leaking of classified information as in the public interest. His activities provoked an international discussion about privacy, surveillance and national security, with the United Nations General Assembly adopting a motion to protect online privacy in the context of extraterritorial surveillance (Williams, 2013).

Nunan and Di Domenico do not argue that Snowden was justified, or not, in leaking the information. Rather they look at the case as an example of a data accident. They see the Snowden case as sharing some aspects of a normal accident. It was a failure of a system that was designed primarily to protect sensitive data and, once underway, the leaked data spread quickly (tight coupling). The leak occurred because unpredicted interactions within the system allowed a significant leak of data; in this case, a junior employee was able to access and remove large amounts of disparate data (interactive complexity). Where a data accident differs from NAT is that it was only apparent that an accident had occurred when the data was put to use. The first sign that an accident had occurred was with the (mis)use of data. However, the key question raised by this case is, according to Nunan and Di Domenico:

> If individual members of staff in a high-security organisational environment are able to remove and publicly distribute large

amounts of unstructured data, much of it, at least in the Snowden case, classified 'Top Secret', then to what extent can it be assumed that commercial applications of big data will not suffer from the same issue?

(Nunan and Di Domenico, 2017, p. 487)

5 Cybersecurity and social harm

While some technological incidents can be thought of as 'normal accidents', many other events are considered to be intentional cybersecurity incidents. Moreover, the intentionality shows how closely connected parts of our digital technology are. We all take for granted our digital privacy and security until deliberate activities reveal these things to be fragile. In this section, we consider the relations between *people and things* along with what happens when harm occurs as a result of a breach of security.

For example, in a domestic situation, you probably access the internet in your home by using a local Wi-Fi network that will be protected by a password and firewall. You probably also have a variety of digital devices such as a smartphone, digital tablet, wireless printer or laptop. These will also be protected by passwords and anti-malware software. For many people, the security settings they have on their digital devices give rise to insecurities. For example, maybe they do not use passwords or re-use the same password multiple times. These all contribute to making digital things insecure and could allow a cybersecurity incident to occur. If you do not have up-to-date security settings or use easy-to-guess passwords on objects that can connect to the internet, these devices could be hacked and co-opted into what is called a 'botnet'. Peter W. Singer and Allan Friedman describe a botnet in the following extract:

> More recently, malware has been used not only to take control of a computer system but to keep control of that computer in order to exploit its computational and network resources. By capturing victims' systems and coordinating their behavior, attackers can assemble armies of "zombie" computers. Millions of machines can be controlled by a single actor through a range of different command and control mechanisms. These are referred to as "botnets," and most computer users will never know if they are part of one.
>
> Botnets are powerful resources for a host of nefarious activities. Regular access to the victims' machines allows monitoring to capture valuable data. Botnet controllers can also leverage the network connections of their victims' systems to send spam, host websites to sell illegal products, or defraud online advertisers.

Perhaps most insidiously, botnets can launch a "distributed denial of service" (DDoS) attack.

DDoS attacks target the subsystems that handle connections to the Internet, such as web servers. ... If someone were to call your phone incessantly, you would first lose the ability to concentrate and then lose the ability to use your phone for any other purpose. Similarly, in the cyber world, if the attacker can overwhelm the connection link, the system is effectively removed from the Internet. It is fairly easy to defend against a single attacker from a fixed source: one just has to block the sender, just like blocking an annoying caller's number.... In a distributed denial-of-service attack, the attacker uses a botnet of thousands or even millions to overwhelm the victim. It's the equivalent of having thousands or even millions of people trying to call your phone. Not only would you get nothing done, but the calls you actually want to receive wouldn't easily get through.

(Singer and Friedman, 2014, p. 44)

An example of a Denial of Service attack was the 'Dyn botnet' attack in 2016. In this attack, a botnet was made up of a large number of unsecured digital devices, such as wireless printers, internet-connected cameras, domestic routers and baby monitors. These were all maliciously taken over and used to access around 70 popular websites and online services, including the BBC, Facebook, Twitter, Amazon, The New York Times and Netflix. The high volume of devices in the botnet repeatedly accessing these services meant that these sites crashed or were taken offline. This had the effect of denying access to these sites, and services, by those who were legitimately trying to access them.

Incidents like the Dyn botnet tend to be merely inconvenient for people trying to watch their favourite show online or post a picture of their friends on social media. Other cybersecurity incidents have more troubling consequences. Take, for example, the WannaCry incident in 2017, where a virus was developed to exploit computers running on older, vulnerable software and systems that were no longer supported by Microsoft security updates. When the virus reached a computer it became locked until the unlucky user paid a ransom to the hackers who designed the virus. This virus seems annoying and innocuous until it is revealed that it infected tens of thousands of devices on the UK's National Health Service (NHS) network. This attack disabled medical scanners, blood-storage refrigerators and some of the computers in operating theatres. Also, the WannaCry attack meant that some people in England and Scotland were unable to access non-emergency medical resources until the problem was resolved.

Figure 11.4 The WannaCry ransom message.

As was discussed earlier in the chapter, normal accident theory (NAT) gives us a framework to understand how a virus such as WannaCry can rapidly spread through a number of disparate systems and cause widespread disruption. These are easy to consider in hindsight, once the accident (or incident) has already happened. Nevertheless what cybersecurity incidents such as WannaCry reveal is that neglect of digital devices connected to complex tightly coupled systems can result in accidents where vital health services become temporarily out of action. But how do you see cyber-attacks such as these? Are they an example of social harm, or are they criminal acts? Or, at the more serious end of the scale, could they be considered to be terrorist acts? How cyber-attacks are framed will impact how we respond to them. As sociologists, we should consider how we frame cybersecurity in terms of how it might relate to *individuals and society* and *power and inequality*.

6 Who is responsible and involved in cyber-attacks?

It is often tricky to determine who is responsible for a cyber-attack since the software and hardware used by the criminals involved in financial cybercrime can often be bought relatively cheaply and used by people with a surprisingly small amount of technical expertise. In larger attacks, such as the Dyn botnet attack and the WannaCry attack described previously, it can be difficult to determine who is behind the attack; it could be an individual, an activist group or a nation-state. Sometimes the people involved might deliberately obscure or hide their identity. In the case of the WannaCry attack, no group or nation-state has claimed responsibility, although the US and UK governments have publicly stated that they believe North Korean actors were responsible (Nakashima and Rucker, 2017).

In the case of the Dyn botnet attack, which denied users access to many websites, it is unclear who was responsible, because the botnet was based on a virus called Mirai, which is simple to use for people with little technical skill. People who carry out attacks with these kinds of tools are often labelled as 'script kiddies' to reflect the fact that it is possible for people who are inexperienced at hacking to achieve significant disruption. With hacking tools (such as pre-written code that can be easily deployed) being easy to purchase and use, it can difficult to find out who is responsible for a cyber incident and their motivation for doing so. While some large-scale incidents are politically motivated, others such as small cases of credit card fraud may be financially motivated. Indeed, data sets containing personal or sensitive data of citizens, such as addresses or credit card numbers, are sold on the **dark web**.

The rhetoric around large-scale, coordinated cybersecurity incidents such as the WannaCry incident mentioned previously poses a problem for governments. How can you confidently identify who is behind a cybersecurity attack? Attribution is difficult because there are technologies such as virtual private networks (VPNs) that can disguise the location of the device being used to connect to the internet. But even if a government could attribute a cybersecurity incident to an organisation or nation-state, what would, or should their response be? As a homeland security advisor acknowledged after the WannaCry attack, 'the United States has few options to retaliate against North

Korea and to pressure the isolated nation to change its behaviour, short of starving its people or attacking it. North Korea is already one of the most heavily sanctioned countries in the world' (Nakashima and Rucker, 2017). Would it be wise for a government to retaliate if they were not completely sure who initiated the attack? These are pressing questions for governments and their respective security agencies as they work to defend countries from cyber incidents and prevent them from happening in the first place.

In previous chapters, we have looked at the relations between *people and things*. How might we consider cybersecurity incidents with some of the ideas introduced to you in previous chapters? We can start by asking questions to help us think about responsibility in situations such as the Dyn botnet attack. Who or what is at fault: the person who purchased the internet-connected object for not maintaining its security? The manufacturer for making the object easy to install and use (commonly known as 'plug and play') and yet difficult to modify the security settings without expertise? Or is the person hacking the object to blame for taking advantage of these insecure objects? It is entirely possible that all three are implicated in these situations and that each could take action to avoid this situation.

7 Are all hackers malicious?

Despite what you have read so far, not all hackers are malicious. Many people with technical skills work as 'ethical hackers' or 'white hat hackers' to prevent cyber-attacks or help organisations and individuals who have been affected as part of a cyber-attack. Many of these ethical hackers do preventative testing of networks, devices and websites to highlight vulnerabilities and show where security could be improved. An example of how this testing works is the annual cyber-security conference called Def Con. During this conference, hackers present their work to others and take part in challenges to hack other objects or systems. At the 2018 Def Con conference, a challenge occurred where conference attendees were asked by Jake Braun, one of the organisers, to hack into voting machines commonly used in US elections:

> Braun and a group of other cybersecurity researchers created Def Con's first-ever Voting Village, a conference within the conference, devoted to election security and its evil twin, election insecurity. Def Con would bring more than twenty-five thousand of the most avid hackers in the world together, jamming the halls of Caesars Palace, and organizers saw an opportunity to show the American public, still reeling from news of Russian interference in the 2016 Presidential election, how easily voting machines could be compromised. For last year's conference, Braun and his colleagues purchased roughly two dozen voting machines from government auction sites and eBay, and every single one was successfully hacked, some within minutes.
>
> (Halpern, 2018)

The actions of ethical hackers uncover the potential for a normal accident to occur, and encourage manufacturers or authorities to do the necessary maintenance to prevent an incident happening. Cybersecurity incidents like these challenge the notion that digitising and connecting processes or activities is a positive act. When deciding whether to introduce a new technology that promises to improve a process, there also needs to be serious thought given to the inequality or power imbalances that may occur if or when the technology fails. For instance, the UK and many other countries have chosen to retain a voting system where citizens use a pencil to check the box of their preferred candidate. Alternatively, in other countries, such as the United States, India and Brazil, electronic voting is allowed in some or all elections. Users select their preferences from a screen, and the machines cast a vote. In the US, we have seen that the use of voting machines has been critiqued for their potential to be hacked. This becomes especially important when the results are close and calls into question whether democracies are robust enough in the digital age.

8 Conclusion

In this chapter, we have used normal accident theory to consider the complexity of keeping digital infrastructure and systems secure. The cybersecurity incidents mentioned throughout this chapter reiterate the need for individuals and organisations to be vigilant when it comes to keeping devices, data sets, log-ins and processes secure. But who is ultimately responsible: individuals or society? As you will have seen in the examples from this chapter, it can difficult to assign complete responsibility for maintaining cybersecurity to one individual or organisation.

The networked and distributed nature of the internet makes it difficult for governments to manage the internet like they would other utilities or infrastructures. But government organisations attempt to give guidance to individuals, businesses, public sector organisations and cybersecurity professionals to allow everyone to be aware of what cybersecurity looks like. However, as evidenced by the Dyn botnet attack, individuals have a responsibility to take care of security settings on not only their accounts but also on all their connected devices. But with the uptake in installing internet-enabled devices such as speakers, doorbells, cameras and lighting, the onus also falls on manufacturers to make it easy to install and update the security settings on these devices. Indeed, both *individuals and societies* are responsible for cybersecurity.

References

Halpern, S. (2018) 'Election-hacking lessons from the 2018 Def Con Hackers Conference', *The New Yorker*, 31 January. Available at: https://www.newyorker.com/news/dispatch/election-hacking-lessons-from-the-2018-def-con-hackers-conference (Accessed: 16 November 2020).

Metcalfe, H. (2018) 'Cybersecurity'. Interview with Harry Metcalfe. Interviewed by Jessamy Perriam for *DD218 Understanding Digital Societies*. 19 October.

Nakashima, E. and Rucker, P. (2017) 'U.S. declares North Korea carried out massive WannaCry cyberattack', *The Washington Post*, 31 January. Available at: https://www.washingtonpost.com/world/national-security/us-set-to-declare-north-korea-carried-out-massive-wannacry-cyber-attack/2017/12/18/509deb1c-e446-11e7-a65d-1ac0fd7f097e_story.html (Accessed: 2 June 2018).

Nunan, D. and Di Domenico, M. (2017) 'Big data: a normal accident waiting to happen?', *Journal of Business Ethics*, 145(3), pp. 481–491.

Perrow, C. (1999) *Normal accidents: living with high-risk technologies.* Princeton, NJ: Princeton University Press.

Singer, P.W. and Friedman, A. (2014) *Cybersecurity and cyberwar: what everyone needs to know.* Oxford: Oxford University Press.

Williams, C. (2013) 'U.N. votes to protect online privacy; Edward Snowden leaks credited', *Los Angeles Times*, 21 November. Available at: https://www.latimes.com/world/worldnow/la-fg-wn-un-surveillance-privacy-rights-edward-snowden-20131219-story.html#axzz2nzV4bWSn (Accessed: 10 March 2020).

Chapter 12

Too much, too young? Social media, moral panics and young people's mental health

Peter Redman

Contents

1 Introduction

In 2017 the UK's Royal Society for Public Health (RSPH), in association with the Young Health Movement, published *#StatusofMind: social media and young people's mental health and wellbeing* (Royal Society for Public Health, 2017). Although *#StatusofMind* drew attention to some of the positive benefits of social media it was mainly concerned with apparently worrying evidence suggesting they can cause young people harm. For example, readers were told, 'The evidence is clear that increased use of social media can be detrimental to some aspects of the health and wellbeing of young people' (p. 24); that '[s]ocial media addiction is thought to affect around 5% of young people [Jenner (2015) cited in original]' (p. 6); that 'young people who … spend … more than two hours per day on social networking sites … are more likely to report poor mental health, including psychological distress (symptoms of anxiety and depression) [Sampasa-Kanyinga and Lewis (2015) cited in original]' (p. 8); and that '[i]ncreasingly … young people are reporting that FoMO [fear of missing out from what's happening on social media] is causing them distress in the form of anxiety and feelings of inadequacy' (p. 12).

Given that evidence it was small wonder the report's Foreword claimed that social media pose 'risks which have already opened the door to significant problems for [young people's] mental health and wellbeing' and warned, 'it is vitally important that we put safeguards in place' (Royal Society for Public Health, 2017, p. 5).

The RSPH was not alone in raising the alarm about social media and digital screen use. Although concern about their impact on mental health and well-being had been rising and falling for some time, the years 2017–19 saw an upsurge of anxiety in the UK and elsewhere. Inevitably, some of that concern could be found in inflated news stories with headlines such as 'Ban your toddler from TV and iPads' (Allen, 2019). However, as *#StatusofMind* indicated, it was not only journalists who expressed worries about social media and digital screen engagement. Researchers, psychiatrists, politicians, youth organisations and others drew attention to their perceived harmful effects, often calling for them to be more tightly regulated. Such was the pressure for action, the Secretary of State for Health and Social Care in England called on the Chief Medical Officer (CMO) to 'draw up guidance to help parents ensure children don't use social media in a way that harms

Figure 12.1   The RSPH's headquarters. The RSPH co-authored *#StatusofMind*.

their mental health' (Department of Health and Social Care, 2018). Equally, an All-Party Parliamentary Group (APPG) on Social Media and Young People's Mental Health and Wellbeing was established with the aim of 'driv[ing] policy change that mitigates the bad and maximises the good of social media for young people' (All-Party Parliamentary Group, 2019, p. 6).

But how justified were those concerns? Did the evidence really support the level of anxiety they revealed and, if not, what was causing that anxiety? It is precisely those questions this chapter seeks to answer. In the following pages, you will consider the relevant research literature and explore a sociological explanation ('**moral panic** theory') of how and why new media technologies frequently generate social anxiety. In light of those investigations you will also reflect on the questions: what does anxiety about social media and digital screen use tell us about social harm?; what does it tell us about the relationship between *individuals and society*?; and, how do the social and technical shape each other?

Throughout the chapter, the term 'social media' is used to refer to online applications – at the time of writing Facebook, Instagram, WhatsApp and Twitter were popular examples – that allow users to create and share content and engage in social networking. Terms such as 'digital screen use' will be used to refer to activities (such as internet surfing) involving digital screens more generally.

Figure 12.2 How justified were concerns about young people's use of social media and digital screens?

1.1 Teaching aims

The aims of this chapter are for you to:

* assess the evidence available in the years 2017–19 about the possible harmful effects of social media and digital screen use on young people's mental health and well-being

* investigate the extent to which anxiety about social media and digital screen engagement in those years can be understood as a 'moral panic'

* reflect on what that social anxiety tells us about social harm

- consider what it indicates about the relationship between *individuals and society*

- revisit the question 'how do the social and technical shape each other?'.

2 Evaluating research on social media

Concern about the possible harmful effects of social media and digital screens was not without foundation. For instance, a study by Jean Twenge and colleagues, which drew on two nationally representative surveys of over 500,000 US adolescents, found that:

> Adolescents who spent more time on screen activities were significantly more likely to have high depressive symptoms or have at least one suicide-related outcome [e.g. suicidal thoughts, plans, or attempts], and those who spent more time on nonscreen activities were less likely. … [A]dolescents using electronic devices 3 or more hours a day were 34% more likely to have at least one suicide-related outcome than those using devices 2 or fewer hours a day, and adolescents using social media sites every day were 13% more likely to report high levels of depressive symptoms than those using social media less often.
>
> (Twenge *et al.*, 2018, p. 9)

Findings from other studies suggested links between young people's screen-based digital activities, including use of social media, with among other things: anxiety, depression, low self-esteem, sleep-loss, negative body-image, and poor psychological well-being (see, for example, Kalpidou, *et al.*, 2011; Meier and Gray, 2014; Hoare, *et al.*, 2016; Woods and Scott, 2016; McRae, *et al.*, 2017; Kelly *et al.*, 2018).

Taken on its own, that evidence would seem to justify the concerns raised in *#StatusofMind*, the report mentioned in the chapter's Introduction. Yet, the UK's CMOs, who had commissioned a review of the evidence, concluded:

> Scientific research is currently insufficiently conclusive to support UK CMO evidence-based guidelines on optimal amounts of screen use or online activities (such as social media use).
>
> (Davies *et al.*, 2019, p. 2)

Figure 12.3 Research has linked young people's use of social media and digital screens to a range of mental health problems.

Equally, a House of Commons Science and Technology Committee report noted 'the limited quantity and quality of academic evidence available' on the effects social media and screen time have on children and young people and went on to say 'there is not yet a well-established body of research in this area' (House of Commons Science and Technology Committee, 2019, p. 3). Why did the CMOs and the Science and Technology Committee express caution about research findings on the impact of social media and digital screen engagement on young people's mental health and well-being?

A number of reasons stand out. Most obviously, the findings were contradictory. True, numerous studies had identified potentially negative effects from the use of digital screens and social media but, in many other cases, the findings were mixed or neutral, or the effects identified were actually positive (Erfani and Abedin, 2018). For instance, Amy Orben and Andrew Przybylski's (2019a) rigorous research on digital screen engagement and adolescent well-being, often seen as the gold standard in the field, found 'little substantive statistically significant and negative associations between digital screen engagement and well-being in adolescents' and concluded that any negative effect present was 'miniscule ... when compared with other activities in an adolescent's life' (p. 693).

There were also concerns about the quality of much of the research on young people's use of social media and digital screens. The Science and Technology Committee's report discussed this matter in detail, and, in the following reading, you will explore three things it identified as being particularly noteworthy:

- the lack of attention paid to social context in much of the existing research

- its over-reliance on cross-sectional studies

- the fact that, where negative effects were found, they were often relatively trivial.

Now read Reading 12.1, 'House of Commons Science and Technology Committee, "Research on social media and screen-use"'. Don't worry if some of the points made are unclear to you. They will be discussed in more detail in the paragraphs following the reading.

Reading 12.1

House of Commons Science and Technology Committee, 'Research on social media and screen-use'

The evidence we received during our inquiry detailed a wide range of possible effects, both positive and negative, that social media and screen-use may have on the physical and mental wellbeing of young people. A note of caution, however, was sounded by some witnesses about the reliability and validity of the evidence base.

...

The need for research to focus more on the *context* in which social media use occurred was ... emphasised by Dr Vicky Goodyear from the University of Birmingham. Dr Goodyear told us that her research showed that "school physical education, parents and other family members and peers played a key role in how much time [young people] spent on social media, but also what they were looking at and why". She added that "evidence from broader samples of young people in different contexts and different demographics" was needed "to be able to understand what the influence is and define an effective response".

...

An additional limitation, linked to research design, concerned the reliance on studies that were "almost always correlational in nature" when examining the effects of social media. Professor Peter Fonagy, National Clinical Adviser on children and young people's mental health at NHS England, explained that these studies encounter the "chicken and egg problem"; namely that it is difficult to "untangle causation" since it is not possible to determine whether a health effect is the cause or consequence of using social media. As Dr Mark Griffiths, Professor of Behavioural Addiction, from Nottingham Trent University told us:

> What we have is a lot of what we call cross-sectional snapshot research, which is not longitudinal [...] There is no good causal evidence. We have lots of correlational evidence. I would add that there have now been over 100 studies of Facebook addiction. Most of them have very poor-quality data. There are very few nationally representative samples. There is almost nothing in terms of longitudinal research.

...

Where associations between social media and mental health had been found, some witnesses emphasised that the effects were "small". According to Amy Orben, a lecturer in psychology at the University of Oxford:

> Oftentimes, we do not find any effects. When we do find effects, they are extremely small. When we take the whole picture into account, they become vanishingly small. From the perspective that there has not been any really good quality evidence, I do not see that that link can be said to be present.

(House of Commons Science and Technology Committee, 2019, pp. 9, 11–12)

As Vicky Goodyear explained to the committee, much of the research on young people's social media use and digital screen engagement had not explored the extent to which their possible effects are filtered through the social context in which they are used. For instance, a 13-year-old girl who receives a sexually explicit message on social media is likely to experience that event differently if she is alone from when in the company of her mother or a group of friends. Goodyear also alluded to the question of 'demographics'. Her point was that research had often failed to explore how digital screens are used differently by different social groups and with what consequences. Perhaps the use of social media by some groups is unproblematic, but not for others – for instance, those with a pre-existing mental health problem. Reliance on 'tick-box' answers to quite generalised survey questions (for example, 'How often do you use social media?' Never; once a week; up to 1 hour a day; 1–2 hours a day; more than 2 hours a day'), meant that much of the research on social media and digital screen engagement had not been good at capturing the kind of nuance to which Goodyear drew attention.

Figure 12.4 Studies frequently ignore the social context in which social media and digital screens are used.

What of the second limitation discussed by the report, its over-reliance on cross-sectional studies? As its name implies, **cross-sectional research** gathers information from a cross-section of people at a single point in time. As Peter Fonagy explains in the reading, because cross-sectional research provides a snapshot of a particular moment, it can usually only establish associations (or '**correlations**') between the things being studied, not whether or how they are causally related. For instance, even when it is established that an apparent association between social media use and depression has not occurred through random chance, the association might indicate variously that:

- using social media causes depression

- being depressed causes the young people concerned to use social media (perhaps because they are more isolated or because using social media helps their depression)

- each reinforces the other.

Alternatively, the association might be the result of a third, unknown factor.

In order to establish **causality** , it is usually necessary to conduct '**longitudinal research**', that is research following a population over a period of time. To explain that point, imagine a study in which participants are assessed at points A and B, with each point separated by 12 months. Now imagine that at point A some participants' social media use is dramatically higher compared to others in the study and, at point B, their level of depression has dramatically increased compared to others in the study. That finding would allow researchers to say with more certainty that higher levels of social media use caused the observed increase in the level of depression rather than depression causing increased use of social media.

As Mark Griffiths notes in the reading, evidence from longitudinal studies on the effects of young people's use of social media and digital screens was limited. Moreover, findings from the studies that were available were inconsistent. For instance, a study by Cara Booker and colleagues (2018) found that high social media use at a young age caused problems with girls' well-being later in adolescence; Taylor Heffer and colleagues (2017) found that pre-existing mental health problems caused younger female adolescents to use social media more than their peers; and Orben and colleagues (2019) found very little effect from digital screen engagement at all.

The final limitation discussed in the reading – concerning '**effect sizes**' – is perhaps the most important of all. As its name suggests, effect size is a statistical measure of the size of the effect being studied.

Imagine cross-sectional research shows a relationship between time spent using digital screens (say, more than two hours in one sitting) and reduced well-being. Imagine also it has ruled out the possibility that that relationship occurred by random chance. Even though you would be unsure which way the relationship works (does more screen time lead to reduced well-being or reduced well-being lead to more screen time?) you would still have preliminary grounds for thinking too much screen time might be harmful. But before doing further research to establish the direction of the relationship you would obviously want to know its strength – was using a digital screen for more than two hours in one go associated with a large reduction in well-being or only a very small reduction? If the reduction were very small, you might well decide that worrying about screen time is unnecessary.

Here is where effect size as a statistical measurement comes in. A large effect size would indicate that using screens for more than two hours was associated with a large reduction in well-being; a small effect size would indicate it was associated with a small reduction. As the reading indicates, a frequent criticism made of research on young people's use of social media and digital screens was that, where associations were found between these and mental health problems, the effect sizes identified were often only moderate or small. In reality, then, although it was relatively common for research to find above-chance associations between using social media or digital screens and reduced psychological health or well-being, the extent of the harm identified was often limited.

Figure 12.5 (left) Amy Orben and **(right)** Andrew Przybylski.

With that problem in mind, Orben and Przybylski (2019b) looked at data from three large-scale surveys. They sought to investigate, first, whether the data revealed an association between young people's digital screen use and well-being and, second, what the effect size was for that association. To compare the potential importance of the effect size found, they also compared it to the effect size of associations between well-being and other activities in the young people's lives. Their findings were surprising. Although they found a small but above-chance relationship between screen-use and reduced well-being, they also found that 'the association of well-being with regularly eating potatoes was nearly as negative as the association with technology use … and wearing glasses was more negatively associated with well-being' (p. 178). Another way to put that would be to say that any possible risk to adolescent well-being posed by digital screen use was similar in size to that from eating potatoes and actually smaller than the risk posed by wearing glasses. In other words, according to Orben and Przybylski's study, the effect of digital screen use on young people's well-being was very small indeed. It should be noted that Orben and Przybylski's interpretation of their data has been criticised (Twenge, 2020, pp. 92–93). Nevertheless, it is evident that claims about the harmful consequences of screen engagement were, at the very least, open to doubt.

In light of those problems, it will be apparent why the CMOs and the Science and Technology Committee expressed caution about research into the effects of social media and digital screen engagement on young people's mental health and well-being. To summarise, at the time the report was written:

- findings from the research literature were contradictory, with some showing negative associations, some positive associations and some no discernible associations at all

- there was a growing recognition of the need for a more nuanced understanding of how social media and digital screens are actually used

- causality had not been established

- concerns had been raised about the small effect sizes observed in many studies and the conclusions drawn from these.

Those points inevitably put into question claims made about social media and digital screen use of the kind outlined in the chapter's Introduction. For example, the Foreword to *#StatusofMind's* unequivocal assertion that social media pose 'risks which have already opened the door to significant problems for [young people's] mental health and wellbeing' (Royal Society for Public Health, 2017, p. 5) seems premature and based on a curiously partial reading of the research. A more balanced reading of the evidence was provided by Orben *et al.* (2019) when they wrote: 'the unknowns of social media effects still substantially outnumber … the knowns' (p. 10227).

How had the RSPH and many others come to conclusions that were so out of step with the actual evidence available at the time? An obvious sociological response to that question would be to wonder if their conclusions were fuelled by a 'moral panic'.

3 Moral panics

Although he did not invent the term, the concept of moral panic was first developed by Stanley Cohen in his book *Folk Devils and Moral Panics: The Creation of the Mods and Rockers*, originally published in 1972. Cohen's point of departure was a clash between groups of youths that occurred over a wet Easter weekend in 1964 in Clacton, a small English seaside town. Although disagreeable, the events in Clacton were not unprecedented. As Cohen (2011) noted, 'Disturbances of various sorts, variously called "hooliganism", "rowdyism" or "gang fights", had occurred frequently throughout the late fifties and early sixties' (p. 43). What was unprecedented however was the reaction to the disturbances in Clacton and, subsequently, in a number of other seaside towns. A chain reaction of public anxiety, excitement and outrage was set in motion. Newspapers ran sensationalised stories about the events; people started clamouring for changes in the law; speeches were made in parliament; and a bill was introduced to amend legislation on 'malicious damage' (Cohen, 2011, pp. 153–155). It was this chain reaction that Cohen identified as a 'moral panic'. But what exactly did he mean by the term?

Figure 12.6 Mods invading the beach at Margate, Kent in 1964.

Here is Cohen's much quoted definition from the opening paragraph of the book's first chapter:

> Societies appear to be subject, every now and then, to periods of moral panic. (1) A condition, episode, person or group of persons emerges to become defined as a threat to societal values and interests; (2) its nature is presented in a stylized and stereotypical fashion by the mass [news] media; (3) the moral barricades are manned by editors, bishops, politicians and other right-thinking people; (4) socially accredited experts pronounce their diagnoses and solutions; (5) ways of coping are evolved or (more often) resorted to; (6) the condition then disappears, submerges or deteriorates …

> (Cohen, 2011, p. 1, numbers added)

Over the years, Cohen's definition has been subject to various criticisms, not least the possibility that, in the digital age, the priority given to conventional news media (television, radio and newspapers) is outdated (McRobbie and Thornton, 1995; Hier, 2019). However, the concept remains widely used in sociology and many of the features Cohen describes continue to be viewed as core to it (see Thompson, 1998; Critcher, 2008; Goode and Ben-Yehuda, 2009; Cohen, 2011, pp. xxvi–xxvii). These features can be summarised in the following terms:

Threat

As the title of Cohen's book indicates, moral panics involve the creation of 'folk devils' – something or someone perceived to pose a threat to the moral order of those sections of society among which the panic spreads. In the Mods and Rockers panic, the threat was considered to come from youth subcultures, but numerous other groups or things have been the subject of panics over the years: people with HIV and AIDS, drugs, immigrants, comic books, and many others.

Overreaction

Cohen did not seek to trivialise the events in Clacton and elsewhere. However, he saw the media's coverage of these disturbances, the scale of public outrage that followed, and the fact that they led to changes to the criminal law as an overreaction. Consequently, as the term 'panic' itself implies, moral panics can be said to be characterised by responses that are disproportionate to the imagined threat that starts them off.

Agents

As already noted, Cohen saw the news media as playing a crucial role in generating moral panics. However, he also argued that 'moral entrepreneurs' ('editors, bishops, politicians and other right-thinking people') fanned the flames of the panic, and knee-jerk responses from the 'control culture' (the police, courts, government officials and parliament) made things worse still (these knee-jerk responses occur in stage 5 of Cohen's model). As that implies, panics do not just happen but are actively created by social actors or agents.

Escalation and spread

Escalation refers to the chain reaction by which, in Cohen's definition, one stage in a panic sparks the next. As Cohen (2011) himself warned, stage-by-stage models should not be applied over-rigidly (p. 227). Nevertheless, the idea that, in some form, moral panics escalate is central to the concept. As they grow, they also spread, pulling in an increasing range of people and groups. Moral panics may not permeate society as a whole, but neither are they purely localised.

Volatility

As stage 6 of Cohen's definition implies, moral panics sometimes blow over leaving little trace of their existence. Alternatively, they can lead to more profound regulatory or legal changes. In either case, they are relatively short-lived. Even if they persist for a number of years – perhaps flaring up and dying down a number of times – they are clearly distinct from more stable and permanent features of the social world.

Underlying social anxieties

Cohen (2011) argues that it was not youth misbehaviour itself that
sparked the Clacton panic but what the images and reports of that
misbehaviour stirred up in the minds of the newspaper-reading
public. Pictures of youth behaving badly, Cohen suggested, roused
fears about the pace of post-war social change. The young people
seemed to symbolise a society in which old certainties were
crumbling in the face of consumer affluence, sexual permissiveness
and a hedonistic youth culture that appeared to flout traditional
ideas about the work ethic (p. 218).

Figure 12.7 Carnaby Street 1965. Consumer affluence and a hedonistic
youth culture raised anxieties about changing social values.

Armed with that understanding of moral panics, it is now possible to
answer the question posed earlier: were concerns such as those
expressed in *#StatusofMind* evidence that, in the UK, sometime
between 2017 and 2019, young people's use of social media and digital
screens was the subject of a moral panic?

4 Was there a moral panic about social media?

If you look back at earlier sections of this chapter you will see that not everything about the anxiety surrounding young people's use of social media and digital screens fits exactly with Cohen's definition of moral panics. In particular, in contrast to the Mods and Rockers panic, concern about social media and digital screen engagement was generated less by the news than by 'socially accredited experts' – in this case, psychological researchers. In Cohen's definition 'socially accredited experts' do not appear until stage 4. Similarly, anxiety was not amplified by the kind of 'moral entrepreneurs' Cohen identified in stage 3 of his model. Politicians certainly played a role in this process, but it was not 'editors, bishops … and other right-thinking people' who were involved but, instead, professional bodies (such as the RSPH) and interest groups advocating for young people (such as the Young Health Movement, co-publishers of *#StatusofMind*). As such, the panic about young people's digital screen use was closer to the model of moral panics described by Erich Goode and Nachman Ben-Yehuda (2009) in their influential book *Moral Panic: The Social Construction of Deviance*, first published in 1994. For Goode and Ben-Yehuda, it is interest groups who start panics with the media and others then fanning the flames (pp. 142–143).

That said, evidence explored earlier in the chapter certainly bears many of the hallmarks of a moral panic understood in broad terms. Looking at the key features of moral panics outlined a moment ago, we can say:

- young people's use of social media and digital screens was identified as a threat to society's interests

- anxiety about social media and digital screen use was arguably an overreaction given the evidence available

- that overreaction was generated by key agents, most obviously academics and bodies such as the RSPH

- anxiety escalated from initial concern in academic papers to the point where the UK government felt impelled to respond (for example, by commissioning guidelines on screen use)

- that escalation implied anxiety had spread from the academic community, to professional bodies such as the RSPH, and out into the media, and parts of government and the general public.

Those points provide clear evidence a moral panic had occurred. However, it is questionable whether the panic ever developed into one that was full-blown, at least in the years under discussion here. Concern about young people's use of social media and digital screens had certainly escalated and spread but did not result in comprehensive and well-established public consensus. Moreover, by moral panic standards, the responses it generated were comparatively limited. For example, the CMOs' advice for parents on children's and young people's screen and social media use, and a UK government White Paper on 'Online Harms' were relatively muted in their response to calls for regulation. The CMOs' guidelines were restricted to commonplaces such as 'Keep moving! Everyone should take a break after a couple of hours sitting or lying down using a screen' (Davies *et al.*, 2019, p. 10). Meanwhile the White Paper focused mainly on specific risks such as those posed to young people from cyberbullying, underage sharing of sexual imagery, and coming across advice on how to commit suicide. To the extent the White Paper addressed social media use and digital screen time as things that might have a detrimental impact in themselves, it merely noted the need for further research and repeated the CMOs' guidance to parents (Department for Digital Culture, Media and Sport, 2019, pp. 19–21, 84). In short, both handled social media use and screen time in ways far removed from #*StatusofMind*'s (Royal Society for Public Health, 2017, pp. 24–25) calls for mandatory 'heavy usage' pop-ups and compulsory school lessons on the risks of 'social media addiction' – a term widely used but whose existence was not clearly established (Kardefelt-Winther, 2017).

The main reason anxiety did not develop into a full-blown panic seems to lie in the active resistance it faced. For example, in 2017, *The Guardian* newspaper published an open letter signed by 81 academics and researchers in the field, questioning the idea that digital screen engagement is inherently harmful to young people and calling for policy to be based on sound evidence (Etchells, *et al.*, 2017). Similarly, researchers such as Amy Orben and Andrew Przybylski made frequent media appearances challenging the evidence for the negative impact of social media and digital screen use (see, for instance, Orben and Przybylski, 2019c). Additionally, academics and researchers went out of their way to give evidence to inquiries likely to inform legislation. For instance, a report produced by the APPG (a body mentioned in the Introduction) noted the group 'was repeatedly made aware [by researchers] of the lack of robust scientific research evidencing whether social media actually causes mental health problems' (All-Party Parliamentary Group, 2019, p. 12). This did not stop the APPG recommending that 'the Government publishes evidence based guidance for those aged 24 and younger to avoid excessive social media use' (p. 5) but it seems likely it would have gone much further had researchers not challenged the evidence on such things as 'social media addiction' and the supposedly harmful effects of intensive screen use.

As those examples suggest, for every academic and professional caught up in the moral panic, another seems to have remained profoundly sceptical. Moreover, among the sceptics, many seem to have been willing to go public and question claims such as those made in *#StatusofMind*. That point brings us to the question of volatility, another of the features of moral panics discussed in the previous section. The fact that sceptical academics and professionals seem to have succeeded in deflating the 2017–19 panic underlines how volatile anxiety about young people's social media and digital screen use was. Faced with concerted resistance, it went into retreat.

5 Moral panic and social anxiety

As you saw in Section 3, Cohen argued that moral panics tap into and express underlying social anxieties. Media reports of the disturbances in Clacton and elsewhere, Cohen argued, stirred up underlying anxieties about the pace of post-war social change. Were similar anxieties being stirred up by young people's use of social media and digital screens?

To answer that question, we should begin by noting the long history of social anxiety about new media technologies and types, much of which focused on their supposed effects on young people. For example, the 1950s saw anxieties about the risks television and comic books were thought to pose to the young while, in the UK, the 1980s saw parallel anxieties about the availability of a genre of violent movies on VHS video cassettes – so-called 'video nasties' (Gilbert, 1986; Thompson, 1998; Mahendran, 2012). In fact, as you are about to read, anxieties of that kind go back at least as far as the 18th century.

Now read Reading 12.2, 'The media's first moral panic' by Frank Furedi. The extract examines anxieties aroused in the 18th century by the novel, *The Sorrows of Young Werther*. As you will see, reactions to the novel had surprising similarities with the moral panics discussed in this chapter.

Reading 12.2

Frank Furedi, 'The media's first moral panic'

When cultural commentators lament the decline of the habit of reading books, it is difficult to imagine that back in the 18th century many prominent voices were concerned about the threat posed by people reading too much.

…

The emergence of commercial publishing in the 18th century and the growth of an ever-widening constituency of readers was not welcomed by everyone. Many cultural commentators were apprehensive about the impact of this new medium on individual behaviour and on society's moral order.

... The consensus that emerged was that unrestrained exposure to fiction led readers to lose touch with reality and identify with the novel's romantic characters to the point of adopting their behaviour. The passionate enthusiasm with which European youth responded to the publication of Johann Wolfgang von Goethe's novel *The Sorrows of Young Werther* (1774) appeared to confirm this consensus.

The Sorrows of Young Werther is an epistolary novel, which recounts the tortured love of a young man, Werther. His letters reveal an intense passion for Lotte, who is already betrothed to another man. Werther cannot reconcile himself to his predicament and concludes that he has no choice but to take his life. ...

The publication of *The Sorrows of Young Werther* turned into an almost instant media event. It became the first documented literary sensation of modern Europe. The novel was translated into French (1775), English (1779), Italian (1781) and Russian (1788) and was repeatedly republished in different editions. There were more than 20 pirated editions published within 12 years of its appearance in Germany. It also enjoyed remarkable success in the United States. ...

The scale of the reaction to *Werther* perturbed authorities throughout Europe. Many officials and critics perceived the vivid and sympathetic manner with which Goethe described Werther's descent into self-destruction as legitimating the act of suicide. They condemned the novel as a danger to the public, particularly to impressionable young readers. The novel was blamed for the unleashing of an epidemic of copycat suicides throughout Europe among young, emotionally disturbed and broken-hearted readers. The numerous initiatives to ban the novel indicated that the authorities took these claims very seriously. In 1775 the theological faculty of the University of Leipzig petitioned officials to ban *Werther* on the grounds that its circulation would lead to the promotion of suicide. ... The novel was also banned in Italy and Denmark.

...

While there is no evidence that *Werther* was responsible for the promotion of a wave of copycat suicides, it evidently succeeded in inspiring a generation of young readers. ...

The association of the novel with the disorganisation of the moral order represented an early example of a media panic. The formidable, sensational and often improbable effects attributed to the consequences of reading in the 18th century provided the cultural resources on which subsequent reactions to the cinema, television or the Internet would draw …. In that sense *Werther* fever anticipated the media panics of the future.

(Furedi, 2015, pp. 46–48)

It is unclear why new media technologies (such as television) and types (such as the novel), frequently arouse social anxiety. One possibility is they are highly visible and therefore appear emblematic of wider changes in society. The furore surrounding *The Sorrows of Young Werther* certainly seems to fit that likelihood. The novel was published as the industrial revolution was gathering pace and political revolution was in the air (the American Revolutionary War began in 1775, only a year after the book's publication). At another time, its apparent endorsement of romantic suicide might have caused a minor scandal. In the heightened state of nervousness then pervading Europe, it seems to have provoked something akin to a continent-wide moral panic.

That panic was doubtless made worse by the book's popularity with younger people. As Kenneth Thompson (1998) argued, young people occupy an ambiguous or **liminal** position in the social order (p. 43). Not quite adults – and therefore not 'full' members of society – they are simultaneously inside and outside society's boundaries. As such, they are unsettling and difficult to place: liable to be seen as a threat to the social order (as in the case of the Mods and Rockers panic); as under threat (as in the 2017–19 moral panic surrounding young people's use of social media and digital screens); or an uneasy combination of the two (as was perhaps the case in *The Sorrows of Young Werther* panic).

Applied to the 2017–19 panic surrounding young people's use of social media and digital screens, those arguments suggest a number of points. First, the 2017–19 panic was clearly a recent twist in a very long tale, one in which new media technologies and types have repeatedly been seen as threatening to young people's sanity, well-being and general standards of behaviour. Second, it is arguable that the novelty of the

Figure 12.8 An engraving illustrating Goethe's novel *The Sorrows of Young Werther*.

technology, its enthusiastic adoption by young people and the possibility of reading it as something with the potential to cause individual, social and moral harm made social media and digital screens ideal vessels through which to channel anxieties about wider social transformation.

Although the first decades of the 21st century may seem far removed from the period in which *The Sorrows of Young Werther* was written, we too are living through a time of rapid social change. During the 1990s, sociologists such as Ulrich Beck (1992) and Zygmunt Baumann (2000) began to identify a new phase of development in advanced industrialised societies. Economic globalisation, neo-liberal reform of labour markets and public services, and the forces unleashed in earlier stages of modernisation were, they argued, reshaping social life in ways that meant it was increasingly characterised by uncertainty, instability, and risk. In the intervening period, little has changed to modify that view. If anything, the financial crisis of 2008, the rise of right-wing populism, the gathering climate emergency, the Covid-19 pandemic and the ongoing digital revolution have intensified the processes they described. For moral panic theory, these are precisely the conditions in which panics are liable to thrive. Perhaps we should not be surprised that, as the internet and social media spread in the first decades of the 21st century, their use by young people became the object of so much concern.

6 Social harm, individuals and society and the social and technological

What do the preceding arguments tell us about social harm, the relationship between *individuals and society*, and the ways in which the social influences technology and technology influences the social? First, anxiety about social media and digital screen use was clearly motivated by genuine concern about their possible harmful consequences. In effect, interest groups such as the RSPH, co-authors of *#StatusofMind*, were identifying social media and digital screens as causes of social harm – things that, although not criminalised, might nevertheless result in real damage and distress. However, the exaggerated nature of their anxiety meant it risked causing harmful consequences of its own. Most obviously, it risked elevating public concern about social media and digital screen use to an extent that was unnecessary. More importantly, calls for tighter regulation of social media and attempts to limit time spent on digital screens also risked undermining social media's widely recognised potential as a source of useful help and information. (See, for example, Harper *et al.* (2015) on the internet as a positive resource in LGBTQ+ (lesbian, gay, bisexual, trans, queer, plus) young people's identity development and mental health.)

An interesting example of that problem was highlighted by Anna Lavis and Rachel Winter (2019). They noted that, under pressure from the UK government and the CMO for England, 'Instagram … altered its search engine so that it [was] no longer possible to search for hashtags relating to self-harm.' As they went on to say, this meant that 'searching for #selfharmsupport also return[ed] no results.' Lavis and Winter did not deny the disturbing and potentially dangerous nature of some of the material related to self-harm available on the internet. Their point was that, unless great care is taken, attempts to regulate such material can have consequences that cause harm in other ways. In this instance, an intervention undertaken with the best intentions also blocked access to sources of support for people at risk of harming themselves.

The second question, concerning the relationship between *individuals and society*, can be addressed via a further question: if the authors of *#StatusofMind*, and others like them, were caught up in a moral panic, should they have known better? For example, should they have taken a more balanced view of the research literature on social media and

digital screen use? There is certainly a case to be made that
#StatusofMind should have been more rigorous in reviewing the
evidence. However, we should not ignore how easy it is to be swept up
in a moral panic. Even the most seasoned and critical observers – even
sociologists of moral panics – can retrospectively find that, what they
had assumed to be genuine concern about an objective problem, was
exaggerated and ill-founded. Moral panics are powerful things and, as
such, they illustrate something important about the relationship
between *individuals and society*. How we see and experience the world is
profoundly shaped by social forces, often in ways of which we are not
wholly aware. None of us can stand outside the society of which we
are a part and our ability to see it objectively will always be partial.

That point brings us to the third and final question, how does the
social influence technology and technology influence the social? The
moral panic surrounding young people's use of social media and digital
screens seems to have involved what was referred to earlier in the
book as a 'technologically determinist' point of view. In other words,
something in the design or functionality of social media and digital
screens was assumed to be inherently harmful to young people, as if
using social media and digital screens would, on its own, cause
depression or anxiety. In another version, that assumption was
modified such that behaviours associated with the use of social media
and digital screens (such as poor sleep quality or comparing yourself to
others apparently more successful than you) were thought to cause
harm. In either case, the technology or a behaviour it promoted was
positioned as 'determining' or the direct cause of the harmful
consequence. Technological determinism is, in fact, a common theme
in many of the techno-panics that have occurred over the years. For
example, responses to *The Sorrows of Young Werther* appeared to
assume that the mere act of reading the novel drove young people to
suicide. Parallel fears were expressed in response to the comic craze of
the 1950s and 'video nasties' in the 1980s.

It was precisely technological determinism that Vicky Goodyear,
someone you met in Reading 12.1, was seeking to counter. From her
more sociological point of view, in order to understand technology's
meanings and consequences, it is always necessary to investigate the
social context in which it is used. As is explored elsewhere in this
book, this point does not mean the technology plays no part in those
meanings and consequences. To take a simple example, social media
allow us to be in contact with far larger numbers of people than earlier

technologies did. That capacity is built into the technology itself. Goodyear's point is that different young people do very different things with that capacity, some of which are positive (for example, sustaining and enhancing friendship networks; providing help and support); some of which are negative (for example, cyberbullying or circulating potentially harmful information). As a result, what young people do with social media, what this means to them, and the consequences it has cannot be assumed in advance or simply 'read-off' from the technology. Each must be established context by context, social group by social group. Consequently, as with other examples explored in this book, we can say the technical and the social influence each other: they are 'co-constructed'.

7 Conclusion

As you have seen, the main argument advanced in this chapter was that, roughly in the years 2017–19, the UK saw a moral panic over young people's use of social media and digital screens. That moral panic never became full-blown in the sense that the agents promoting the panic (academics, public health experts, youth advocacy groups, elements of the news media and government) did not succeed in establishing a comprehensive public consensus on the nature and severity of the threat posed by social media and digital screen use. Neither did they succeed in enacting their preferred regulatory responses (such as official guidance on limiting screen time). Nevertheless, many of the criteria for judging the existence of a moral panic were met. Most important, fears about the threat social media and digital screen use were said to pose can be shown to have been exaggerated. Although not without foundation, they were clearly in excess of the evidence available at the time.

References

Allen, V. (2019) 'Ban your toddler from TV and iPads', *Daily Mail*, 25 April, p. 1.

All-Party Parliamentary Group (2019) *#NewFilters to manage the impact of social media on young people's mental health and wellbeing.* Available at: https://www.rsph.org.uk/our-work/policy/wellbeing/new-filters.html (Accessed: 3 February 2020).

Bauman, Z. (2000) *Liquid modernity.* Cambridge: Polity.

Beck, U. (1992) *Risk society: towards a new modernity.* Translated from the German by M. Ritter. London: Sage.

Booker, C., Kelly, Y.J. and Sacker, A. (2018) 'Gender differences in the associations between age trends of social media interaction and well-being among 10-15 year olds in the UK', *BMC Public Health*, 18(321), pp. 1–12. doi: 10.1186/s12889-018-5220-4.

Cohen, S. (2011) *Folk devils and moral panics: the creation of the mods and rockers.* 3rd edn. Abingdon: Routledge Classics.

Critcher, C. (2008) 'Moral panic analysis: past, present and future', *Sociology Compass*, 2(4), pp. 1127–1144. doi: 10.1111/j.1751-9020.2008.00122.x.

Davies, S.C., Atherton, F., Calderwood, C. and McBride, M. (2019) *United Kingdom Chief Medical Officers' commentary on 'Screen-based activities and children and young people's mental health and psychosocial wellbeing: a systematic map of reviews'.* Department of Health and Social Care. Available at: https://www.gov.uk/government/publications/uk-cmo-commentary-on-screen-time-and-social-media-map-of-reviews (Accessed: 6 February 2020).

Department for Digital, Culture, Media and Sport (2019) *Online Harms White Paper* (CP 57). Available at: https://www.gov.uk/government/consultations/online-harms-white-paper (Accessed: 3 February 2020).

Department of Health and Social Care (2018) *Matt Hancock warns of dangers of social media on children's mental health* [Press Release]. 2 October. Available at: https://www.gov.uk/government/news/matt-hancock-warns-of-dangers-of-social-media-on-childrens-mental-health (Accessed: 27 September 2019).

Erfani, S.S. and Abedin, B. (2018) 'Impacts of the use of social network sites on users' psychological well-being: a systematic review', *Journal of the Association for Information Science and Technology*, 69(7), pp. 900–912. doi: 10.1002/asi.24015.

Etchells, P. *et al.* (2017) 'Screen time guidelines need to be based on evidence, not hype', *The Guardian*, 6 January. Available at: https://www.theguardian.com/science/head-quarters/2017/jan/06/screen-time-guidelines-need-to-be-built-on-evidence-not-hype (Accessed: 31 October 2019).

Furedi, F. (2015) 'The media's first moral panic', *History Today*, 65(11), pp. 46–48.

Gilbert, J. (1986) *A cycle of outrage: America's reaction to the juvenile delinquent in the 1950s*. Oxford: Oxford University Press.

Goode, E. and Ben-Yehuda, N. (2009) *Moral panic: the social construction of deviance*. 2nd edn. Chichester: Wiley-Blackwell.

Harper, G.W., Serrano, P.A., Bruce, D., Bauermeister, J.A. and the Adolescent Trials Network for HIV/AIDS Interventions (2015) 'The internet's multiple roles in facilitating the sexual orientation identity development of gay and bisexual male adolescents', *American Journal of Men's Health*, 10(5), pp. 359–376. doi: 10.1177/1557988314566227.

Hier, S. (2019) 'Moral panics and digital-media logic: notes on a changing research agenda', *Crime, Media, Culture*, 15(2), pp. 379–388. doi: 10.1177/1741659018780183.

Hoare, E., Milton, K., Foster, C. and Allender, S. (2016) 'The associations between sedentary behaviour and mental health among adolescents: a systematic review', *International Journal of Behavioral Nutrition and Physical Activity*, 13(1), p. 108. doi: 10.1186/s12966-016-0432-4.

House of Commons Science and Technology Committee (2019) *Impact of social media and screen-use on young people's health: Fourteenth Report of Session 2017-19*. London: House of Commons, pp. 9–12. Available at: https://www.parliament.uk/business/committees/committees-a-z/commons-select/science-and-technology-committee/publications/ (Accessed: 30 October 2019).

Kalpidou, M., Costin, D. and Morris, J. (2011) 'The relationship between Facebook and the well-being of undergraduate college students', *CyberPsychology, Behavior, and Social Networking,* 14(4), pp. 183–189. doi: 10.1089/cyber.2010.0061.

Kardefelt-Winther, D. (2017) *How does the time children spend using digital technology impact their mental well-being, social relationships and physical activity? An evidence-focused literature review.* . Innocenti Discussion Paper 2017-02. Florence: UNICEF Office of Research – Innocenti. Available at: https://www.unicef-irc.org/publications/pdf/Children-digital-technology-wellbeing.pdf (Accessed: 22 Nov 2019).

Kelly, Y., Zilanawala, A., Booker, C. and Sacker, A. (2018) 'Social media use and adolescent mental health: findings from the UK millennium cohort study', *EClinicalMedicine*, 6, pp. 59–68. doi: 10.1016/j.eclinm.2018.12.005.

Lavis, A. and Winter, R. (2019) 'Self-harm and social media: a knee-jerk ban on content could actually harm young people', *The Conversation*, 7 February. Available at: https://theconversation.com/self-harm-and-social-media-a-knee-jerk-ban-on-content-could-actually-harm-young-people-111381 (Accessed: 28 February 2020).

Mahendran, K. (2012) 'Describing childhood intimacies', in Banks, M. and Barnett, C. (eds) *The uses of social science*. Milton Keynes: The Open University, pp. 15–52.

McCrae, N., Gettings, S. and Purssell, E. (2017) 'Social media and depressive symptoms in childhood and adolescence: a systematic review', *Adolescent Research Review*, 2(4), pp. 315–330. doi: 10.1007/s40894-017-0053-4.

McRobbie, A. and Thornton, S.L. (1995) 'Rethinking "moral panic" for multi-mediated social worlds', *British Journal of Sociology*, 46(4), pp. 559–574. Available at: https://www.jstor.org/stable/591571 (Accessed: 3 February 2020).

Meier, E.P. and Gray, J. (2014) 'Facebook photo activity associated with body image disturbance in adolescent girls', *Cyberpsychology, Behavior, and Social Networking*, 17(4), pp. 199–206. doi.org/10.1089/cyber.2013.0305.

Orben, A. and Przybylski, A.K. (2019a) 'Screens, teens and psychological well-being: evidence from three time-use-diary studies', *Psychological Science*, 30(5), pp. 682–696. doi:10.1177/0956797619830329.

Orben, A. and Przybylski, A.K. (2019b) 'The association between adolescent well-being and digital technology use', *Nature Human Behaviour*, 3(2), pp. 173–182. doi: 10.1038/s41562-018-0506-1.

Orben, A. and Przybylski, A.K. (2019c) 'We're told that too much screen time hurts our kids. Where's the evidence?', *The Guardian*, 7 July. Available at: https://www.theguardian.com/commentisfree/2019/jul/07/too-much-screen-time-hurts-kids-where-is-evidence (Accessed: 24 October 2019).

Orben, A., Dienlin, T. and Przybylski, A.K. (2019) 'Social media's enduring effect on adolescent life satisfaction', *PNAS*, 116(21), pp. 10226–10228. doi: 10.1073/pnas.1902058116.

Royal Society for Public Health (2017) *#StatusofMind: social media and young people's mental health and wellbeing*. Available at: https://www.rsph.org.uk/our-work/campaigns/status-of-mind.html (Accessed: 3 February 2020).

Thompson, K. (1998) *Moral panics*. London: Routledge.

Twenge, J.M. (2020) 'Why increases in adolescent depression may be linked to the technological environment', *Current Opinion in Psychology*, 32(1), pp. 82–94. doi: 10.1016/j.copsyc.2019.06.036.

Twenge, J.M., Joiner, T.E., Rogers, M.L. and Martin, G.N. (2018) 'Increases in depressive symptoms, suicide-related outcomes, and suicide rates among US adolescents after 2010 and links to increased new media screen time', *Clinical Psychological Science*, 6(1), pp. 3–17. doi: 10.1177/267026177333376.

Woods, H.C. and Scott, H. (2016) '#Sleepyteens: social media use in adolescence is associated with poor sleep quality, anxiety, depression and low self-esteem', *Journal of Adolescence*, 51(1), pp. 41–49. doi: 10.1016/j.adolescence.2016.05.008.

Chapter 13
Algorithms

Jessamy Perriam

Contents

1 Introduction

In 1999, a BBC reporter interviewed rock star, David Bowie. Among other achievements, Bowie was an early adopter and innovator of the internet, setting up a website and an internet service provider in 1998. The interviewer asked Bowie what he thought of the internet; more than 20 years later it reads somewhat like prophecy:

> Bowie: I don't even think we've seen the tip of the iceberg. I think the potential of what the internet is going to do to society, both good and bad is unimaginable. I think we're actually on the cusp of something exhilarating and terrifying.
>
> Interviewer: It's just a tool though, isn't it?
>
> Bowie: No it's not, no. No it's an alien life form.
>
> Interviewer: It's simply a different delivery system there. You're arguing about something more profound.
>
> Bowie: Oh yeah, and I'm talking about the actual context and the state of content is going to be so different to anything that we can really envisage at the moment. Where the interplay between the user and the provider will be so in simpatico it's going to crush our ideas of what mediums are all about.
>
> (BBC Newsnight, 2016, 10:35)

In this final chapter of *Understanding Digital Societies*, we examine the role of algorithms in society. Much as the interview with David Bowie indicated, algorithms have the potential to be both good and bad in almost unimaginable ways.

Algorithms can be difficult to describe, partly because people from a range of professional backgrounds and interests describe them differently. This difficulty in defining algorithms results in confusion about what is specifically being discussed, debated and problematised. This presents us with a confusing picture, which often deters members of the public from considering the impact of algorithms on society. But algorithms are being increasingly used in everyday life, from what we buy, what we watch and listen to and, the search results we are presented with when we look up something online.

In this chapter, you will explore how *people and things* have an impact on *individuals and society*, increasing *power* for some and *inequality* for others. To be sure, while some algorithms have a positive influence on the world, matching people with partners, donor organs and the perfect song, it is not always a story of convenience and connection. Algorithms need to be critically examined because they combine all of the sociological threads in a perfect storm of personal troubles and public issues. Throughout the chapter, you will encounter readings and case studies that will help you understand algorithms and their impact on society.

While reading this chapter, you are encouraged to think sociologically about the issues raised, considering what you have read throughout the book. What are the personal troubles and public issues being described? Where might social harm be occurring and how might we observe it?

1.1 Teaching aims

The aims of this chapter are for you to:

- define what an algorithm is

- understand how algorithms work

- recognise the impact algorithms have on society

- appreciate that algorithms raise issues of power and inequality.

2 Defining algorithms

You may have heard many definitions of algorithms. One of them possibly describes algorithms as a big mathematical problem. Other definitions might try to relate an algorithm to a recipe, where ingredients get mixed together and cooked with a certain product or outcome in mind. While others try to define algorithms as a series of 'If ... then ...' statements, much like a flow chart where the outcome depends on the answer given to certain questions.

Algorithms rely on data to work. If there is no data available, there is nothing to run an algorithm on. In theory, the more data there is available, the more questions you can ask of it.

Figure 13.1 We can think of flow charts as basic representations of algorithms. Algorithms ask certain questions of the data given to them and make decisions based on the responses.

The advent of big data has also given rise to larger, more complex datasets. These are processed and used by corporations and governments to make decisions that impact the lives of users and citizens. Algorithms are often used to process these datasets in real-time – so when you are shopping online, the store may suggest items that you might like based on analysis of past customer preferences or target you with customised advertisements. Alternatively, police datasets may be processed to suggest places or people who may be at risk or likely to commit offences. Some people think that there should be more clarity and transparency when it comes to defining how algorithms use this data. In the following reading, Rosenblat and colleagues describe the problem in further detail.

Reading 13.1

Alex Rosenblat, Tamara Kneese and danah boyd, 'Algorithmic Accountability'

Algorithms can be hugely beneficial in sorting through vast troves of information to deliver what is potentially the most useful sort. Automated algorithms can use a sequence of well-defined steps and instructions to generate categories for filtering information based on a combination of motives about a desirable outcome. In the final expression of that combination, the elements of uncertainty, subjective interpretation, arbitrary choice, accidents, and other ingredients in the mix are rendered invisible, and what is displayed to the end-user who interfaces with the algorithm's product is just the functionality of the technology. ...

Designing software to mobilize and unlock the supposed power of the "big data" phenomenon is often focused on the best technical ways to achieve a particular outcome, like personalizing search results so that a user gets information that is tailored to their interests. Algorithms break down information into certain constituent parts, and reconfigure it into a new production of information to fulfil particular goals. This can have huge societal benefits. For example, a Microsoft Research team has come up with an algorithm to help medical researchers sort through data on 120,000 individuals in a few hours, in contrast with current algorithms that cannot make computations on such large datasets. This algorithm has the potential to identify a patient's risk for diseases, and even which drugs might be best suited to them.

Can any problem be resolved using an algorithm? The social, cultural, and political impact of an algorithmic solution has consequences that play out far beyond the technical innovation behind the restructuring of information. Does an algorithmic-orientation to solving technical problems mitigate or downplay the social, political, or ethical issues at stake? For example, one study found that Google's AdSense algorithm, which automates targeted advertising to serve users the adverts that are most relevant to them, is more likely to suggest possible arrest records for racially associated names that are being queried, like Trevon Jones, than for Caucasian names like Geoffrey. How can this association affect someone's job prospects, or their application to rent an apartment?

Negative adverts linked to a person's name are likely to get more clicks than neutral or positive adverts. Higher click-rates increase the value of those adverts, which makes them appear more often, thereby reproducing the prejudicial impact. The discrimination produced in the search results is unintentional, but do companies have an obligation to correct for prejudice? If an algorithmic solution is being presented, it is useful to examine how the problem is being framed? Is it possible to build an algorithm that is either bias-free, or has corrective measures built in for explicit biases? What kind of mechanisms should exist for evaluating discriminatory or prejudicial outcomes, and what criteria would they use? Are there methods other than reverse engineering for evaluating allegedly prejudicial outcomes?

(Rosenblat *et al.*, 2014, pp. 1–2)

In this excerpt from a short paper about algorithmic accountability, you can see a working definition. Algorithms are described as having an ability to process vast amounts of information that would otherwise take humans a large amount of time to complete. The authors of the paper also describe how algorithms solve technical problems. But crucially, the paper also calls into question whether it is necessary to solve every problem with an algorithm, or whether the creators consider the potential for negative outcomes when devising an algorithm. In this sense, the authors are asking whether the people and companies developing the algorithms have adequately considered the potential social harm that may result from this data being acted upon and processed.

In the next reading, anthropologist Nick Seaver draws upon **ethnographic fieldwork** to look at whether algorithms consist of more than a set of instructions. Seaver investigated how recommendation algorithms were used at a music streaming company, and as he explains in the reading below, we can consider how people contribute to algorithms. He also highlights that many of the people working to produce algorithms have trouble deciding a common definition to focus their work. As with many readings you may have encountered, it is not vital for you to have a complete understanding of every portion of the reading, rather you need to understand Seaver's main argument.

Reading 13.2

Nick Seaver, 'Algorithms as culture: some tactics for the ethnography of algorithmic systems'

A straightforward solution to our definitional crisis would be to take some expert definition as decisive: let computer scientists define "algorithms" and then examine how those things interact with our own areas of expertise. Like many straightforward solutions, this one has complications. As Paul Dourish has noted, "the limits of the term algorithm are determined by social engagements rather than by technological or material constraints" (2016: 3). That is to say, different people, in different historical moments and social situations have defined algorithms, and their salient qualities, differently. A data scientist working at Facebook in 2017, a university mathematician working on a proof in 1940, and a doctor establishing treatment procedures in 1995 may all claim, correctly, to be working on "algorithms," but this does not mean they are talking about the same thing. An uncritical reliance on experts takes their coherence for granted and runs the risk of obscuring a key interest of critical scholars: what happens at the edges of knowledge regimes.

Given this instability and diversity, Dourish advances an anthropological case for taking on a "proper" expert definition of algorithms: we should do it not because this definition offers "a foundational truth of the nature of algorithms as natural occurrences," but because it is what engineers do (2016: 2). […]

But what exactly is the emic definition of "algorithm," and where should we find it? Dourish's argument hinges on a definition of group boundaries. He writes:

> When technical people get together, the person who says, "I do algorithms" is making a different statement than the person who says, "I study software engineering" or the one who says, "I'm a data scientist" and the nature of these differences matters to any understanding of the relationship between data, algorithms, and society. (Dourish, 2016: 3)

The boundaries of the "algorithm" are social boundaries: between algorithm people and other "technical people," and between technical people and their non-technical others, who may not understand the definitions in play. Now imagine an ethnographer encountering these technical people; if she did not know what an algorithm was supposed to be, she would have to suss it out from how they speak and act. ("*These* people say 'algorithm' whenever they want those people to stop talking…" "*Those* people talk about algorithms like precious intellectual property, while *these* people talk about them like plumbing…") Dourish suggests that, if an ethnographer does this, she will end up where he begins: "In computer science terms, an algorithm is an abstract, formalized description of a computational procedure" (2016: 3).

This is, however, an empirical question: Do the people who "do" algorithms today actually treat them according to this "proper" definition?

Reference

Dourish P (2016) Algorithms and their others: Algorithmic culture in context. *Big Data & Society* 3(2): 1–11.

(Seaver, 2017, p. 2–3)

From the readings in this section, you can see how it becomes helpful to consider that there are many definitions of what an algorithm is. And it is also the case that differing definitions help us to understand how people with different interests work with them in slightly different ways to achieve different ends.

For the remainder of this chapter, our focus turns away from defining algorithms to considering the outcomes of algorithms in society and how they might relate to the concept of social harm. We also consider some of the arguments around seeking accountability when algorithms go wrong.

3 Algorithms, racism and oppression

In the following extract, you will read about racism and sexism embedded within algorithms. Of course, there is nothing inherently racist or sexist about algorithms or technology, but these things are produced by people who may or may not be aware of their own biases. In the following reading, Safiya Noble describes how it is important to consider *who* is creating algorithms and *how* their values and standpoints become ingrained in what they create. Sometimes these values are deliberately included and other times they may be included unknowingly as a form of unconscious bias. As you read this excerpt from the introduction to Noble's book *Algorithms of Oppression*, consider the potential for social harm to occur. Additionally, consider where *power and inequality* lie in algorithms. Please be advised, the reading contains language that some readers may find offensive.

Reading 13.3

Safiya Umoja Noble, 'Algorithms of oppression: how search engines reinforce racism'

Part of the challenge of understanding algorithmic oppression is to understand that mathematical formulations to drive automated decisions are made by human beings. While we often think of terms such as "big data" and "algorithms" as being benign, neutral or objective, they are anything but. The people who make these decisions hold all types of values, many of which openly promote racism, sexism, and false notions of meritocracy, which is well documented in studies of Silicon Valley and other tech corridors.

For example, in the midst of a federal investigation of Google's alleged persistent wage gap, where women are systematically paid less than men in the company's workforce, an "antidiversity" manifesto authored by James Damore went viral in August 2017 [Matsakis 2017], supported by many Google employees, arguing that women are psychologically inferior and incapable of being as good at software engineering as men, among other patently false and sexist assertions. ... What this antidiversity screed has underscored for me as I write this book is that some of the very people who are developing search algorithms and architecture are willing to promote sexist and racist attitudes openly at work and beyond while we are supposed to believe that these same employees are developing "neutral" or "objective" decision-making tools. Human beings are developing the digital platforms we use, and as I present evidence of the recklessness and lack of regard that is often shown to women and people of colour in some of the output of these systems, it will become increasingly difficult for technology companies to separate their systematic and inequitable employment practices, and the far-right ideological bents of some of their employees, from the products they make for the public.

...

I situate my work against the backdrop of a twelve-year professional career in multicultural marketing and advertising, where I was invested in building corporate brands and selling products to African Americans and Latinos (before I became a university professor). Back then, I believed, like many urban marketing professionals, that companies must pay attention to the needs of people of colour and demonstrate respect for consumers by offering services to communities of colour, just as is done for most everyone else. After all, to be responsive and responsible to marginalized consumers was to create more market opportunity. I spent an equal amount of time doing risk management and public relations to insulate companies from any adverse risk to sales that they might experience from inadvertent or deliberate snubs to consumers of colour who might perceive a brand as racist or insensitive. Protecting my former clients from enacting racial and gender insensitivity and helping them bolster their brands by creating deep emotional and psychological attachments to their products among communities of color was my professional concern for many years, which made an experience I had in fall 2010 deeply impactful. In just a few minutes while searching on the web, I experienced the perfect storm of insult and injury that I could not turn away from. While Googling things on the Internet that might be interesting to my stepdaughter and nieces, I was overtaken by the results. My search on the keywords "black girls" yielded HotBlackPussy.com as the first hit.

Hit indeed.

Since that time, I have spent innumerable hours teaching and researching all the ways in which it could be that Google could completely fail when it came to providing reliable or credible information about women and people of color yet experience seemingly no repercussions whatsoever. Two years after this incident, I collected searches again, only to find similar results …

In 2012, I wrote an article for *Bitch* magazine about how women and feminism are marginalized in search results. By August 2012, Panda (an update to Google's search algorithm) had been released, and pornography was no longer the first series of results for "black girls"; but other girls and women of colour, such as Latinas and Asians, were still pornified. By August of that year, the algorithm changed, and porn was suppressed in the case of a search on "black girls". I often wonder what kind of pressures account for the changing of search results over time. It is impossible to know when and what influences proprietary algorithmic design, other than that human beings are designing them and that they are not up for public discussions, except as we engage in critique and protest.

Reference

Matsakis, L. (2017, August 5). Google Employee's Anti-Diversity Manifesto Goes "Internally Viral." Motherboard. Retrieved from https://motherboard.vice.com.

(Noble, 2018, pp. 1–4)

From the excerpt above, you can identify the inequality that occurred with Google's search results. Two questions become apparent: how did the algorithm become biased for the inequality to occur? How might what Noble describes be considered socially harmful, and to whom does it present social harm? To answer the first questions, we need to look at the excerpt from a *people and things* perspective and we are required to examine whether it is the algorithm (the thing) or the people who, in creating the algorithm, coded in bias when putting it together.

When we talk about bias in the technology industry, it is important to consider the diversity of those working on algorithms. The demographics of Silicon Valley companies skew heavily towards white and Asian men from middle-to-high socio-economic backgrounds. In the years 2014–15, technology companies such as Apple, Google, Yahoo and Facebook disclosed their diversity statistics, with most companies stating that 15–20% of their workforce comprised of women, while 1–2% of staff identified as Black, as this quote from a USA Today article explains:

> By 2040, the U.S. will be a minority majority, with 42% of the country black or Hispanic.
>
> "I bet we'll be able to do some really interesting business case studies in 10 years and see what companies did and didn't make it — and who had the most diverse teams from top to bottom," Kelly said.
>
> With the technology sector fueling the U.S. economy, the low rate of participation in high tech also threatens to drive up the unemployment rate for blacks and Hispanics, which is already three times the national average.
>
> Computer science jobs are the fastest growing and command the highest salaries. Yet just one in 14 technical employees in Silicon Valley is black or Hispanic.
>
> "The numbers are not where we want them to be," said Sarah Stuart, manager of global diversity and talent inclusion at Google.
>
> Nationally, blacks make up 12% of the U.S. workforce and Hispanics 14%.
>
> At Google, 3% of the staff are Hispanic and 2% black. At Yahoo and Facebook 4% are Hispanic and 2% black
>
> (Guynn and Weise, 2014)

While this does not mean that technology companies are inherently racist, classist or sexist, it does mean that they have blind spots. In particular, it means that decisions about issues and values are being made that impact on people who are not present in the decision-making process. How these tools then work in practice will consequently have an influence on people's lives. In settings where women of colour and other minority groups are not represented in the teams making crucial decisions about technology, we see situations where technology produces inequalities. The people affected by these crucial decisions have not been taken into consideration either through ignorance or deliberate act.

Once Safiya Noble highlighted the algorithmic bias that had occurred with those search results, Google corrected the algorithm. But it is not the first time, nor will it probably be the last, that technologies reflect the unconscious biases or blind spots of their creators.

4 Algorithms and the digital sociological imagination

As has been already discussed in this chapter, it is easy to know when an algorithm has produced a harmful outcome, but it is difficult to examine the processes that contributed to that particular outcome occurring. This difficulty in understanding the processes that have happened to data is often referred to as **black-boxing**. But while we as sociologists cannot examine the algorithm itself, we can use our sociological imaginations (see Chapter 1) to observe, analyse and bring to light the personal troubles and public issues that are implicated in algorithmic use.

In 2019, the United Nations' special rapporteur on extreme poverty and human rights, Philip Alston, described the problematic use of algorithms in welfare systems around the world. In his report, Alston highlights examples of the public issues that some of the world's poorest are facing as a result of the rollout of digitally-enabled welfare systems (such as Universal Credit in the UK).

> [T]he embrace of the digital welfare state is presented as an altruistic and noble enterprise designed to ensure that citizens benefit from new technologies, experience more efficient government, and enjoy higher levels of well-being. Often, however, the digitization of welfare systems has been accompanied by deep reductions in the overall welfare budget, a narrowing of the beneficiary pool, the elimination of some services, the introduction of demanding and intrusive forms of conditionality, the pursuit of behavioural modification goals, the imposition of stronger sanctions regimes, and a complete reversal of the traditional notion that the state should be accountable to the individual.
>
> These other outcomes are promoted in the name of efficiency, targeting, incentivizing work, rooting out fraud, strengthening responsibility, encouraging individual autonomy, and responding to the imperatives of fiscal consolidation. Through the invocation of what are often ideologically-charged terms, neoliberal economic policies are seamlessly blended into what are presented as cutting edge welfare reforms, which in turn are often facilitated, justified,

and shielded by new digital technologies. Although the latter are presented as being 'scientific' and neutral, they can reflect values and assumptions that are far removed from, and may be antithetical to, the principles of human rights. In addition, because of the relative deprivation and powerlessness of many welfare recipients, conditions, demands and forms of intrusiveness are imposed that would never have been accepted if they had instead been piloted in programs applicable to better-off members of the community.

Despite the enormous stakes involved not just for millions of individuals but for societies as a whole, these issues have, with a few notable exceptions, garnered remarkably little attention. The mainstream tech community has been guided by official pre-occupations with efficiency, budget-savings, and fraud detection. The welfare community has tended to see the technological dimensions as separate from the policy developments, rather than as being integrally linked. And those in the human rights community concerned with technology have understandably been focused instead on concerns such as the emergence of the surveillance state, the potentially fatal undermining of privacy, the highly discriminatory impact of many algorithms, and the consequences of the emerging regime of surveillance capitalism

(Alston, 2019, pp. 3–4)

This excerpt outlines some of the motivations for governments around the world to implement digital welfare systems. These include economic reasons where governments believe that they can make cost reductions in providing welfare to citizens. In other circumstances, governments may believe that they can use a digitised service to track citizens in more efficient ways and therefore disincentivise fraud and incentivise citizens to re-enter the workforce, even if for many reasons they may not be able to take part in work.

As sociologists, our concern begins to emerge when discrimination, inequality and power imbalances occur. The main problem with algorithms – along with other digital solutions – being deployed in welfare systems is that these digital systems make it difficult to seek accountability or ask questions of those responsible for maintaining the system. In this way, algorithms in welfare systems become a problem of *people and things* being implicated with *power and inequality*. And this can lead to dire circumstances. Consider a person who has problems accessing digital services due to a lack of economic capital. What happens when they need to use a digital service urgently to respond to a problem with their welfare payment?

In the Ken Loach film, *I, Daniel Blake* (2016) we see a fictionalised example of this happening when the main character Daniel Blake is unemployed due to a heart condition. For the first time in his life, he is forced to interact with the UK's Department for Work and Pensions to receive a regular welfare payment until he is well enough to return to work. In one scene, Daniel Blake is in his local library using a computer to fill out a form to ensure he receives his welfare payment. Having spent most of his life as a carpenter, he has not needed to learn how to use a computer or the internet. We see him attempt to follow the librarian's instructions to fill out the online form and realise that digital literacy – or a lack of – is a barrier towards people accessing welfare that they are legally entitled to.

Figure 13.2   In *I, Daniel Blake* we see the film's main character having trouble accessing the UK's welfare system using digital means.

While *I, Daniel Blake* questions the inequality involved in requiring citizens to use 'digital-by-default' systems to access welfare, there are more indications that we need to be concerned about automation and algorithms in the welfare state. Consider this extract from an article in *The Guardian*:

Benefits system automation could plunge claimants deeper into poverty

The UK government is accelerating the development of robots in the benefits system in a digitisation drive that vulnerable claimants fear could plunge them further into hunger and debt, the Guardian has learned.

The Department for Work and Pensions has hired nearly 1,000 new IT staff in the past 18 months, and has increased spending to about £8m a year on a specialist "intelligent automation garage" where computer scientists are developing over 100 welfare robots, deep learning and intelligent automation for use in the welfare system.

As well as contracts with the outsourcing multinationals IBM, Tata Consultancy and CapGemini, it is also working with UiPath, a New York-based firm co-founded by Daniel Dines, the world's first "bot billionaire" who last month said: "I want a robot for every person." [...]

The DWP is also testing artificial intelligence to judge the likelihood that citizens' claims about their childcare and housing costs are true when they apply for benefits.

It has deployed 16 bots to communicate with claimants and help process claims and is building a "virtual workforce" to take over some of the jobs of humans. One recent tender document requested help to build "systems that ... can autonomously carry out tasks without human intervention".

[...]

The DWP believes welfare transactions could be handled more quickly, accurately and cheaply using robotic process automation and is developing it for use in UC.

But claimants have warned the existing automation in UC's "digital by default" system has already driven some to hunger, breakdown and even attempted suicide. One described the online process as a "Kafka-like carousel", another as "hostile" and yet another as a "form of torture". Several said civil servants already appeared to be ruled by computer algorithms, unable to contradict their verdicts.

"We are striking the right balance between having a compassionate safety net on which we spend £95bn, and creating a digital service that suits the way most people use technology," said a DWP spokesperson. "Automation means we are improving accuracy, speeding up our service and freeing up colleagues' time so they can support the people who need it most."

But Frank Field, chairman of the Commons work and pensions select committee, warned that vulnerable claimants "will be left at the mercy of online systems that, even now, leave all too many people teetering on the brink of destitution".

(Booth, 2019)

Considering the article above, what do you think are the social harms that could arise from automating parts of the UK's welfare state with the use of algorithms? If as the article states, 'certain tasks would be carried out without human intervention', how then could a citizen challenge adverse outcomes? To examine this further, we need to visit Australia, where this scenario has already taken place.

5 Algorithms and accountability

While algorithms that recommend purchases or a new song to listen to can be quite innocuous and sometimes even helpful, there are times when algorithms can change lives with drastic consequences. One example of this is the increase of algorithms used in welfare systems across the world. Our focus turns to one example of the algorithms used in Australia's welfare system that has impacted some of their poorest and disadvantaged citizens.

Sociologist Paul Henman describes the situation in which Centrelink – Australia's welfare agency – chose to replace human checks on welfare recipients' income with an algorithm.

Reading 13.4

Paul Henman, 'The computer says "DEBT": Towards a critical sociology of algorithms and algorithmic governance'

In the lead up to Christmas 2016 and into the New Year, several media outlets published a series of exposés about Australia's social security delivery agency, Centrelink, automated issuance of about 20,000 'debt' letters a week to current and former clients. These letters had been automatically issued to people following "discrepancies" algorithmically found in data-matching income data held by Centrelink with that held by the Australian Tax Office (ATO). The letters asked individuals to log into their government account and confirm or correct their income for the financial year in question, their response was then used to algorithmically determine if a debt was owed, and then automated recovery processes, either by withholding social security benefits or by referring the matter to private debt collectors, with an automatic ten percent debt collection charge added to the alleged debt (Pett & Cosier 2017).

This media coverage was not driven by a fascination of government's use of automation in new ways, but by a concern of its effects on many vulnerable Australians and of what seemed to be an error-riddled, unaccountable and politically-driven process.

Dubbed 'Robodebt', this case study of government by algorithm demonstrates the urgent need for a critical analysis of algorithms that interrogates both the socio-technical design and development of algorithms, as well as the socio-organizational location of their operation. From a government practitioner perspective, Robodebt demonstrates the need for governments' development and use of algorithms to be acutely aware of the social-embeddedness of their use – that algorithms interface with complex social circumstances that are not readily encoded – and not just to think of algorithms as a technical challenge of algorithmic design for administrative efficiency.

...

Analyzing government by algorithm is tricky because of limited awareness of an algorithm's presence, the highly technical and complex nature of algorithms that are often impenetrable 'black boxes', and government sensitivity around administrative processes, particularly when algorithms are developed and operated by third party contractors. Accordingly, government by algorithm can typically only be analyzed by their reported effects and by abstract accounts of what government and others say about them.

...

To be sure, Robodebt is more than one algorithm, but an automated system that involved input from Centrelink clients, a system akin to Bovens and Zouridis' (2002) concept of 'system level bureaucracy'. While several elements in this process had been previously automated (Henman 1997), there was also considerable human involvement by government officials and had not been joined-up. With 'Robodebt', once the algorithm started, the chain of events operated without input from government officials.

Did the Robodebt algorithm perform as intended, or as publicly described? Based on media reports and an understanding of the *Social Security Act*, the short answer is 'no'. In short, individuals who had correctly reported their income to both Centrelink and the ATO, and had their entitlements appropriately assessed on that information, subsequently had debts raised by the Robodebt system. ...

In some cases the name of the employer organization was listed differently in the ATO and Centrelink databases, yet were the same employer (Pett & Cosier 2017). This may have been due to differences in publicly recognized names reported by Centrelink clients to Centrelink, compared to formally registered business names reported to ATO by businesses. In such cases, the client had accurately reported income, but Robodebt concluded that the individual had exactly double the income than they had declared; the same income from two employers which were in fact the one. A more sophisticated algorithm could have been designed to detect that the two different names were the same organization.

...

Algorithms typically automate pre-existing administrative practices undertaken by other means including humans and paper forms. Such automation has effects. Algorithms change administrative processes, be it speeding them up, reducing ambiguity, increasing consistency, and removing (some) humans from the process. They can also enable new forms of administration possible (Henman 1997; 2010) and disrupt administrative principles (c.f. Henman 2005). These dynamics were evident in the Robodebt debacle in several ways.

... Prior to Robodebt, outcomes of data-matching suggestive of possible 'overpayment' were reviewed by Centrelink officers for checking. With Robodebt, not only did human checking of possible 'overpayments' cease, but Centrelink officers were directed to not intervene to halt Robodebt procedures even when human officers suspected the algorithm had incorrectly raised a debt (Knaus 2017a). This extraordinary (non-)intervention fundamentally breached public administrative principles of good administration and public governance.

Centrelink officers in walk-in offices and telecall centres were also directed not to engage with clients who sought to challenge their debts but direct the clients to the online system to contest their alleged debt, even when that system would not work for clients (McGrath 2017b). At its best, this practice constitutes poor public service delivery.

... In addition to removing Centrelink officers from the process, clients could only engage in very limited ways with Robodebt notices. In the initial directive for clients to confirm, correct or contest their income, clients' responses were limited and processes complex and hard to understand. The ability of clients to lodge an appeal to an alleged debt was also heavily constrained; it had to be done online through a newly constructed webpage that was reported to have been inoperable at times and very difficult to follow when operable. Clients were not able to lodge it with human Centrelink officers. ...

... Robodebt reversed the legal principle of innocent until proven guilty in several ways. Once an income discrepancy was observed and a letter was sent to a client to confirm, correct or explain the discrepancy, clients had 21 days to respond. In the case of no response, the Robodebt system automatically assumed the algorithm's calculations were correct and automatically raised a debt, which was automatically garnished from future social security payments (for ongoing clients) and automatically sent and on sold to private debt collectors in the case of former clients (Ombudsman 2017: 1-2).

References

Bovens, M., & Zouridis, S. 2002. From street-level to system-level bureaucracies: how information and communication technology is transforming administrative discretion and constitutional control. *Public administration review*, 62(2): 174-184.

Glenn, R. 2017. *Centrelink's automated debt raising and recovery system: A report about the Department of Human Services' online compliance intervention system for debt raising and recovery*, Report 02/2017, Canberra: Commonwealth Ombudsman.

Henman, P. 1997. Computer technology–a political player in social policy processes. *Journal of Social Policy*, 26(3): 323-340.

Henman, P. 2005. E-government, targeting and data profiling: policy and ethical issues of differential treatment. *Journal of E-government*, 2(1): 79-98.

Henman, P. 2010. *Governing electronically: E-government and the reconfiguration of public administration, policy and power*. Basingstoke: Palgrave.

Knaus, C. 2017a. Centrelink staff told not to fix mistakes in debt notices - whistleblower. *The Guardian*, 19 January.

McGrath, P. 2017b. Leaked Centrelink memo shows staff told not to process debt disputes in person. *ABC News*, 12 January.

Pett, H. & Cosier, C. 2017. We're all talking about the Centrelink debt controversy, but what is 'Robodebt' anyway?. *ABC News, Background Briefing*, 3 March.

(Henman, 2017, pp. 1–3)

From this excerpt of Henman's paper on algorithm use in the Australian social services, we learn a few things about the relations between power, inequality and technology. Firstly, we learn that the quality of data that goes into algorithms matters greatly to the outcomes for those who are impacted by the decisions made. In frank terms, the 'garbage in, garbage out' rule applies for the data that goes into algorithms and the potentially dire outcomes that may follow. Secondly, Henman outlines the assumptions made by the algorithm and, by extension, the people who have created and configured the way it works.

He also highlights a critical problem, one that is worth focusing on for a while. In the case of Robodebt, there was no clear path to gain accountability from the social services if a citizen suspected that there was an error and they were not liable for the debt. Further, there was an active discouragement of citizens challenging the algorithmic decision with welfare staff. This placed citizens in a terrible position. Individuals who found that the algorithm (or set of algorithms in this case) had incorrectly indicated they owed the government money were treated as if the problem was a private trouble. Yet as more and more stories of errors and inability to seek accountability from the human staff came to light, it became clear that the private trouble was in fact a public issue. But what does this mean in practice? It meant that many Australians had to experience the shock of receiving a letter demanding money that they likely did not have, and then endure the frustration of attempting to engage with an unresponsive digital system. Many would have experienced financial stress and reduced mental health. The Robodebt event is an issue because it calls us to questions our values as a society. Do we value digital systems that place those in need of assistance under greater stress? Or do we value digital systems that ensure fairness and trust?

6 Finding a way forward

The increasing use of algorithms in society seems concerning, especially when considering it from the standpoint of *power and inequality*. How do we go from recognising algorithm use in some parts of society as problematic, to taking steps to ensure that inequality and social harm is not furthered in society?

Many technology companies, academics and public sector organisations have been considering how algorithms might be made fair, ethical and accountable. But returning to the UN special rapporteur on extreme poverty and human rights' report, we can see questions arise as to whether these efforts will result in a genuine prevention of social harm for citizens on the receiving end of erroneous algorithmic decisions.

> **Reading 13.5**
>
> **Philip Alston, *Report of the Special rapporteur on extreme poverty and human rights***
>
> In response to growing calls for effective governmental regulation, the industry has gone into high gear in producing, influencing and embracing 'codes of ethics' and other non-binding standards purporting to 'regulate' digital technologies and their developers. Most, but by no means all, of these codes contain a reference to human rights, but the substance of human rights law is invariably lacking. Instead the token reference to human rights serves only to enhance claims to legitimacy and universality. Meanwhile, the relevant discussions of ethics are based on almost entirely open-ended notions that are not necessarily grounded in legal or even philosophical arguments, and can be shaped to suit the needs of the industry. As a result, there are serious problems of conceptual incoherence, conflicts among norms are rarely acknowledged, meaningful input is rarely sought from stakeholders, and accountability mechanisms are absent.[81] Even industry-employed ethicists acknowledge that "[i]f ethics is simply absorbed within the logics of market fundamentalism, meritocracy, and technological solutionism, it is unlikely that the tech sector will be able to offer a meaningful response to the desire for a more just and values-driven tech ecosystem."[82] Against this background, it is unsurprising that there are few public or

scholarly discussions of the *human rights* implications of digital welfare states.

...

The processes of digitization and the increasing role played by automated decision-making through the use of algorithms and artificial intelligence have, in at least some respects, facilitated a move towards a bureaucratic process and away from one premised on the right to social security or the right to social protection. Rather than the ideal of the State being accountable to the citizen to ensure that the latter is able to enjoy an adequate standard of living, the burden of accountability has in many ways been reversed. To a greater degree than has often been the case in the past, today's digital welfare state is often underpinned by the starting assumption that the individual is not a rights-holder but rather an applicant. In that capacity, a person must convince the decision-maker that they are 'deserving', that they satisfy the eligibility criteria, that they have fulfilled the often onerous obligations prescribed, and that they have no other means of subsistence. And much of this must be done electronically, regardless of the applicant's skills in that domain.

The right to social security encompasses the right "to access and maintain benefits, whether in cash or in kind, without discrimination"[99]. The imposition of technological requirements can make it impossible or very difficult for individuals to effectively access that right, thus making it effectively unaffordable.[100]

...

Digital technologies in general, and especially those central to the digital welfare state, are often presented as being both unavoidable and irresistible. If a country wants to be seen to be at the technological cutting edge, if its government wants to have the most efficient, economical and flexible welfare system available, and if its citizenry wants all of the convenience that comes from not having to provide ID in order to undertake various transactions, then a transition to a digital welfare state must be pursued. But quite apart from the choices that citizens and governments might make if they were fully informed and adequately consulted, the reality is that such decisions are all too often taken in the absence of sophisticated cost–benefit analyses. And when such analyses are undertaken, they consist of financial balance sheets that ignore what might be termed the fiscally invisible intangibles that underpin human rights. Values such as dignity, choice, self-respect, autonomy, self-determination, privacy, and a range of other factors are all traded off without being factored into the overall equation, all but guaranteeing that insufficient steps will be taken to ensure their role in the new digital systems.

Notes

81. Karen Yeung, Andrew Howes, and Ganna Pogrebna, 'AI Governance by Human Rights-Centred Design, Deliberation and Oversight: An End to Ethics Washing', forthcoming in M Dubber and F Pasquale (eds.), *The Oxford Handbook of AI Ethics* (2019), at https://ssrn.com/abstract=3435011, p. 22.

82. Jacob Metcalf, Emanuel Moss, and danah boyd [sic], 'Owning Ethics: Corporate Logics, Silicon Valley, and the Institutionalization of Ethics', 82 Social Research (2019) 449, at 473.

99. Committee on Economic, Social and Cultural Rights, The Right to Social Security, General Comment No. 19 (2007), para. 2.

100. Committee on Economic, Social and Cultural Rights, The Right to Social Security, General Comment No. 19 (2007), paras. 24-27.

(Alston, 2019, pp. 12, 14–15, 17; some notes omitted.)

Through this report, we can see that industry attempts to self-regulate against social harm and uphold human rights have not been as successful as the hype around setting up "codes of ethics" would suggest. But legal action has been tested as one way of preventing social harm from occurring. In the Netherlands, a court ruled that use of a system of algorithms to score fraud risk in welfare recipients was illegal:

The Dutch government's System Risk Indication (SyRI) legislation uses a non-disclosed algorithmic risk model to profile citizens and has been exclusively targeted at neighborhoods with mostly low-income and minority residents. Human rights campaigners have dubbed it a 'welfare surveillance state'.

A number of civil society organizations in the Netherlands and two citizens instigated the legal action against SyRI — seeking to block its use. The court has today ordered an immediate halt to the use of the system.

The ruling is being hailed as a landmark judgement by human rights campaigners, with the court basing its reasoning on European human rights law — specifically the right to a private life that's set out by Article 8 of the European Convention on Human Rights (ECHR) — rather than a dedicated provision in the EU's data protection framework (GDPR) which relates to automated processing.

(Lomas, 2020)

7 Conclusion

This chapter, much like the rest of this book, has traversed a lot of ground. In this chapter, we have discussed the difficulty in defining algorithms in a way that is meaningful to all: technologists, ethicists and citizens. This, in turn, makes it tricky to critique and interrogate a digital object that has not entirely been agreed upon or defined. This chapter also addressed the role diversity has to play in creating algorithms that take into account the needs and perspectives of many in society, rather than just those of the people who have written the code and engineered a solution to a design problem. We have also highlighted the common inability to unpack the decisions and actions that have taken place within an often black-boxed algorithm when there may be reasons to dispute the result.

Throughout this chapter, you have also seen real-life (or empirical) examples from welfare states around the world of what is at stake when algorithms produce unexpected or unjust outcomes. Through using the sociological imagination, you can see that it is important to gather accounts of the personal troubles experienced at the automated, digital hands of algorithms. This makes it possible to articulate the public issue of algorithmic inequality so that some better form of accountability might result.

This book has aimed to better equip you with the sociological theory necessary to begin to explore real-life examples of the evolving relations between society and technology. While many technologies make life connected, convenient and hope-filled, there is also the double-edged sword of those technologies that punish, surveil and cause inequality amongst some of the planet's most vulnerable. To give the final word in part to Philip Alston:

> … technologies are not the inevitable result of 'scientific' progress, but instead reflect political choices made by humans. Assuming that technology reflects pre-ordained or objectively rational and efficient outcomes risks abandoning human rights principles along with democratic decision-making
>
> (Alston, 2019, p. 19)

References

Alston, P. (2019) *Report of the Special rapporteur on extreme poverty and human rights.* The Office of the High Commissioner for Human Rights. Available at: https://www.ohchr.org/Documents/Issues/Poverty/ A_74_48037_AdvanceUneditedVersion.docx (Accessed: 20 January 2020).

BBC Newsnight (2016) *David Bowie speaks to Jeremy Paxman on BBC Newsnight (1999).* 11 January. Available at: https://www.youtube.com/watch? v=FiK7s_0tGsg (Accessed: 10 February 2020).

Booth, R. (2019) 'Benefits system automation could plunge claimants deeper into poverty', *The Guardian,* 14 October. Available at: https://www. theguardian.com/technology/2019/oct/14/fears-rise-in-benefits-system-automation-could-plunge-claimants-deeper-into-poverty (Accessed: 10 February 2020).

Guynn, J. and Weise, E. (2014) 'Opportunity is not created equal in Silicon Valley for African Americans, Hispanics', *USA Today,* Available at: https:// www.usatoday.com/story/tech/2014/06/26/black-hispanic-tech-silicon-valley-diversity-google-facebook/1 (Accessed: 25 November 2020).

Henman, P. (2017) 'The computer says "DEBT": Towards a critical sociology of algorithms and algorithmic governance', *3rd Data for Policy Conference: Government by Algorithm?,* London, 6–7 September. Available at: https:// zenodo.org/record/884117 (Accessed: 20 January 2020).

I, Daniel Blake (2016) Directed by K. Loach. [Feature film]. UK: Sixteen Films, Why Not Productions, Wild Bunch.

Lomas, N. (2020) *Blackbox welfare fraud detection system breaches human rights, Dutch court rules.* Available at: https://techcrunch.com/2020/02/06/blackbox-welfare-fraud-detection-system-breaches-human-rights-dutch-court-rules/? guccounter=1 (Accessed: 10 February 2020).

Noble, S.U. (2018) *Algorithms of oppression: how search engines reinforce racism.* New York: New York University Press. pp. 1–4.

Rosenblat, A., Kneese, T. and boyd, d. (2014) *Algorithmic Accountability.* Available at: https://papers.ssrn.com/abstract=2535540 (Accessed: 6 February 2020).

Seaver, N. (2017) 'Algorithms as culture: Some tactics for the ethnography of algorithmic systems', *Big Data & Society,* 4(2), p. 2053951717738104. doi: 10.1177/2053951717738104.

Glossary

Affordances

This term refers to the particular uses objects or technologies offer to people. Affordances are not always intentional design features of objects or technologies. Take the example of the chair. It is designed for sitting, however, it also affords its users a place to hang their coats or a step that could be used to change a light bulb.

Agency

The capacity to act freely according to one's own choices, intentions and desires.

Alt-right

Abbreviated from 'alternative right', this is a largely online populist political movement which rejects traditional conservatism, instead promoting white nationalism, anti-feminism and other far right ideas.

Always-on lifestyles

Characterised by people being networked through digital connections (e.g. access to the internet and social networks). While the term does not mean that people's activities are always focused on the digital, it emphasises that people are available to connect with others or are aware of their networks' activities through digital technology.

Austerity policies

A programme of reduction of government spending to make savings to the national budget.

Autonomy

Autonomy is an important concept in sociology, one whose origins derive from the 18th and 19th century philosophies of Immanuel Kant and John Stuart Mill. For Kant, autonomy refers to a person's ability to make choices and take actions unaffected by forces external to themselves. For Mill, autonomy involves a person being able to direct their actions in accordance with their own values and desires. In contrast to these ideas, some would argue that autonomy is an illusion and that people are heavily constrained by such things as their position in the economic structure or their biological make-up.

Big data

This term is commonly used to describe large sets of information and the potential for organisations to analyse that data for many commercial (such as advertising) and non-commercial purposes (such as decision-making or scheduling).

(Bio)politics

[Also biopolitics] The term biopolitics has various definitions and usages but in sociology it often refers to the works of Michel Foucault. For Foucault, the terms biopolitics and biopower are closely related and refer to an extension of power over the physical and political bodies of a population. In the modern period, biopolitics represents a new form of power or control over people, populations and even life itself. An example could be the state regulation of women's reproductive rights, the patenting of the human genome or even to the collection of government demographic statistics.

Black-boxing

In the social sciences, black-boxing refers to situations where a process or its parts have been hidden away from view, meaning that researchers cannot investigate or analyse it.

Causality

Causality refers to the process by which one thing causes another. Since correlations only identify the existence of a relationship between two phenomena (e.g. when A goes up, B goes down), it is usually important to identify which of the two causes that relationship. For example, when the temperature goes up this causes the number of people wearing warm coats to go down. The reverse is not true.

Cloud computing

This term refers to on-demand computer system resources, such as data storage or computing power, that are available to people or organisations to use without their direct active management. Often these services will be in locations remote from their users.

Correlation

In statistics, correlation refers to an association or relationship identified between two phenomena under investigation that does not occur by random chance (e.g. when A goes up B goes down). Correlation does not tell us which of the phenomena causes that relationship or whether a third, unknown factor has caused it. It is important to remember that correlation does not always imply causation [*see* Causality].

Cross-sectional research

Cross-sectional research involves studying a cross-section of a particular population at a single point in time.

Cyborg

The term 'cyborg' was coined in 1960 by Manfred Clynes and Nathan Kline as shorthand for 'cybernetic organism'. Cyborgs feature heavily in science fiction writing and film, frequently appearing as terrifying blends of the artificial and the organic such as the Daleks or the Borg. However, artificial implants such as pacemakers and cochlear implants, which establish feedback loops between the body and the implanted device, are cyborg enhancements and quite commonplace.

Dark web

A corner of the internet where users can access often illegal or frowned upon goods and services, such as malware or drugs.

Diaspora

The term diaspora comes from the Greek word meaning to scatter. It is used to refer to the dispersal around the world of people from the same origins or homeland. Originally referring to the forced displacement of the Jews in antiquity, the term is now used to describe any large group of people who have become dispersed around the globe.

Disenchantment

According to the sociologist Max Weber, disenchantment is the process in which science has replaced religious, supernatural and magical explanations with rational, mechanistic ones, and the loss of existential meaning that results from it (Weber, M. (1946) *From Max Weber: essays in sociology*. Edited by H.H. Gerth,. Translated from the German by C. W. Mills. New York, NY: Oxford University Press).

Disinformation

The term disinformation is usually used to refer to information known to be false by those promoting it and that is disseminated with the intention of manipulating or harming others.

Effect size

Effect size provides a statistical measure of the magnitude or size of an observed effect.

Empirical research

This term refers to research based on observation, experiences or the collection of original data about the social world.

Ethnographer

An ethnographer is someone who conducts ethnographic research [*see* Ethnographic research].

Ethnographic fieldwork

See Ethnographic research.

Ethnographic research

Ethnographic research is a qualitative research method, with small research samples, often based on participant observation. It is interested in social phenomena and often focuses on understanding the insider perspective of people involved in particular social groups. Ethnographic research also often involves observation or participant observation in digital, in particular social media, environments.

Fetishism

The term 'fetishism' was coined in the late 18th century by Charles de Brosses (1709–1777) to describe the religion of West Africa. The fetish was a made object said to possess magical or sacred power and believed capable of enchanting the unwary or unprotected. The term subsequently became a staple of early anthropological and sociological theories of the origins of religion including Emile Durkheim (1858–1917), Herbert Spencer (1820–1903) and Sigmund Freud (1856–1939).

First Nation

People whose ancestors lived in regions before the arrival of Europeans. It typically refers to the indigenous peoples of Canada.

Frame

The term 'frame' has various meanings but, in Goffman's usage, refers to 'definitions of the situation [that] are built up in accordance with the principles of organization which govern events – at least social ones – and our subjective involvement in them' (Goffman, E. (1974) *Frame analysis: an essay on the organization of experience.* Cambridge, MA: Harvard University Press). Framing here refers to how experiences are socially organised, so that issues become defined in terms not immediately connected to them. Thus 'active travel' becomes redefined as a public health issue rather than a transportation issue.

Framed

See Frame.

Global North

After the Second World War, the world began to be seen as divided into 'developed' (wealthy) and 'undeveloped' (poor) countries. Today, the terms 'Global North' and 'Global South' are used, which still geographically divides the world into wealthier and poorer regions but removes the ideas of an ideal or 'Western' state of development that countries must strive to obtain. It is important to note that these are not necessarily geographical spaces but rather conceptual divisions. Australia, for example, as a wealthy country, would be considered part of the Global North, even though it is in the southern hemisphere.

Global South

See Global North.

Holocaust

The Holocaust involved the persecution, torture, genocide (or the mass murder), of European Jews between 1941 and 1945 across countries occupied by Germany. Also known as the Shoah, Nazi Germany and its collaborators systematically murdered six million Jews or two thirds of Europe's Jewish population.

Imagined Community

The term Imagined Community was coined by Benedict Anderson and refers to the many ways in which citizens imagine national belonging. The concept is used to explain how modern national identities were shaped and forged by communications technologies. Print technologies, in particular, helped people imagine themselves living within the same territorial boundaries, feeling a sense of solidarity with fellow citizens even though they would never meet most face-to-face, sharing a culture and future destiny, and in these ways belonging to the same nation.

Liminal

A person or object is said to be liminal when it is in transition between one physical or cultural state and another. The concept derives from Arnold van Gennep's (1873–1957) work on rites of passage.

Longitudinal research

Longitudinal research involves studying a group or population over time. It is more effective at identifying causality than cross-sectional research.

Moral panic

Moral panics involve episodes of social anxiety in which a 'folk-devil' (e.g. a youth subculture) is identified as being a threat to the wider society. For something to count as a moral panic, the level of concern generated must be exaggerated or unjustified on objective grounds.

Normative

Something that is concerned with ideas about desirable standards and values, and what ought to be considered normal and accepted – even if this is currently not the case.

Nudge

Nudge theory is a relatively recent development in the overlapping fields of behavioural science, behavioural economics and political theory. Based on the work of Richard Thaler and Cass Sunstein, nudge theory argues that positive reinforcements can be used to adapt behaviour by playing on 'assets' that people already value – assets may be existing beliefs, economic interest or simple convenience (e.g. putting fruit at eye level in self-service food outlets). The nudge concept is itself based on the somewhat contradictory idea of 'libertarian paternalism': people need help to live healthy lives (paternalism) but such help should be not meddlesome (libertarian). The focus is on designing social environments that make 'good' choices 'easier'.

Patents

Legal documents that describe inventions that people have come up with. The purpose of a patent is to make a legal claim that you have invented something so another person cannot legally profit from that invention. Patents are helpful historical artefacts that can help researchers understand what people in the past considered important.

Qualitative research

Research that aims to understand particular aspects of social life in depth, and using a range of non-numerical narrative research methods, such as in-depth interviews, semi-structured interviews, and participant observation. Ethnographic research is a type of qualitative research.

Radicalisation

The process through which an individual comes to adopt increasingly radical views, such as extremist religious or political ideologies, and particularly when these involve support for terrorism.

Remittances

Resources that migrants send back home to their families and friends. These can be used by family members to secure their survival or improve their material position or status in the home community.

Secularised

The term secularised (or secularism) refers to political and social systems in which religious ideas have ceased to be the principal source of public authority.

Settler

The word settler is sometimes used when considering the relations between first nations communities and those who share the land due to migration. Settlers often bring with them various privileges which they then pass on to their descendants. Consequently, the term settler is often used in contexts where it is important to capture the impact of colonialism with specific reference to privilege and inequality.

Social harm

Social harm refers to harms and injuries caused by the way society is organised or such things as the state, large corporations or the criminal justice system itself. Although the harms they involve are often significant, social harms tend not be criminalised.

Social institutions

Social institutions are sets of patterned and relatively enduring arrangements of people in groups that come together for a common purpose. They may be governed by both informal or formal rules and expectations. Examples of major social institutions include the family, education, religion, the economy and work, government, and health care.

Social structures

Social structures are stable and enduring social institutions, organisations or arrangements that make up the social world, and that appear to exist independently of individuals and their agency. Social scientists think of class, gender, ethnicity and nationality as social structures.

Sociology of health and illness

The study of health and illness by sociologists has been a major growth area of research and teaching in sociology, and in terms of membership it represents the largest sub-section of both the British and American Sociological Associations. The sociological study of health and illness critically addresses many of the concepts within medicine and public health as problematic and political. It is concerned with: understanding how patients experience and give meaning to health and illness; analysing the enduring health inequalities within society; and is critical of the medicalisation of everyday social problems.

Symbolic interactionism

Associated with the Chicago School in America and particularly the works of George Herbert Mead (1863–1931), symbolic interactionism focuses on social interaction as the process through which human beings create, ascribe and transmit meanings, typically according to established, underlying codes of behaviour and feeling. The approach has been criticised for its neglect of issues of power and inequality and, more recently, for its tendency to regard things and objects as passive vehicles of human meaning rather than as agentive in their own right.

Technological determinism

A technological determinist perspective suggests that technology will take society to a distinctly positive or negative endpoint. More generally, it describes any viewpoint arguing that the functionality of a technology (what it can do) causes or 'determines' particular outcomes. In contrast, sociological viewpoints tend to argue that outcomes are the result of an interaction between the technology, how it is used in a particular social context and the meanings given to it by the people who use it.

Technological optimism

A technological optimist (also known as a technological utopian) perspective suggests that technology can be liberating and produces only positive outcomes for individuals and society.

Technological utopianism

See Technological optimism.

Technoscientific

[Also Technoscience] In sociological studies of science and technology, the expression technoscientific or technoscience refers to how science and technology are intertwined against the background of a social context. In other words, science and technology both affect each other and are situated in a social and historical context and are made durable by material and human networks.

Transnationalism

Transnationalism refers to a wide range of practices – not all related to migration – that transcend national physical borders or symbolic boundaries. As an analytical perspective, transnationalism examines the many ties and connections that bypass national belonging, citizenship or identity – especially the new kinds of interconnectivity afforded in the digital age. Transnational ties might be economic, political, cultural and social or a combination of all of these. Transnationalism examines the declining importance in some spheres of life and activity of national boundaries. Some uses of the term have been criticised for underestimating the enduring significance of the nation and of national borders and citizenship in an age of global migration.

Unconscious bias

Unconscious bias is when someone forms a stereotype or acts in a discriminating way without being consciously aware that they are doing so. An example of this could be with a job advertisement being written in masculine language which discourages women from applying.

Acknowledgements

Grateful acknowledgement is made to the following sources.

Introduction

Figure 1: Wellcome Collection. This file is licensed under the Creative Commons Attribution License https://creativecommons.org/licenses/by/4.0; Figure 2: Cover from Becker, H. S (1982). Art worlds. Berkeley, University of California Press; Figure 3: Kristoffer Tripplaar/Alamy.

Section 1

Figure 1.1: Archive Photos/Stringer/Getty Image; Figure 1.2: Punch Cartoon Library/TopFoto; Figure 1.3: Dr Kat Jungnickel. This file is licensed under the Creative Commons Attribution-NonCommercial-ShareAlike 4.0 International License https://creativecommons.org/licenses/by-nc-sa/4.0/; Figure 1.5: HASPhotos/Shutterstock; Figure 1.6: Kodak; Reading 1.1: ©2014 National Public Radio, Inc. Excerpt from NPR news report titled "How Kodak's Shirley Cards Set Photography's Skin-Tone Standard" by Mandalit Del Barco as originally published on npr.org on November 13, 2014, and is used with the permission of NPR. Any unauthorized duplication is strictly prohibited; Figure 2.1: Julie, Dave & Family. This file is licensed under the Attribution-ShareAlike 2.0 License https://creativecommons.org/licenses/by-sa/2.0/; Chapter 2 photo of Pierre Bourdieu: Ulf Andersen/Getty Images; Reading 2.1: Weale, S. (2018) 'An Education Arms Race': Inside the Ultra-Competitive World of Private Tutoring, The Guardian; Reading 2.2: Savage, M. (2015) Social class in the 21st century. London: Pelican, an imprint of Penguin Books (A Pelican introduction); Figure 2.2: Photo by Oleg Magni from Pexels.

Section 2

Introduction to Section 2, Figure 1: David Cardinez/Shutterstock; Introduction to Section 2, Figure 2: Alexandros Michailidis/Shutterstock; Introduction to Section 2, Figure 3: Trismegist san/Shutterstock; Figure 3.1: Trinity Mirror/Mirrorpix/Alamy; Figure 3.2: Jim Jarvie. Tweet reproduced with permission from Ryan McGoverne; Figure 3.3: Dedi Grigoroiu/Shutterstock; Figure 3.4: Source: Office for

National Statistics, 2018; Reading 3.1: van Deursen, A. J. and van Dijk, J. A. (2019) 'The first-level digital divide shifts from inequalities in physical access to inequalities in material access', New Media & Society, 21(2), pp. 354–375. doi: 10.1177/1461444818797082. This file is licensed under the Creative Commons Attribution-Non-commercial Licence http://creativecommons.org/licenses/by-nc/3.0/; Reading 3.2: Faith, R. (2016). How does the use of mobile phones by 16-24 year old socially excluded women affect their capabilities? PhD thesis, The Open University; Figure 3.5: Photo Vault/Alamy; Figure 3.6: © British Library Board. All Rights Reserved/Bridgeman Images; Figure 3.7: 'Where is Milton Keynes', 1972, commissioned by Milton Keynes Development Corporation, agency Minale Tattersfield. © Victoria and Albert Museum, London; Figure 3.8a: 'Concrete Jungle', commissioned by Milton Keynes Development Corporation, agency Cogent Elliott. The Advertising Archives; Figure 3.8b: 'The Back Streets', commissioned by Milton Keynes Development Corporation, agency Cogent Elliott; Figure 3.9a: City Discovery Centre, Milton Keynes; Figure 3.9b: Simon Phipps; Figure 3.10: Milton Keynes Development Corporation; Quote on pp. 105–106: Albrecht, C. (2019) ArticulATE Q&A: Why starship's delivery robots are as wide as your shoulders. Available at: https://thespoon.tech/articulate-qa-why-starships-delivery-robots-are-as-wide-as-yourshoulders/ (Accessed: 11 February 2020); Figure 3.11: Leon Neal/Getty Images News; Figure 3.12: Liz McFall; Figure 3.13: Delta-NC; Figure 3.14: Liz McFall; Figure 4.1: Sam Tarling; Figure 4.2: Knut Bry; Poem on pp. 130–131: @MattAbbottPoet; Reading 4.1: Leurs, K., and Smets, P. (2018) "Five questions for digital migration studies: Learning from digital connectivity and forced migration in (to) Europe." Social Media + Society. doi:10.1177/2056305118764425; Figure 4.3: Jillian Kay Melchior/National Review; Figure 4.4: Marie Gillespie; Figure 5.1: Ariel Skelley/Getty Images; Figure 5.2: Rey Borlaza/Shutterstock; Figure 5.3: Pius Utomi Ekpei/AFP via Getty Images; Figure 5.4: © Jonathan Thacker. This file is licensed under the Creative Commons Attribution-ShareAlike license https://creativecommons.org/licenses/by-sa/2.0/; Quote on p. 175: RCCG (Redeemed Christian Church of God) http://rccg.org/who-we-are/mission-and-vision/.

Section 3

Introduction to Section 3, Figure 1: Bletchley Park Trust; Introduction to Section 3, Figure 2: Just AI; Figure 6.1: chalermphon_tiam/ Shutterstock; Quote on p. 202: Graham, J., Molina, B. (2017) 'Waze sent commuters toward California wildfires, drivers say', 7 December 2019, USA today, (c) Gannett 2018; Reading 6.2: Rammert, W. (2012) 'Distributed agency and advanced technology: Or: how to analyze constellations of collective inter-agency', in Passoth, J.-H., Peuker, B., and Schillmeier, M. (eds) Agency Without Actors?: New Approaches to Collective Action. London: Routledge; Figure 6.2: Timitrius. This file is licensed under the Creative Commons Attribution-ShareAlike Licence https://creativecommons.org/licenses/ by-sa/2.0/; Figure 6.3: Reproduced with permission of Jeppesen Sanderson, Inc. NOT FOR NAVIGATIONAL USE © Jeppesen Sanderson, Inc. 2019; Figure 6.4: Mikko Ryynanen/Shutterstock; Figure 7.1: IanDagnall Computing/Alamy; Figure 7.2: TCD/Prod.DB/ Alamy; Figure 7.3: TCD/Prod.DB/Alamy; Figure 7.4: KOKUYO. This file is licensed under the Creative Commons Attribution-ShareAlike 4.0 International Licence https://creativecommons.org/ licenses/by-sa/4.0/; Figure 7.5: Quino, 1986; Figure 7.6: University of Hertfordshire; Figure 7.7: Source: "Donna Haraway: Story Telling for Earthly Survival," a film by Fabrizio Terranova, Courtesy Icarus Films. Photo: Kjell Ove Storvik/North Norwegian Art Centre; Figure 8.1: Rosie. This file is licensed under the Creative Commons Attribution-NonCommercial-NoDerivs License https://creativecommons.org/ licenses/by-nc-nd/2.0/; Figure 8.2: Cover design: Sam Schwartz Engineering and America Walks. Photo: Tracie7779, Sam Schwartz Engineering, Matt Bernstine, Chicago Department of Transportation (CDOT), Ed Yourdon, Paul Lowry; Figure 8.3: Cover design: SWITCH Consortium (editor) (2016) The SWITCH Campaign Guide – Practical advice for campaigns to promote a switch from car-based travel to active modes of travel. Cologne. Photo: Alex Proimos; Figure 8.4: Dedi Grigoroiu/Shutterstock; Quote on pp. 268–269: ©2019 Fitbit, Inc; Figure 8.6: New York City Department of Transport. This file is licensed under the Creative Commons Attribution-NonCommercial-NoDerivs Licence https://creativecommons.org/licenses/by-nc-nd/ 2.0/.

Section 4

822/822.pdf. Parliamentary Copyright material is reproduced under Licence Number P2005000031, with the permission of the Controller of HMSO on behalf of Parliament; Figure 12.4: Tyler Olson/ Shutterstock; Figure 12.5: (left) Amy Orben, (right) Oxford Internet Institute; Figure 12.6: Keystone/Getty Images; Figure 12.7: Pictorial Press Ltd/Alamy Stock Photo; Reading 12.2: Furedi, F. (2015) The media's first moral panic, History Today; Figure 12.8: The Granger Collection/Alamy; Figure 13.1: Rawpixel.com/Shutterstock; Reading 13.1: Rosenblat, A. et al. (2014) Algorithmic Accountability, A workshop primer produced for: The Social, Cultural & Ethical Dimensions of "Big Data" March 17, 2014 - New York, NY. https:// datasociety.net/pubs/2014-0317/AlgorithmicAccountabilityPrimer.pdf. This file is licensed under the Creative Commons Attribution Licence http://creativecommons.org/licenses/by/3.0/; Reading 13.2: Seaver, N. (2017) 'Algorithms as culture: Some tactics for the ethnography of algorithmic systems', Big Data & Society. https://journals.sagepub. com/doi/full/10.1177/2053951717738104. This file is licensed under the Creative Commons Attribution Licence http://creativecommons. org/licenses/by/3.0/; Reading 13.3: Noble, S. U. (2018) Algorithms of oppression: how search engines reinforce racism. New York: New York University Press; Quote on p. 438: Guynn, J. and Weise, E. (2014) 'Opportunity is not created equal in Silicon Valley for African Americans, Hispanics', USA Today. Available at: https://eu.usatoday. com/story/tech/2014/06/26/silicon-valley-tech-diversity-white-asian- black-hispanic-google-facebook-yahoo/11372421/ (Accessed: 25 November 2020); Quote on pp. 440–441: Alston, P. (2019) Report of the Special rapporteur on extreme poverty and human rights. Geneva. Available at: https://www.ohchr.org/Documents/Issues/Poverty/ A_74_48037_AdvanceUneditedVersion.docx; Figure 13.2: TCD/Prod. DB/Alamy. Quote on pp. 443–444: Booth, R. (2019) Benefits system automation could plunge claimants deeper into poverty, The Guardian; Reading 13.4: Henman, P. (2017) The computer says 'DEBT': Towards a critical sociology of algorithms and algorithmic governance. https:// zenodo.org/record/884117#.XbkqLUYzZPZ. This file is licensed under the Creative Commons Attribution Licence http:// creativecommons.org/licenses/by/3.0/; Reading 13.5: Alston, P. (2019) Report of the Special rapporteur on extreme poverty and human rights. Geneva. Available at: https://www.ohchr.org/Documents/Issues/ Poverty/A_74_48037_AdvanceUneditedVersion.docx; Quote on p. 453: Lomas, N. (2020) Blackbox welfare fraud detection system breaches human rights, Dutch court rules, TechCrunch.

Every effort has been made to contact copyright holders. If any have been inadvertently overlooked the publishers will be pleased to make the necessary arrangements at the first opportunity

Index

Page references in **bold** refer to figures.